CODES FOR HOMEOWNERS

5th Edition

Electrical • Plumbing • Construction • Mechanical
Current with 2021–2023 Codes

Bruce A. Barker

COOL SPRINGS PRESS

Inspiring | Educating | Creating | Entertaining

Brimming with creative inspiration, how-to projects, and useful information to enrich your everyday life, quarto.com is a favorite destination for those pursuing their interests and passions.

© 2015, 2019, 2023 Quarto Publishing Group USA Inc.

First published in 2015 by Cool Springs Press, an imprint of The Quarto Group, 100 Cummings Center Suite 265D, Beverly, MA 01915 USA. This edition published in 2023. T (978) 282-9590 F (978) 283-2742 www.Quarto.com

Cool Springs Press titles are also available at discount for retail, wholesale, promotional, and bulk purchase. For details, contact the Special Sales Manager by email at specialsales@quarto.com or by mail at The Quarto Group, Attn: Special Sales Manager, 100 Cummings Center Suite 265D, Beverly, MA 01915 USA.

10 9 8 7 6 5 4 3 2 1

ISBN: 978-0-7603-8164-9

Digital edition published in 2023
eISBN: 978-0-7603-8165-6

Acquisitions Editor: Mark Johanson
Art Director: Brad Springer
Layout: Danielle Smith-Boldt
Author: Bruce Barker
Illustration: Bruce Barker
Additional Illustration: Mark Abdellah, Christopher R. Mills
Photography: Rau + Barber
Photo Assistance: Jon Hegge

Printed in China

NOTICE TO READERS

For safety, use caution, care, and good judgment when following the procedures described in this book. The publisher, author, and BLACK+DECKER cannot assume responsibility for any damage to property or injury to persons as a result of misuse of the information provided.

The techniques shown in this book are general techniques for various applications. In some instances, additional techniques not shown in this book may be required. Always follow manufacturers' instructions included with products, since deviating from the directions may void warranties. The projects in this book vary widely as to skill levels required: some may not be appropriate for all do-it-yourselfers, and some may require professional help.

Consult your local building department for information on building permits, codes, and other laws as they apply to your project.

Contents

Codes for Homeowners

Contents (Cont.)

Maximum gap 4⅜"

Handrails at least 34" but not more than 38" above stair treads

Nosing radius ≤ ⁹⁄₁₆"

Riser height ≤ 7¾"

Tread depth ≥ 10"

Introduction

The purpose of the 2021 International Residential Code (IRC), and of all building codes for that matter, is expressed in IRC Section R101.3: "The purpose of this code is to establish minimum requirements to provide a reasonable level of safety, health and general welfare through affordability, structural strength, means of egress, stability, sanitation, light and ventilation, energy conservation and safety to life and property from fire and other hazards and to provide a reasonable level of safety to fire fighters and emergency responders during emergency operations." This statement provides important information about building codes and code inspections. Building codes are minimum requirements. A house built to minimum requirements is not necessarily a high-quality house built by craftsmen according to best practices. Code inspections are about safety and health. They are not about fit, finish, and other cosmetic issues. They are not even about functional issues that are not specifically addressed in the code. Understanding the purpose of building codes helps you set realistic expectations about the limits of building codes and code inspections.

Building codes change; most do so on a three-year cycle. Many code changes are little more than rewording or reorganization in an attempt to make code provisions easier to understand and easier to find. Many code changes and additions are substantive, and homeowners should be aware of these as they perform repairs and remodeling projects. Substantive additions and changes are the reasons for this updated edition of *Codes for Homeowners*.

Trying to condense a 900-page code book that is mostly text and tables in very small print into significantly fewer pages filled with pictures and illustrations is a challenge. We have not included many code provisions, because homeowners are unlikely to use them. The provisions we include have been simplified to make them easier to understand. This means that *Codes for Homeowners* is not your local building code. Your local building code, as interpreted by your building inspector, is the code with which you must comply. You must do so even if you do not obtain a building permit for your work. **If you have any doubts or questions about how a building code provision applies in your area, you should ask your local building inspectors.** In almost every case, if you approach them as a resource and not as an obstacle, you will find your local inspectors to be friendly, knowledgeable, and eager to help.

Codes + Permits: The Basics

In just the United States you will find hundreds of code books describing thousands upon thousands of building code provisions. On top of this, there are even more books that look and feel like code books but are really only attempting to describe best practices. Almost all of these have their own inherent value. But almost none of them apply to a typical homeowner living in a typical single-family home. As a homeowner and DIYer, perhaps the hardest thing about building codes is learning how to tell which one applies to you and, if there is a disagreement, which takes precedence. As an introduction, here are some brief biographies of the more common codes and enforcement agencies you're likely to encounter.

The International Residential Code

The IRC 2021 is one of an extensive collection of model building codes published by the International Code Council (ICC). A model building code is a recommended building code developed by a national organization that specializes in writing building codes. When adopted by a government agency, the IRC regulates the construction, renovation, maintenance, and repair of buildings used as homes. The IRC, by itself, has no formal legal status. A government agency must first adopt the IRC before it has any legal status in a local area.

State + Local Building Codes

Almost all areas of the United States have adopted some version of a building code. Some states, such as California, Florida, and New York, have a state building code. Some large cities, such as Chicago and New York City, have a city building code. Many of these state and local building codes are based on model building codes from the ICC.

Smaller cities and counties often use ICC model building codes, such as the IRC. Some rural areas may not have adopted a building code, but this is becoming a rare situation. If you do any work that is regulated by the local building code, you are responsible for knowing, or for hiring someone who knows, the applicable building code where the building is located. Ignorance of the code is no excuse.

Local Code Amendments

Most building departments that use the IRC adopt local changes to the IRC. Many of these changes are minor and help to adapt the IRC to local conditions and needs. Some of these changes can significantly alter IRC provisions. The building department should publish, in writing, any changes adopted by the local government. You are responsible for knowing and complying with all local changes. Ask the building official if there are any local code changes.

Other Building Codes

The IRC is not the only building code. Others commonly used include: The International Building Code (IBC), The International Mechanical Code (IMC), The International Plumbing Code (IPC), The Uniform Plumbing Code (UPC), The International Fuel Gas Code (IFG), The National Electrical Code (NEC), and The International Energy Conservation Code (IECC). Each of these building codes regulates a different aspect of building construction.

The IBC regulates the structural aspects of all buildings, although it is not commonly applied to residential buildings. The IBC usually applies to commercial, industrial, and multi-family buildings, such as apartments. The IRC references the IBC and the IECC when a part of a residential building is not addressed by the IRC.

Each major system in a building has its own code. The IMC regulates heating, ventilation, and air conditioning systems; the IPC regulates plumbing systems; and the IFG regulates gas piping and gas equipment. These codes usually apply to commercial-type buildings. The UPC is a separate code, published by another code-writing organization, that also regulates plumbing systems. It may replace the IRC plumbing chapters in areas that adopt the UPC. The NEC regulates electrical systems. The IRC contains an adapted version of the NEC in the IRC electrical chapters. When the IRC does not address an electrical situation in a home, the NEC usually applies.

The IECC regulates energy-related aspects of all buildings. These aspects include: insulation, air infiltration, and window and door energy efficiency. The IRC contains a simplified subset of the IECC.

You should know which codes apply to your construction project. Ask your local building official which codes apply in your area.

Zoning Ordinances

Many areas, particularly the more densely populated ones, have land use and zoning ordinances that control what you can build on your property. You are responsible for knowing and complying with them. In larger jurisdictions, the planning and zoning department may be separate from the building inspection department, and sometimes one does not know what the other is doing. It is possible that the building inspection department might issue a permit that would create a zoning violation. Projects that might run afoul of zoning ordinances include new, free-standing buildings, basement remodels that add a bedroom, bathroom, and kitchen, and any project that adds an additional full kitchen on property zoned for single-family use.

Buildings Governed by the IRC

Apply the IRC to buildings containing one or two individual residential dwelling units in one building. Duplex is a common term for one building containing two individual dwelling units.

Apply the IRC to townhouses. A townhouse contains at least three individual dwelling units in one building.

Each dwelling unit in any building within the scope of the IRC must have a separate means of egress. This is often interpreted to mean that each dwelling unit must have a separate door to the outside.

Apply the IRC to residential buildings with not more than three stories above grade plane. A story above grade plane is: (a) one where the finished floor is entirely above grade plane, (b) is more than 6 feet above grade plane, or (c) is more than 12 feet above finished ground level at any point. The definition of grade plane is complex and is measured at the lowest point 6 feet from each building foundation wall. Refer to the definitions in the IRC and consult the local building official if there is a question about whether a basement is a story above grade plane.

Apply the IRC to owner-occupied guest accommodations (such as a bed and breakfast) if the building contains not more than five guest rooms and if a fire suppression system is installed in the building.

Do not apply the IRC to buildings used for business, office, commercial, industrial, or other residential purposes, such as a fraternity house. This is true even if the building was once used as a residence. You may apply the IRC to an office in the home if the office is incidental to the residential use of the building. Refer to the IBC and other applicable codes for code provisions governing buildings not governed by the IRC.

Apply the IRC to all single-family homes.

Apply the IRC to multi-family buildings, such as duplexes and townhomes.

Building Departments

A local building department enforces the building code in its jurisdiction. The technical term often used to describe this department is the Authority Having Jurisdiction (AHJ). The term used to describe the person responsible for enforcing the code is the Building Official or Chief Building Official. The public name for the local building department varies by jurisdiction. Many building departments will have the terms "building" or "safety" somewhere in the name. In some larger jurisdictions, the building department may be a division of a larger agency that is also responsible for land planning, zoning, and development. Some building department names may not sound like they have anything at all to do with building code enforcement. If you do any work that requires a building permit, you are responsible for finding and contacting the building department. Work done without a permit can have serious legal and financial consequences.

Consider your local building department to be a friendly place with extremely valuable resources to help you get your projects done correctly.

Working with Government Building Inspectors

The building official is the king of his building jurisdiction. Don't mess with the king. He can make your life very difficult. If you must disagree with him, do so respectfully and with facts that support your position. The building official has the right to interpret any code provision. While he does not have the right to waive code provisions or to require more than the code requires, interpretations can sometimes have that effect. Even if his interpretation seems unreasonable, eventually it will probably prevail. In almost all cases, you should just smile and do what he tells you.

Most building officials and inspectors are honest, hardworking people who want to ensure that your project is safe and complies with local building codes. They can be a valuable resource. Take advantage of that resource. Ask questions and work with them. Most will, in turn, work with you.

Who Is Responsible for Code Compliance?

The general answer is that everybody associated with the project is responsible for code compliance, but with one exception. The primary responsibility usually falls on the permit holder, which is one reason why it is a warning signal if a contractor asks the property owner to pull the permit. A contractor who does not want to pull a permit may not have an active license, may have a bad reputation with the building inspectors, or there may be other reasons, few of which are good.

The one exception is the building inspectors. Building inspectors are not responsible for code compliance. They are responsible for inspecting to catch code violations, but they are usually not responsible if they do not catch a violation. Thus, passing an inspection and obtaining a certificate of occupancy is not a guarantee of code compliance.

Manufacturer's Instructions

The IRC requires installing all components, equipment, and appliances according to the manufacturer's instructions. This requirement is so important that it is repeated many times in the IRC. Manufacturer's instructions are an enforceable extension of the IRC. This means that it is a code violation to install something in a manner that does not conform to manufacturer's instructions.

Manufacturer's instructions are an important part of ensuring that components are safe. Independent organizations test many components used to build homes. This includes almost all manufactured

Time is not the friend of government building inspectors. From an eight-hour day, they must subtract doing paperwork, discussing inspections with stakeholders, traveling between inspections, and performing other duties. Divide the remaining time by 20 to 30 inspections per day, or more, and they may have only a few minutes to perform each inspection. It's a credit to government inspectors that they find many major code violations. Most will admit, however, that they cannot find all code violations. They will also admit that they are not even looking for issues that, although they are not code violations, can have a significant negative impact on the cost to operate and maintain the home.

Private building inspectors fill this quality control gap for many people. People building homes and people performing major remodeling projects hire a private inspector who helps the government inspector and the contractor provide quality construction. A private inspector can perform a far more thorough inspection than a government inspector, because a private inspector can invest more time on each inspection. In addition, a private inspector usually inspects areas such as attics and roofs, where government inspectors rarely go.

Private building inspectors (such as the author, seen here) may be hired by a client to check the contractor's work at key points.

When building a new home or during a major remodeling project, a private inspector is often most useful at two critical points. The most critical point is just before insulation and drywall are installed. This inspection is sometimes called the pre-drywall inspection and is the most important inspection a home will ever have. At this time, an inspector can see many important components that will be covered by finish materials and, in most cases, will never be visible again. The other critical point is at the end of construction. At this time, an inspector can see and test important systems in the home.

Private inspectors are increasingly common on construction sites. While some contractors welcome private inspectors, many do not. Even if you decide not to engage a private inspector, it is wise to discuss the option with the contractor before signing a contract, and it is wise to agree, in writing, to how the contractor will work with the private inspector during construction.

components. The tests are conducted under defined conditions that include using the manufacturer's instructions to install the component. The testing organization certifies that the component is safe when installed and used according to manufacturer's instructions. The testing organization places the certified components on a list maintained by the testing organization. This process is called listing, and the components are referred to in the IRC as listed.

The IRC cannot anticipate every possible building component and every possible way the component could be installed. As such, the IRC relies on the manufacturer's instructions to specify how components should be installed.

When a difference between the IRC and the manufacturer's instructions occurs, the IRC assumes that the manufacturer is in a better position to know its product and how it should be installed in a given situation. This is why the IRC usually defers to the manufacturer's instructions. Ask the local building

official for an interpretation if there is a difference between the manufacturer's instructions and the IRC.

Grandfathering Existing Work

In almost all situations, you are not required to abandon, remove, or alter existing work that is lawfully in existence and safely functioning. Lawfully in existence means the work was inspected and complied with the code when installed and/ or modified.

In almost all situations, when updating, modifying, or repairing existing work, you are required to perform the update, modification, or repair according to the code in force when the work is performed. You are usually not required to make the existing work comply with current code.

Building Permits + Inspections

Contact your local building officials to determine which construction activities require a building permit and to determine the documents and procedures required to obtain a permit. The building official you speak with may not enforce some building permit requirements contained in the IRC, but may add building permit requirements not contained in the IRC.

You must wait until the required permit is issued before beginning work. Beginning work before the permit is issued may result in fines, and the building official could require removal of the work.

Comply with the building code applicable to where the building is located. The applicable building code is usually the code in force when the permit is issued. If you do not obtain a building permit, comply with the building code in force when the work is performed. The building code applies whether or not you obtain a building permit. This is important. Lack of a building permit does not relieve the building owner or the contractor of responsibility for code compliance.

Required Inspections

Contact the building official to determine the required inspections for a construction project. Each jurisdiction has its own rules for inspections. These rules include: which inspections it performs, what work must be complete before requesting the inspection, how and when to schedule the inspection, and how it handles inspections of work that fails inspection.

Note that some jurisdictions conduct a separate inspection for each trade, some jurisdictions conduct one inspection when all trade work is complete, and some jurisdictions conduct trade inspections during the framing inspection. Check with the building official to determine if other inspections are required. Further required inspections may include flood plain and elevation, roof coverings, insulation and energy efficiency, interior drywall, and exterior wall coverings, such as stucco and masonry.

Final Inspections

Prior to final inspection, you should: Install all plumbing, HVAC, and electrical fixtures, equipment, and appliances and install all required safety components, such as stair handrails and guards,

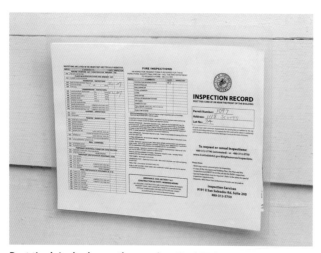

Post the job site inspection card so the inspector can see it.

CERTIFICATES OF OCCUPANCY

A certificate of occupancy is issued by your building official to affirm that your structure is safe to inhabit. Do not move into or occupy a building until after the building official issues a certificate of occupancy. Do not change the use of a building without a new certificate of occupancy. Example: do not use a building as an office if the building was once a home without receiving a new certificate of occupancy. The new certificate of occupancy may require changes to the building that reflect its new commercial use. You are not required to obtain a certificate of occupancy for accessory structures.

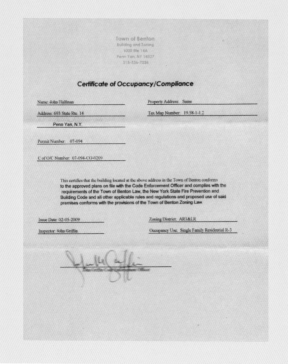

safety glazing, and smoke alarms. Note that jurisdictions have different rules about whether you must install finish components, such as floor coverings, before the final inspection. Jurisdictions also differ on whether tasks such as final grading and landscaping must be installed.

Do not assume that passing an inspection or receiving a certificate of occupancy is a waiver of any code violations. The building owner and contractor are responsible for any code violations regardless of whether the building has passed inspections.

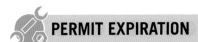

PERMIT EXPIRATION

Verify building permit expiration rules with your local building official. A building permit may expire if more than 180 days lapse without an inspection or without some other evidence that work is progressing on the project.

WHEN IS A PERMIT REQUIRED?

You typically will need a building permit for:

- Construction of new buildings

- Additions and structural modifications to existing buildings

- Structural repairs to existing buildings

- Replacement of or major repairs to building components, such as roof coverings and exterior wall coverings

- Movement and demolition of existing buildings

- Changes to building occupancy. A change to building occupancy means changing how the building is used. Example: using a single-family home as a place of business is a change in occupancy that may require a building permit and may require a zoning change or zoning waiver.

- Additions to, major changes to, and/or replacement of electrical, plumbing, gas, and HVAC components

You may not need a building permit for:

- Building or installation of one-story detached accessory structures (such as storage sheds and playhouses) with a floor area not more than 200 sq. ft.

- Fences not more than 7' tall

- Retaining walls not more than 4' tall measured from the bottom of the footing to the top of the wall and not supporting a surcharge (a surcharge is a vertical load in addition to and/or above the retained ground)

- Driveways and sidewalks

- Painting, papering, floor covering installation, cabinet and countertop installation, and similar finish work

- Installation of portable plug-and-cord connected decorative lights and similar plug-and-cord connected electrical equipment

- Replacement of fuses and circuit breakers

- Low-voltage lights and other electrical wires and equipment operating at less than 25 volts and not more than 50 watts

- Installation of portable gas heating, cooking, and clothes-drying equipment

- Installation of portable HVAC equipment (such as window air conditioners)

- Clearing of plumbing stoppages and repair of plumbing leaks and removal and reinstallation of toilets if the repairs do not involve replacement or rearrangement of valves, pipes, or fixtures

- Decks that are not more than 30" aboveground, are not more than 200 sq. ft. in area, are not attached to the building, and do not serve the required egress door

You usually do not need a building permit for:

- Routine maintenance of existing buildings, fixtures, and equipment, if the building structure is not affected and if the nature and use of the electrical, plumbing, gas, or HVAC system is not changed

Preparing for Inspections

Concrete footing inspections must be done before concrete is poured. Try to coordinate the inspection for the day before the planned pour, so you leave enough time to make corrections if required.

1. Install, square, and level forms.
2. Dig footing and pier trenches.
3. Install any required reinforcing bars.

Isolated footings, such as those used to support deck columns, must be inspected before the concrete is poured. The footings will be inspected for size and depth. Some footings may require reinforcing bars.

Typical Freestanding Wall Form

- Pull wire
- ¾" plywood
- Spacer
- 2 × 2 frame for stop board
- ¾" plywood
- 2 × 4 frame
- ¾" plywood stop board
- #3 rebar
- Concrete footing
- Stake
- Diagonal bracing
- Stake

Concrete foundation wall inspections will focus on the wall thickness, base preparation, and reinforcement. All forms must be approved prior to the pour.

1. Install, square, straighten, plumb, and secure wall forms.
2. Install any required reinforcing bars.

Plumbing rough-in inspection

1. Install plumbing water supply and drain pipes in the building. The building sewer pipe inspection is usually a different inspection from the interior drainage and water supply pipe inspection. Install fixtures, such as tubs and showers, that may be difficult to install after the wall construction is complete.

HVAC inspection

1. Install HVAC ducts, pipes, and thermostat wires.
2. Install (or have installed) appliances, such as furnaces and air handlers, that may be difficult to install after the construction is complete.

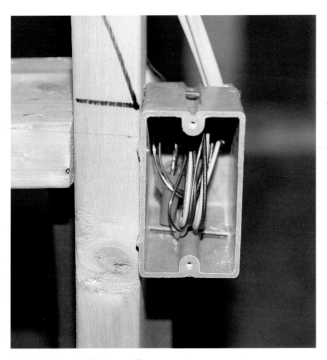

Electrical rough-in inspection

1. Have electrical service panel and subpanel cabinets installed.
2. Install boxes for switches, receptacles, fixtures, and all electrical cables.

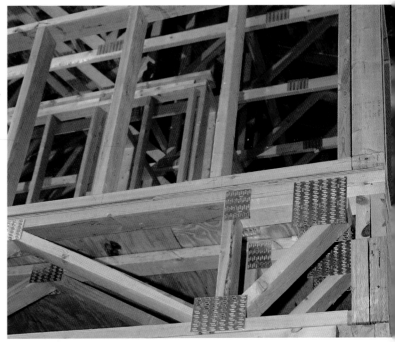

Framing inspection

1. Install all interior and exterior walls, floor joists and subflooring, ceiling joists and rafters, and roof sheathing. Install all required wall bracing, firestops, and draftstops.
2. Note that some jurisdictions may require installation of other components, such as moisture barriers and roofing underlayment, before calling for a framing inspection.

Building Design + Safety

One of the most important reasons for building codes is to promote the health and safety of building occupants. Health issues involve topics such as minimum room size, minimum ceiling height, and requirements for removing moisture and fumes that could damage your home and make you sick. **Safety issues involve topics such as the size and location of emergency escape openings, design and construction of stairs (one of the most dangerous areas in a home), and the location and installation of smoke alarms and carbon monoxide alarms.**

This chapter will help you understand building code requirements that you may encounter when doing projects such as adding rooms and remodeling basements and attics. While this chapter will help you avoid the most common health and safety code violations, it does not address all code requirements. You should refer to other sources for more information before tackling complex projects.

In this chapter:
- Habitable Rooms
- Fire Separations
- Stairways
- Emergency Escape Openings
- Egress Doors
- Exterior Doors
- Door + Window Hazards
- Ventilation + Exhaust
- Smoke Alarms + Carbon Monoxide Alarms

Habitable Rooms

Habitable rooms (also called habitable spaces) are living, sleeping, eating, and cooking rooms. Bathrooms, toilet rooms, closets, hallways, storage, and utility rooms are not habitable rooms. Habitable rooms have their own set of requirements for size, ceiling height, heating, lighting, and ventilation. Rooms that are not habitable do not have these requirements.

Provide at least 84" of clear ceiling height between the finished floor and the ceiling at the center of the room. Ignore lights, fans, and similar fixtures. If the ceiling slopes, only that floorspace where the ceiling height is at least 60" may be considered habitable. Heights less than 60", such as kneewall areas, may be useful for storage, but they aren't considered living space.

Minimum Ceiling Height

1. Provide at least an 84-inch-tall finished ceiling height in habitable rooms and in hallways, including a basement containing habitable rooms and hallways. Measure ceiling height from the finished floor to the lowest projection from the ceiling. Projections usually include components such as joists, beams, and ducts. Projections do not usually include light fixtures and ceiling fans.

2. You may have beams that are at least 78 inches above the finished floor of habitable rooms if there is at least 36 inches between the edges of the beams (not 36 inches between the centers of the beams).

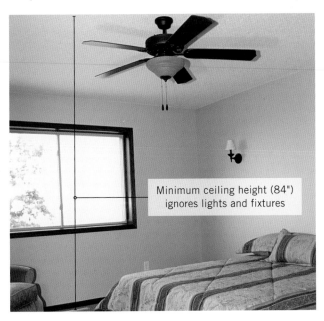

Minimum ceiling height (84") ignores lights and fixtures

Measure between finished floor and the lowest part of the ceiling in most rooms and basements to determine if minimum ceiling height standards are met. Ceiling-mounted lights and fans do not factor into the height measurement.

HABITABLE ROOM AREA REQUIREMENTS

- Provide every habitable room with an area of at least 70 sq. ft.

- Provide every habitable room with a horizontal dimension of at least 84". Kitchens may be excepted: In some conditions you may design a kitchen that is smaller than 70 sq. ft. or with a horizontal dimension less than 84".

3. You may have obstructions that are at least 76 inches above the finished floor in a basement containing habitable rooms and hallways.

4. Provide at least an 80-inch-tall finished ceiling height in a basement that does not contain habitable rooms or hallways. You may have obstructions that are at least 76 inches above the finished floor in these basement areas. Use these basement areas only for mechanical equipment and for storage.

5. Provide at least an 80-inch finished ceiling height in bathrooms and laundry rooms. This does not mean that all of the bathroom must have an 80-inch-tall ceiling. The ceiling height above sinks and toilets may be less than 80 inches high but must be high enough to safely use the fixture. How much less is subject to interpretation by the building inspector.

6. Provide at least an 84-inch-tall finished ceiling height in habitable rooms with a sloped ceiling. Provide this ceiling height for at least 35 square feet of the finished floor area. Do not count any area with a ceiling height less than 60 inches toward the minimum 70-square-foot habitable room floor area.

Bathroom Design Standards

15" from center of toilet to nearest wall or fixture

21" clearance in front of sinks and toilets

22" minimum shower opening

24" clearance in front of shower door

Shower base at least 30" × 30"

Door

Codes (and good design practices) insist on ample space between bathroom fixtures.

Provide at least 80" of finished ceiling height for all of the required floor area in showers and in tubs containing showers.

A toilet that is too close to an obstruction (in this case, the wall) can be inconvenient or dangerous to use.

An opening that is too small can be a slip-and-fall hazard in a wet area.

Shower Size

1. Provide showers with a finished area of at least 900 square inches and a finished minimum dimension of at least 30 inches. Maintain the minimum dimensions from the top of the threshold to at least 70 inches above the shower drain outlet. Measure the shower from the center line of the threshold (curb). You may install valves, shower heads, soap dishes, and grab bars that encroach into the minimum dimensions. You may install a fold-down seat in the shower if the minimum dimensions are maintained when the seat is up.

2. You may provide a shower with a finished minimum dimension of at least 25 inches if the finished area is at least 1,300 square inches.

3. Provide a shower compartment entry opening of at least 22 inches finished width.

4. Swing hinged shower doors out from the shower stall. Hinged doors may swing into the shower stall if they also swing out. Sliding shower doors are also allowed if the 22-inch minimum opening size is maintained.

Fire Separations

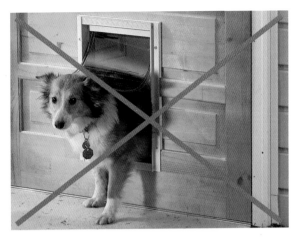

VIOLATION! DO NOT install pet doors in doors that separate the garage from the dwelling.

Fire Separation: Garage + Home

Many fires begin in garages. Unfortunately, garage fires often are more intense than fires that start elsewhere, because gasoline, cardboard, newspapers, and other flammable materials are usually stored in the garage. **Fire safety is an important rationale for many IRC provisions. Because of this the IRC has special requirements to help prevent the spreading of garage fires into the home.**

Fire Separation Doors

In walls that are shared between your dwelling and your garage, use at least a 20-minute fire-rated door. These may be made from solid wood or honeycomb-core steel. Use doors that are at least 1⅜ inch thick.

Doors in a garage wall may not open directly into a bedroom. You also may not install pet doors or other openings in doors or walls from a garage into the home unless the pet door or opening is listed to maintain fire separation. Install self-closing hinges on doors between the garage and the home.

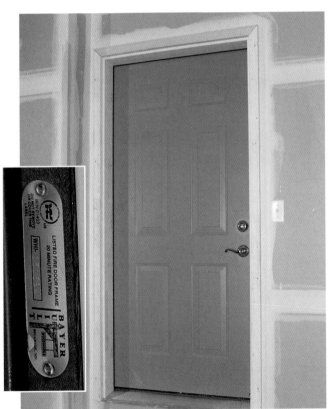

A fire-rated door with a minimum rating of 20 minutes is required in walls shared between a garage and a home.

DEFINITION OF A GARAGE

A garage is defined as a space for parking motor vehicles that is completely closed to the outdoors on three or more sides. It typically has an overhead door, but a structure that meets the requirement but has no door is still considered a garage. A carport is a space for parking motor vehicles that is open to the outdoors on at least two sides. A space with two solid walls (often the house walls), a partially open wall, and an opening without a vehicle door is considered a carport. Garages and carports may be attached to, or detached from, the dwelling. Garage fire separation requirements do not normally apply to carports.

Fire Separation Walls + Ceilings

Walls and ceilings that separate the home from the garage should be covered on the garage side with gypsum drywall that's at least ½ inch thick. A garage must have a ceiling made of Type X drywall that's a minimum of ⅝ inch thick if the garage is beneath a habitable room. (Type X has fibrous reinforcement to help the drywall maintain its integrity when exposed to high heat).

Maintain the same fire separation for drywall penetrations, such as attic scuttle holes, pull-down attic stairs, gas vents, and plumbing pipes, as provided by the gypsum drywall. Many older pull-down attic stairs interrupt the ceiling fire separation, because the panel to which the stairs are attached is thin plywood that has not been treated to be fire-resistant. Seal penetrations between the garage and the home, such as pipes and ducts, with materials that resist the free flow of fire and smoke. Such materials include fire-resistant caulk or foam.

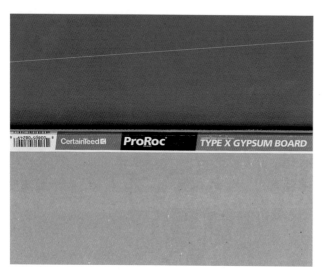

Type X drywall is required on garage ceilings if the space above is habitable.

VIOLATION! Do not install pull-down stairs in a garage ceiling unless they maintain the required fire separation. The standard plywood covers do not maintain fire separation unless they have been treated to be fire-resistant. Fire-resistant stairs should be labeled as such.

HVAC Ducts + Registers in Garages

Use at least 26-gauge sheet steel or other approved material to construct HVAC ducts that are installed in a garage and ducts that pass through garage walls and ceilings. Do not install HVAC supply or return air openings in the garage. This restriction does not apply to an independent HVAC system that serves only the garage. Do not use flexible HVAC duct or duct board to penetrate garage walls and ceilings. Flexible ducts and duct board may attach to steel ducts after the steel ducts penetrate the garage firewall.

Stairways

Interior and exterior stairways are regulated closely by most codes because they are inherently very dangerous parts of a house. Many of the regulations deal with lighting issues, including the type and location of fixtures and switches. The size, grippability, and location of handrails and railing balusters also account for much of the regulatory wording on stairways. Regulations for interior stairways also apply to exterior stairways. They include riser height, tread depth, and handrails and guards. It is important to comply with exterior stairway regulations, because they are used when wet or covered with snow and ice.

Interior Stairway Lighting + Switching

You should install as many light fixtures as necessary to illuminate all stairway landings and treads. The areas at the top and bottom of stairs are landings, so the lights should illuminate them too. For example, a light fixture at the top of a stairway may not provide enough light to illuminate the bottom landing, especially if the stairway changes direction. The light must be capable of illuminating treads and landings to at least 1 foot-candle.

NOTE: A foot-candle is a unit of light measurement approximating the amount of light you receive from a birthday cake candle when it is held 12 inches from your eyes. Photographer's light meters may be used to measure foot-candles.

You must locate a switch for interior stairway lights at the top and bottom of all interior stairs with at least six risers. Only one switch is required for interior stairs with fewer than six risers. Locate all stair switches so they can be used without climbing any steps.

Exterior Stairway Lighting + Switching

Codes for outdoor stairway lighting differ somewhat from interior requirements and recommendations. In exterior areas, you must locate a light fixture near the top landing for stairs providing access to doors above grade level. You must also locate a light fixture near the bottom landing for stairs providing access to doors below grade level. Locate the switch inside the dwelling for exterior stairs.

DEFINITIONS OF STAIRWAY TERMS

Landing: A landing is a flat surface at the top and bottom of a stairway, or it may also occur at points within a stairway. A landing must be at least as wide as the stairway and at least 36" deep.

Nosing: A tread nose (nosing) is the part of a horizontal stair surface that projects outward beyond a solid (closed) riser below.

Riser: A riser is the vertical part of a stair. A closed riser is created with solid material between adjacent treads. An open riser has no material (except for any required guards) between adjacent treads.

Stairway (flight of stairs): A series of risers and treads that is not interrupted by a landing, a flight of stairs includes the landings at the top and bottom of the flight. A stairway with only a top and bottom landing has one flight of stairs. A stairway with a landing in the middle has two flights of stairs.

Tread: A tread is the horizontal part of a stair. A tread is sometimes called the step.

Winder tread: A winder is a tread with one end wider than the other. Winders are often used to change a stairway's direction.

Stairway components include: tread, winder tread, nosing, riser, landing, flight of stairs.

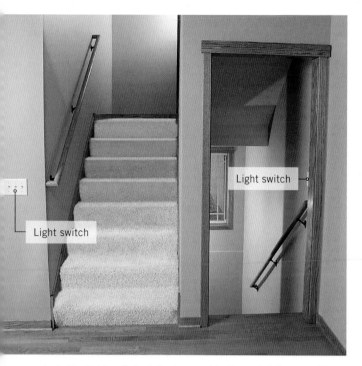

Light switch

Light switch

Install a light switch at the top and bottom of stairways with at least six risers.

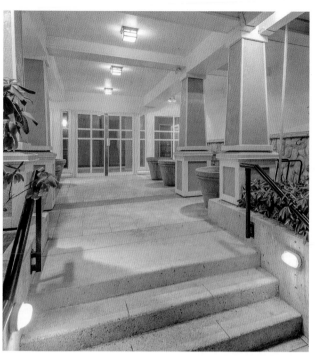

Install a light at the top landing of above-grade exterior stairs.

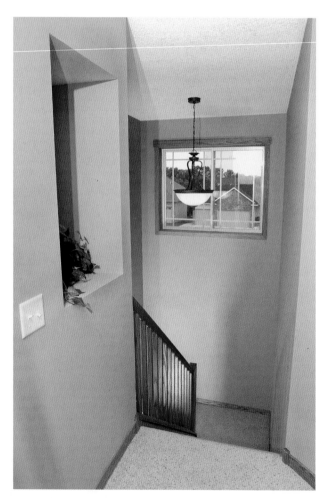

One light at a center landing may not be enough to illuminate the top and bottom landings.

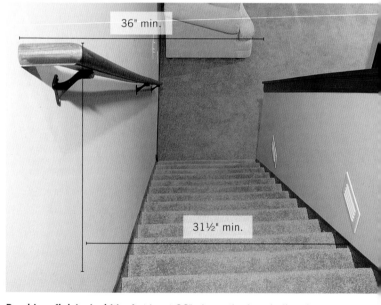

36" min.

31½" min.

Provide a finished width of at least 36" above the handrail and at least 31½" at and below one handrail.

Stairway Width

1. Provide a finished stairway width of at least 36 inches above handrail to the minimum headroom height.

2. Provide a finished stairway width of at least 31½ inches at and below the handrail for stairs with one handrail and at least 27 inches at and below both handrails for stairs with two handrails.

Riser Height

1. Provide a finished riser height of not more than 7¾ inches. Measure riser height vertically from leading edges of adjacent treads. The IRC does not mandate a minimum riser height.

2. Do not exceed ⅜-inch finished riser height difference between any two risers in a flight of stairs.

3. Do not allow open risers to fit a 4-inch-diameter sphere for passthrough. This includes interior stairs and exterior stairs, such as stairs for decks and balconies, but does not include spiral stairs.

4. Do not include the height of carpets, carpet pads, rugs, and runners when measuring riser height.

Maximum riser height is 7¾". Maximum difference between two risers in a flight of stairs is ⅜".

7¾" max.

Open risers have the potential to trap the head of a small child. Do not allow an open riser to pass a 4" diameter sphere. Install filler strips to reduce riser opening size, beginning with the fourth riser.

Filler strip

Nosing

10" min.

Provide a tread depth of at least 10" if treads have a nosing or at least 11" if treads have no nosing.

Tread Depth

1. Provide a finished tread depth of at least 10 inches. Measure tread depth horizontally from the leading edges of adjacent treads and at a right angle to the tread's leading edge.

2. Do not exceed ⅜-inch finished tread depth difference between any two treads in a flight of stairs. This does not apply to consistently shaped winder treads contained within the same flight of stairs.

Tread Nosing

1. Provide a finished tread nosing depth of at least ¾ inch and not more than 1¼ inches for stairs with solid risers. Add the nosing depth to the 10-inch minimum tread depth. Tread nosing is not required if treads are at least 11 inches deep.

2. Do not exceed ⅜-inch finished tread nosing depth difference between any two treads for all treads between two stories, including at floors and landings. Note that this differs from the tread and riser maximum difference. The tread and riser differences are for a flight of stairs, and the nosing depth difference is for all treads between two stories.

3. Do not exceed 9⁄16 inch for the curvature radius of a tread nosing, and do not exceed ½ inch for the bevel of a tread nosing.

Tread Slope

1. Slope treads and landings not more than 2 percent from horizontal in any direction.

2. Slope landings not more than 5 percent in the direction of travel if the landings are required to drain surface water.

Winder Stair Treads

1. Locate the winder tread walk line at 12 inches from the inside of where the winder tread turns. Measure the tread depth at the widest point along the walk line.

2. Provide a finished winder tread depth of at least 6 inches at any point on a winder tread within the finished width of the stairway and at least 10 inches at the walk line.

3. Do not exceed ⅜-inch finished tread depth difference between any two treads in a flight of stairs measured at the walk line.

4. Do not compare the depth of winder treads to the depth of rectangular treads in a flight of stairs if: (a) the winder treads all have a consistent shape, and (b) the winder treads comply with the winder tread depth requirements. Winder treads will not have the same depth as the rectangular treads, so the winder tread depth will not be within ⅜ inch of the rectangular tread depth.

Stairway Headroom Height

1. Provide a finished stairway headroom height of at least 80 inches measured vertically from a sloped plane connecting the tread nosing or from the

OK range ¾" to 1¼"

Provide a tread nosing depth of at least ¾" and not more than 1¼". Do not exceed 9⁄16" radius for a curved nosing or ½" depth for a beveled nosing.

The step up from landings should be not more than 7¾". Measure the step to the top of the threshold. Make landings at least as wide as the stairway and at least 36" deep.

finished floor of a landing. Projections from the ceiling are permitted above the minimum finished headroom height.

Stairway Landings

1. Provide a landing or floor at the top and bottom of most stairs.

2. You are not required to provide a landing or floor at the top of interior stairs, including stairs in an attached garage, unless a door swings over those stairs. This means you may terminate a flight of interior stairs directly into a door if the door swings away from the stairs.

3. Do not exceed 151 inches vertical rise of a flight of stairs without providing a landing or a floor. Example: do not install more than twenty 7⅜-inch-high risers without an intermediate landing.

4. Make rectangular and square landing widths at least as wide as the stairway. Example: if the stairway is 36 inches wide, build the landing at least 36 inches wide.

5. Make rectangular and square landings depth at least 36 inches, measured in the direction of travel.

6. You may make landings with shapes other than rectangular or square if: (a) the depth of the landing at walk line is at least as wide as the stairway and (b) the total area of the landing is at least as large as a ¼ circle with a radius equal to the required width of the landing. The walk line is 12 inches from the narrow side of the landing. The area of a circle is 3.14 multiplied by the circle's radius squared. Example: the minimum area of a curved landing serving a 36-inch-wide stairway is calculated $(36 \text{ in.}^2 \times 3.14) \times .25 = 1,017.9$ square inches.

Guards: Definition

A guard is a barrier that protects occupants from falling from a raised surface, such as a stairway, deck, or balcony. Guards are often call guardrails when the guard also serves as a handrail; however, guards need not be an open rail. A guard may be a partial height solid wall, a partial height wall containing safety glazing, or any other structure that complies with IRC requirements.

Handrails + Guards: Location

1. Provide a handrail on at least one side of every continuous flight of stairs with four or more risers.

2. Provide a guard at raised walking surfaces more than 30 inches above an adjacent interior or exterior surface. Areas that require guards include floors, porches, balconies, decks, hallways, screened enclosures, ramps, and the open sides of stairs with a total rise of more than 30 inches.

Height

1. Install the handrail at least 34 inches and not more than 38 inches above the treads measured vertically from a sloped plane connecting the tread nosing or from the finished floor of a ramp.

2. You may exceed the 38-inch maximum height where a handrail connects with a guard to provide a continuous structure. Example: a handrail connects to a guard at an intermediate stairway landing. The handrail height at the beginning and ending of the intermediate landing guard may exceed 38 inches high.

3. Provide guards at least 36 inches tall at raised surfaces other than the open sides of stairs.

4. Provide guards at least 34 inches high on the open sides of stairs. Measure the guards vertically from the nosing of the treads.

5. Limit the height of guards that are also handrails to not more than 38 inches. The IRC does not limit guard height other than for handrails.

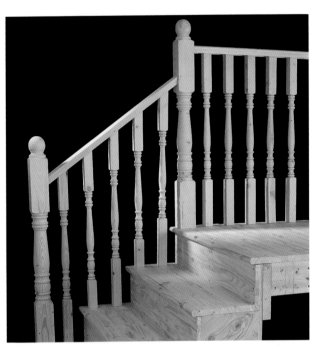

Install a handrail on stairways with at least four risers. Provide a continuous handrail beginning above the first riser and ending at or above the last riser.

34 to 38"

Install handrails at least 34" and not more than 38" above a sloped line connecting the stair treads.

The **maximum space** between guard vertical members is a 4"-diameter sphere. The maximum space for stairway guards is a 4⅜" diameter sphere.

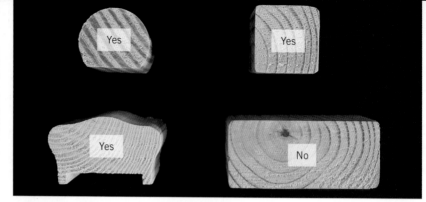

Install handrails that have the required gripping surface dimensions. Three of the above profiles will suffice. Handrails using 2 × 4 and larger lumber are too large to be grippable and thus do not meet the dimensions standard. Note that commonly available 2 × 2 lumber may satisfy the gripping surface requirement but may not satisfy the live-load requirement. These may break under the load.

Continuity

1. Run the handrail continuously from at least a point directly above the top riser of the flight of stairs to at least a point directly above the lowest riser of the flight.

2. Begin and end all handrails with a newel post, volute, starting easing, or starting newel.

3. Project handrails at least 1½ inches and not more than 4½ inches from any adjacent wall.

4. You may interrupt a handrail with a newel post at a turn.

5. Provide continuous guards for open sides of the entire flight of stairs, even if some of the flight is less than 30 inches above an adjacent surface.

6. You need not provide a guard if the entire flight of stairs is less than 30 inches above an adjacent surface. This applies even if a lower flight of stairs connects with an upper flight of stairs at a landing. Example: a landing occurs before the last three risers of a stairway. The last three risers are a separate flight of stairs and do not require a guard or a handrail.

Shape

1. Use material with an outside diameter of at least 1¼ inches and not more than 2 inches for Type 1 circular handrails.

2. Use material with a perimeter dimension of at least 4 inches and not more than 6¼ inches and a cross-section dimension of not more than 2¼ inches for Type 1 non-circular handrails.

3. Provide Type 2 handrails that have a perimeter dimension greater than 6¼ inches with a graspable finger recess on both sides of the profile.

4. Apply handrail shape requirements to interior and exterior stairways, including stairways for decks and balconies.

Openings

1. Do not allow openings in horizontal guards to pass a 4-inch-diameter sphere.

2. Do not allow stair guard openings, such as balusters, to pass a 4⅜-inch-diameter sphere.

3. Do not allow openings under stair guards formed by a riser, tread, and the guard's bottom rail to pass a 6-inch-diameter sphere.

Handrails + Guards Live Loads

1. Install a handrail that also serves as a guard so that it does not fail when a 200-pound load is applied in any direction at the top.

2. Install a guard that does not serve as a handrail so that it does not fail when a 200-pound load is applied at the top from above and from the horizontal direction away from the walking surface.

Emergency Escape Openings

An emergency escape and rescue opening, also called an egress opening, is required in bedrooms and in basements. Codes are very specific concerning the minimum dimensions of the openings and how they can be accessed, as well as the path from the opening to a public area. Rooms that are not intended for sleeping typically do not need to meet egress requirements. **You may use an operable window or a side-hinged or sliding door as the escape opening.**

The 2021 IRC provides several exceptions when dealing with replacement windows, when adding new rooms to an existing home, and when finishing basements. These exceptions make it easier to do remodeling. Verify interpretation and enforcement of these provisions with your local building official.

Egress windows allow emergency exit from a structure and must meet certain minimum size and accessibility codes. They are required primarily in bedrooms and basements.

Escape Opening Locations

1. Provide at least one escape opening in bedrooms, including bedrooms above, at, and below ground level.

2. Provide at least one escape opening in most basements and in habitable attics. You are not required to provide an escape opening in a basement or a storm shelter if: (a) the area is not more than 200 square feet and (b) the area is used only to house mechanical appliances.

3. Provide each basement bedroom with an escape opening. You are not required to provide other escape openings in basements in addition to the bedroom escape openings.

4. Open all escape openings onto an area that leads to a public way or onto a yard, court, or path that leads to a public way. The yard, court, or path must be at least 36 inches wide. This means that escape openings cannot open onto an enclosed courtyard or onto a similar area that does not lead without obstruction to an area that is accessible by the public.

5. You may open an escape opening under a deck or porch if: (a) the escape opening can be opened to the full required dimensions and (b) the space under the deck or porch is at least 36 inches high and 36 inches wide.

⚠ LOCKS + BARS ON OPENINGS

Do not cover or obstruct escape openings, area wells, and bulkhead doors with locks, bars, screens, or similar devices unless they can be operated from the inside without tools, keys, lock combinations, and special knowledge, and can be operated with the same force required to open the escape opening.

Escape Opening Size—New Openings

1. Provide escape openings with a clear opening area of at least 5.7 square feet. This includes escape openings above and below grade level. You may reduce an escape opening at grade level to at least 5.0 square feet.

2. Provide each escape opening with a clear opening at least 24 inches high and at least 20 inches wide.

3. Locate the bottom of each escape opening not more than 44 inches above the finished floor. Measure the sill height from the finished floor to the where the clear opening begins (the bottom of the opening).

4. Measure escape opening height and width using the clear opening area, which does not include obstructions, such as window frames.

5. Escape opening windows may have an opening size control device that complies with ASTM F2090 if the device is located not more than 70 inches above the floor. These devices usually keep the window from opening more than 4 inches unless the device is deactivated.

WINDOW ESCAPE OPENING AREA

≥ 5.7 SQ. FT. CLEAR OPENING

(≥ 5 SQ. FT. AT GRADE LEVEL)

≥ 24"

≥ 20"

≤ 44" OPENING HEIGHT

FINISHED FLOOR

To satisfy building codes for egress, a window must have a minimum opening of 5.7 sq. ft. through one sash, with at least 20" of clear width and 24" of clear height. Casement, double-hung, and sliding window styles may be used as long as their dimensions for width and height meet these minimum requirements.

NOTE: If the window opening is the minimum in both dimensions, it will be too small; at least one dimension must be more than minimum to meet the code requirement.

Escape Opening Size—Replacement Windows

1. You are not required to comply with the escape opening size rules for new openings when replacing an existing window if: (a) the replacement window is the largest standard size window that fits in the existing opening or frame; and (b) the replacement window provides a clear opening area at least as large as the existing window; and (c) there is no change of occupancy of the room where the replacement window is installed.

2. A change of occupancy means a change in how the room is used. For example, changing a room from a den to a bedroom is a change of occupancy.

Escape Openings—Change of Room Occupancy, Existing Windows

1. Provide an escape opening when a room has a change of occupancy, usually to a bedroom.

2. You may use the existing window in the room as the escape opening if: (a) the net clear open area is at least 4 square feet; (b) the net clear open height is at least 22 inches; and (c) the net clear open width is at least 20 inches.

3. You may install a replacement window in the existing window opening if: (a) the replacement window is the largest standard size window that fits in the existing opening or frame; and (b) the net clear open dimensions are at least as large as #2 above.

Escape Openings—New Additions to an Existing House

1. Provide at least one escape opening in new sleeping rooms and in new basements when building an addition to an existing house, unless an exception applies.

2. You are not required to install an additional escape opening in the new basement if the new basement contains a sleeping room with an escape opening.

3. You are not required to install an escape opening in the new basement if the existing basement has an escape opening that is accessible from the new basement.

4. You may install an escape opening that complies with the requirements for Change of Room Occupancy, Existing Windows.

Escape Openings—Remodeling an Existing Basement

1. Provide an escape opening in every new sleeping room when remodeling an existing basement.

2. You are not required to install an escape opening when remodeling an existing basement, unless a new sleeping room is added during the remodel.

Area Wells

1. Provide all below-grade escape windows and doors with an area well.

2. Provide each well with at least a 9-square-foot clear opening area and a depth and width of at least 36 inches in each direction.

3. The well area must allow the escape opening to fully open. The escape opening must not obstruct access to any ladder or steps. These situations might occur when using casement windows, or other windows and doors that open outward into the well area.

4. Install a permanent ladder or steps if the well bottom is more than 44 inches below grade.

5. You may install a permanent ladder with rungs that are at least 12 inches wide, project at least 3 inches from the well wall, are vertically spaced not more than 18 inches apart, and do not encroach more than 6 inches into the minimum well dimensions.

6. You may install permanent steps that are at least 12 inches wide, have treads that are at least 5 inches deep, and have risers that are vertically spaced not more than 18 inches.

Area wells must be at least 36" wide and project 36" from the foundation. Those deeper than 44" must have a means of escape, such as an attached ladder or a tiered design that forms steps. Drainage at the bottom of the well should be connected to the foundation drain or to another approved drainage system.

Egress Doors

The egress door opens to the outside and meets all egress door requirements for accessibility and opening size. Every dwelling must have at least one egress door. The egress door is usually the front door. Other exterior doors need not comply with the egress door requirements.

Egress Door Requirements

1. Provide at least one egress door that: (a) is accessible from all areas of the home and (b) allows people to go directly outside without traveling through the garage.

2. Install a side-hinged egress door that provides a clear opening at least 32 inches wide and 78 inches high. Measure door width between the face of the door when open to 90 degrees and the outer edge of the door stop. Measure door height between the top of the threshold and the bottom of the stop. This means that a 36-inch by 80-inch door is required when using standard-size doors.

3. Provide a landing on the interior and exterior sides of the door. Build each landing at least as wide as the door. Example: if the door is 36 inches wide, then build each landing at least 36 inches wide. Build each landing at least 36 inches deep, measured in the direction of travel.

4. Build the interior and exterior landings not more than 1½ inches below the top of the threshold.

5. You may build the exterior landing not more than 7¾ inches below the top of the threshold, if the egress door does not swing over the landing. You may build the exterior landing with not more than a 5 percent slope away from the door. You may have a storm door or a screen door swing over any landing.

6. Provide a ramp or a stairway to any egress door that is not at grade level.

Build a landing at least 36" deep on both sides of the egress door. You may build the exterior landing not more than 7¾" below the top of the threshold.

EGRESS DOOR LOCK

Do not install a double cylinder dead bolt lock or any other lock or device that requires use of a key, tool, or any special knowledge or effort to open the egress door. This includes screen and security doors.

VIOLATION! Use only thumb-latch deadbolts on egress doors.

Exterior Doors

A landing area is required on both sides of exterior doors.

Exterior Door Landing Requirements

1. Provide a landing on the interior and exterior sides of exterior doors.

2. Build each landing at least as wide as the door served. Example: if the door is 36 inches wide, then build each landing at least 36 inches wide.

3. Build each landing at least 36 inches deep, measured in the direction of travel.

4. Build each landing not more than 1½ inches below the top of the threshold.

SITE ADDRESS

Install approved building address numbers or letters that are clearly legible from the road fronting the property. This is so emergency responders can quickly locate the property. Make the letters and/or numbers Arabic type that are at least 4" tall and at least ½" wide. Make the letters or numbers contrast with the background.

5. You may build the exterior landing with not more than a 5 percent slope away from the door.

6. You are not required to build a landing on the exterior side of a door if: (a) a stairway of not more than two risers is on the exterior side and (b) the exterior door does not swing over the stairway.

7. You may build an exterior landing not more than 7¾ inches below the top of the door threshold if the exterior door does not swing over the landing.

8. Provide a ramp or a stairway to any exterior door that is not at grade level.

9. You may have a storm door or a screen door swing over any stairway and landing serving as a door into the house.

10. You are not required to build a landing on the exterior side of a door that opens to a narrow, above-grade balcony or similar structure.

Door + Window Hazards

You may have seen pictures of people severely cut when they fell or were pushed through doors and windows containing regular glass. Regular glass usually breaks into large pieces that can cause severe injury. Safety glass shatters into very small pieces that are less likely to cause severe cuts.

General codes designate several locations as hazardous, where people could fall or be pushed through glass. These locations are mostly near doors, near water, and near stairs. A large window where the sill is close to the floor is also a hazardous location.

Safety glazing usually means tempered glass; however, other materials also qualify. This is why it is called safety glazing, not safety glass. Most safety glazing should be identified with permanent writing in one corner of the glazing. This writing can be very difficult to see, so look closely before deciding that glazing is not safety glazing.

Another window hazard involves children falling from windows where the sill is close to the floor. Recent general codes require a mechanism that prevents a child from opening these windows enough so that they can climb through them and fall.

Safety glazing and fall hazard rules are complicated and have many exceptions. Our objective here is to introduce the subject and point out some hazardous locations that you might encounter if you remodel or add to your home.

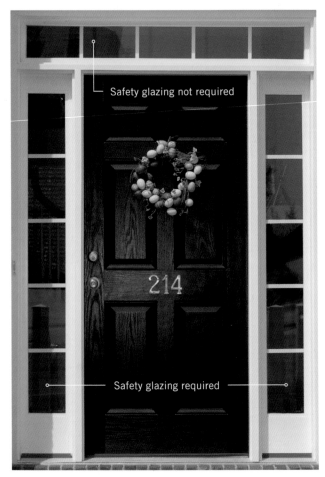

Laminated glass is one type of safety glazing that has a clear membrane in the center layer to keep the shattered glass more or less in place when it breaks. Tempered glass is another common type of safety glazing.

Safety glazing not required

Safety glazing required

The sidelights on both sides of the door should contain safety glazing. Safety glazing is not required in the transom above the door.

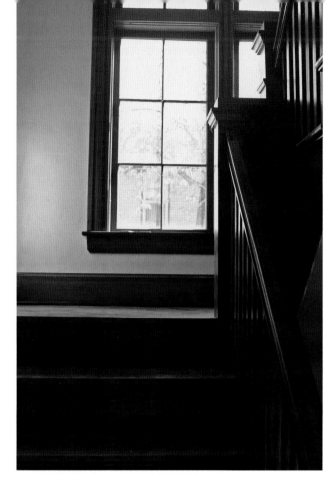

Windows along stairways and at landings should contain safety glazing if the bottom edge of the glazing is less than 36" above the stair walking surface.

Safety Glazing In + Near Doors

1. Use safety glazing in doors, including swinging and sliding doors, outside doors, and interior doors such as French doors. Exceptions include decorative glazing, such as stained glass, and glazing in very small openings in the door.

2. Use safety glazing in windows that are within 24 inches on either side of a door. Exceptions include decorative glazing and windows when the bottom edge of the glazing is located 60 inches or more above the walking surface.

Safety Glazing Near Stairs + In Guards

1. Use safety glazing in guards, including guards at decks, balconies, raised walkways, and similar locations.

2. Use safety glazing in stairway handrail guards.

3. Use safety glazing in windows within stairways when the bottom edge of the glazing is less than 36 inches above the adjacent walking surface. Exceptions include if a handrail is between the

Windows above bathtubs and showers should contain safety glazing unless the bottom of the glazing is located 60" or more above the tub or shower floor.

stairs and the window and if the window is 36 inches or more away from the nearest part of the stairs.

4. Use safety glazing in windows within 60 inches of the last tread at the bottom of a stairway when the bottom of the glazing is less than 36 inches above the adjacent walking surface.

Safety Glazing Near Wet Surfaces

1. Use safety glazing in bathtub and shower doors and enclosures.

2. Use safety glazing in walls, enclosures, and fences that are less than 60 inches horizontally from the edge of bathtubs, showers, swimming pools, whirlpool tubs, hot tubs, saunas, and steam rooms. Exceptions include windows when the bottom edge of the glazing is located 60 inches or more above the walking surface and windows that do not face the bathtub, etc.

Window Fall Protection

1. Install a means to restrict the distance that an operable window can open so that a 4-inch-diameter sphere cannot pass when: (a) the top of the window sill is less than 24 inches above the finished floor and (b) the top of the window sill is more than 72 inches above the exterior surface below.

2. You may comply with this provision by permanently restricting the window opening distance, except where the window serves as an emergency escape and rescue opening.

3. You may comply with this provision by installing a window opening control device that complies with ASTM F2090.

Ventilation + Exhaust

Controlling moisture levels in a home is important for your comfort and health, as well as for the health of your home. Although inadequate moisture levels can cause discomfort for some people and can cause furnishings and some construction materials to become brittle, it is not usually a significant risk to you or to your home, so the IRC has no provisions governing minimum moisture and humidity levels. Too much moisture, however, can be a significant risk to you and your home, so the IRC has several provisions governing the removal of excess moisture. Current indoor air quality best practices also encourage removal of excess moisture and other contaminants from the home.

The greatest threat posed by water vapor is that it provides one of the three things that mold needs to grow. The other two are the correct temperature and food. Mold grows at the same temperatures we humans prefer, so there is little we can do about that. Because mold eats almost any wood-based product and our homes are filled with these products, there is little we can do about the food risk. The one thing we can do something about is moisture.

Water vapor travels in the air. When water vapor condenses on visible surfaces, it provides the moisture that mold needs. We then see what is often called mildew. Mildew is another name for mold. When water vapor travels into attics and wall cavities, it can condense and provide moisture for mold. Mold can grow in these hidden spaces for long periods before it is discovered. Damage to your home and health can be significant when mold grows for long periods of time.

Water vapor is always present in every home. Some water vapor occurs naturally in the air. We introduce some water vapor into the home with every breath we take. Much of the water vapor in a home results from activities such as bathing, cooking, and clothes drying. The IRC has provisions that help remove the excess water vapor caused by these activities.

Mechanical Ventilation

First, the good news: New homes (including new additions to existing homes) are required to be tightly sealed against air leakage. This makes newer homes much more energy efficient compared to older homes. Air sealing can have a greater impact on energy efficiency than insulation.

Now, the bad news: Tight air sealing restricts the air changes between the home and the outdoors. This can cause the air inside the home to become unhealthy. This can also create air quality problems when combustion equipment, such as furnaces, water heaters, and fireplaces, are operating.

Energy codes may require providing tightly sealed homes with mechanical ventilation to maintain a healthy amount of fresh air inside the home. Mechanical ventilation methods vary from an air duct between the outdoors and a forced-air heating/cooling return plenum to energy recovery or heat recovery ventilation systems.

Design and installation of mechanical ventilation systems is far beyond the scope of this book. The point of this discussion is to make you aware of these systems so you can look for them and conduct additional research if you are interested.

Note also that mechanical ventilation may be necessary if you air-seal an older home. This is especially important if combustion equipment is present. Air sealing an older home should include a blower door test and a combustion safety test that is performed by a qualified professional.

Air outlet

Air intake (ventilation fan)

Moisture exhaust requirements generally are met with a combination of natural (windows and doors) and mechanical (ventilation fans) solutions. The bathroom and kitchen are the two rooms where ventilation is most critical.

Air Movement Requirements

1. Provide outdoor light and ventilation to bathrooms, toilet rooms, and similar areas using windows or doors containing glazing. Provide a total glazing area of at least 3 square feet with at least 1½ square feet operable. Open the glazing directly onto a street, public alley, or onto a yard or court located on the same lot. Best practice is to equip every bathroom with a ventilation fan.

2. You may replace the glazing with artificial light and exhaust ventilation. Provide exhaust ventilation of at least 20 cubic feet per minute (cfm) continuous ventilation or at least 50 cfm for a switched ventilation fan.

3. Comply with the ventilation fan manufacturer's instructions or general codes about exhaust duct type and length. Three-inch diameter duct may not be allowed as an exhaust duct. Four-inch diameter or larger duct may be required.

4. Discharge bathroom and toilet room ventilation fan exhaust directly outdoors. Discharging a ventilation fan exhaust duct into or toward an attic, soffit, or crawl space ventilation opening does not comply with this provision.

5. Terminate exhaust fans at least: (a) 3 feet from property lines, gravity air intake openings, operable windows and doors; (b) 10 feet horizontally or 3 feet above mechanical air intake openings (such as for a heat recovery ventilation unit).

6. Do not recirculate air from bathrooms within a residence or into another residence.

7. Provide an automatic or gravity-operated damper for exhaust systems that will close the damper when the system is not operating.

8. Do not direct outdoor exhaust openings, such as from bathroom and kitchen exhaust fans, onto a walkway.

9. Protect outdoor air intake and exhaust openings with a corrosion-resistant screen having openings at least ¼ and not more than ½ inch or by louvers, dampers, or similar means. This does not include clothes dryer exhaust openings. Do not cover clothes dryer exhaust openings with a screen.

10. Protect outdoor openings against local weather conditions, such as rain and snow infiltration and blockage by snow accumulation.

EXHAUST FAN LABELS

HVI
70 C.F.M.
AT .10 WG
4.0
C-K3285 SONES

Check the information label attached to each exhaust fan. Bathroom fans that are switch-operated should be rated at least 50 cfm. Baths over 100 sq. ft., or multiple tubs or showers, should have higher-capacity fans. The sone rating refers to the relative quietness of the unit, rated on a scale of 1 to 7. (Quieter fans have lower sone ratings.)

Terminate exhaust ducts directly outdoors with a cover that protects against weather and pest infiltration.

VIOLATION! Do not terminate exhausts into attic or crawl space areas.

Kitchen Exhaust Requirements

General Installation Requirements

1. You are not required to install either a recirculating or an externally ducted kitchen exhaust hood; however, externally ducted kitchen exhaust hoods are recommended. Verify kitchen exhaust hood requirements with the local building official, because interpretation of kitchen exhaust hood requirements can vary among jurisdictions.

2. Terminate a kitchen exhaust hood duct, if any, to the outdoors when natural or mechanical ventilation is not provided in the kitchen area. Natural ventilation usually means an operable window in the kitchen area. Mechanical ventilation may be provided by a ducted central heating system that is connected to a ventilation opening terminating outdoors. Mechanical ventilation may be provided by a heat recovery or energy recovery ventilation system. Most homes have either natural or mechanical ventilation in the kitchen area, so external discharge of range hoods is rarely required.

3. You may, but are not required to, install a recirculating kitchen hood if the kitchen is provided with natural or mechanical ventilation.

4. Provide a backdraft damper at the duct termination or other approved location. Many kitchen hoods and cabinet-mounted microwave ovens have backdraft dampers integrated into the appliances.

Aboveground Exhaust Duct Construction

1. Discharge the kitchen exhaust fan to the outdoors using a duct. Do not discharge the fan through a framed cavity.

2. Use galvanized steel, stainless steel, or copper to construct kitchen exhaust ducts.

3. Seal the exhaust duct air tight to avoid leaking flammable grease into wall or floor cavities or between the kitchen exhaust hood and the kitchen cabinet.

Use galvanized metal or other approved ductwork for range hood ducts, and be sure to seal the joints very well so the airborne grease doesn't escape into walls and cabinets, where it poses a fire hazard.

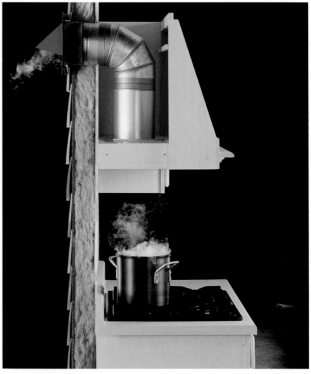

Externally exhausted range hoods are not required by codes except in very rare situations. Typical cabinet-mounted models, such as the one seen here, are quite popular, however, and are recommended whenever practical.

Exhaust Duct Termination

1. Terminate kitchen exhaust hood ducts outside the building. This does not include attics and crawl spaces.

2. Provide a backdraft damper at the duct termination or other approved location. Many kitchen exhaust hoods and cabinet-mounted microwave ovens have backdraft dampers integrated into the equipment.

Kitchen Exhaust Fan Rates

1. Provide an exhaust rate of at least 100 cfm for intermittently operated exhaust hoods or at least 20 cfm for continuously operating exhaust hoods.

2. Provide makeup air for exhaust fans with a capacity of more than 400 cfm. Install a gravity operated or an electrically operated damper to open and close the takeup air duct.

Replacing a Range Hood with a Microwave Oven

This is a popular upgrade that is often installed incorrectly. Failure to read and follow manufacturer's instructions can be a fire hazard and a burn hazard. It can also reduce the microwave's service life. The following address some of the most frequent installation errors.

1. Leave enough space between the microwave and the range top. A typical instruction is to have at least 66 inches between the floor and the top of the microwave, at least 30 inches between the range top and the bottom of the cabinet, and at least 2 inches between the bottom of the microwave and the range control panel.

2. Connect the microwave to a dedicated 120-volt circuit. Most microwaves should be served by a 20-amp circuit.

3. Plug a microwave that comes with an attachment plug into a receptacle. Do not connect the microwave directly to the electrical wires, and do not use an extension cord.

4. Use the size and type of exhaust duct material and termination fittings specified by the microwave manufacturer. Do not exceed the exhaust duct effective length specified by the manufacturer.

Effective length adds for the losses created by elbows and termination fittings.

5. Connect the microwave to the exhaust duct. Do not simply blow the exhaust at the hole in the cabinet where the exhaust duct is located.

6. Install the backdraft damper if one is supplied with the microwave.

Downdraft ventilation is a space-saving alternative to exhaust hoods, often used on kitchen islands with built-in cooktops. It is less efficient but will mitigate some of the cooking vapors and airborne particulate matter.

Many manufacturers recommend at least 66" between the floor and the top of the microwave.

Clothes Dryer Exhaust Requirements

General Installation Requirements

1. Construct, install, and terminate clothes dryer exhaust ducts according to the clothes dryer manufacturer's installation instructions. If the clothes dryer manufacturer is not known during construction, use general requirements.

2. Do not connect clothes dryer exhaust ducts to any other system, such as bathroom exhaust fan ducts, plumbing vents, or fuel-burning equipment vents and flues.

3. Do not install clothes dryer exhaust ducts in or through any fireblocking-, draftstopping-, or fire-resistance-rated assembly, unless the duct is constructed and installed to maintain the code that requires fireblocking or draftstopping.

4. Do not run clothes dryer exhaust ducts into or through other ducts or plenums. Example: do not run a clothes dryer exhaust duct into or through an HVAC supply or return duct or into or through a combustion air duct.

5. Install the clothes dryer exhaust duct during construction if space for a clothes dryer is provided.

6. You may not install a dryer duct booster fan to extend the dryer exhaust duct's length.

Duct Construction

1. Use a 4-inch-diameter, smooth wall metal duct that is at least 28 gauge, unless the clothes dryer manufacturer's instructions allow another diameter.

Use strap hangers to support rigid ducts. Install hangers at joints at intervals not exceeding 12'.

2. Install duct joints so that the inside part of the joint fits into the outside part of the joint in the direction of the air flow.

3. Fasten duct joints with mechanical fasteners, such as screws or pop rivets. Do not use screws or other fasteners that penetrate the duct more than ⅛ inch. Longer fasteners could trap lint.

4. Seal the duct joints with metal tape or mastic.

5. Support the duct at least every 12 feet. Joints and elbows are vulnerable areas for separation.

6. Protect the duct with at least 16-gauge shield plates if the duct is within 1¼ inches from the edge of a framing member. Extend the shield plate at least 2 inches above sole plates and below top plates. Protect the duct with shield plates at any other location where it is likely to be penetrated by fasteners.

Duct Length

1. Do not exceed 35 feet developed length between the beginning of the clothes dryer duct and the duct termination, unless the clothes dryer manufacturer's installation instructions allow a longer length. Developed length means the straight line length of the duct, reduced by bends in the duct. The clothes dryer manufacturer is rarely known during construction, so the manufacturer's installation instruction exception rarely applies.

Transition duct

35' max.

Limit clothes dryer exhaust duct developed length to not more than 35'.

2. Add 2½ feet for every 45-degree bend and 5 feet for every 90-degree bend to the dryer duct's developed length. You may use the manufacturer-provided developed length for smooth radius bends. You may use the IRC table for smooth radius bend developed length if the manufacturer's instructions are not available.

3. Do not include the transition duct in the dryer duct developed length.

4. Locate a permanent label within 6 feet of the clothes dryer exhaust duct connection that shows the exhaust duct's developed length. This requirement applies only when the duct developed length is more than 35 feet.

Duct Termination

1. Terminate clothes dryer exhaust ducts outside the building. Outside the building does not include attics or crawl spaces.

2. Locate the clothes dryer exhaust duct termination at least 3 feet from: (a) the property line and (b) operable and non-operable openings. Operable openings include windows and doors. Non-operable openings include eave ventilation openings and combustion air openings. This provision does not apply if the clothes dryer manufacturer's installation instructions allow other locations. The clothes dryer manufacturer is rarely known during construction, so the manufacturer's installation instruction exception rarely applies.

3. Provide a backdraft damper at the duct termination or at another approved location.

4. Do not install a screen at the exhaust duct termination. A screen will trap lint.

5. Make the open area of the exhaust duct termination at least 12.5 square inches.

Transition Duct

1. The transition duct is the duct (usually flexible duct) between the dryer and the start of the smooth wall dryer exhaust duct.

2. Limit the transition duct length to 8 feet.

3. Use only one piece of transition duct. Do not splice together two or more lengths of transition duct material.

4. Do not run the transition duct through walls or in concealed spaces.

Clothes Dryer Makeup Air

1. Provide makeup air for clothes dryers that exhaust more than 200 cubic feet per minute. General codes do not specify how to provide makeup air or specify that the makeup air come from outdoors.

2. Provide a net free opening of at least 100 square inches when clothes dryers are installed in closets or provide makeup air by other approved means.

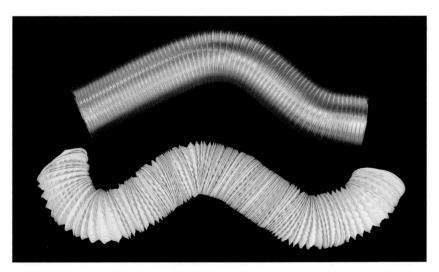

Use and install transition ducts according to the clothes dryer's instructions. Replace plastic transition ducts (bottom) with flexible metal transition ducts (top).

Cut the transition duct to the shortest length possible. Eliminate bends and kinks that will reduce air flow.

Smoke Alarms + Carbon Monoxide Alarms

Smoke alarms and carbon monoxide (CO) alarms have been required in houses for many years. Combination smoke and CO alarms are not preferred, because the service life of the different alarms are different, meaning that one alarm could fail before the other.

You should replace old smoke alarms and carbon monoxide alarms. Smoke alarms have a useful life of about 10 years. Carbon monoxide alarms have a useful life of about 7 years. Install carbon monoxide alarms near all bedrooms and inside bedrooms with a fuel-burning appliance, such as a gas fireplace.

Smoke alarms and carbon monoxide (CO) alarms have been required in houses for many years. Carbon monoxide alarms (A) are triggered by the presence of carbon monoxide gas. Smoke alarms are available in photoelectric and ionization models. In ionization alarms (B), a small amount of current flows in an ionization chamber. When smoke enters the chamber, it interrupts the current, triggering the alarm. Photoelectric alarms (C) rely on a beam of light, which when interrupted by smoke triggers an alarm. Heat alarms (D) sound an alarm when they detect areas of high heat in the room. Also available are combination smoke/CO alarms and ionization/photoelectric smoke alarms. The combination ionization/photoelectric alarms are recommended, because they detect smoke from different types of fires.

Install smoke alarms in and near all bedrooms and on all levels of a home.

Smoke Alarm + CO Alarm Required Locations

1. Locate a smoke alarm: (a) in every bedroom; (b) outside all bedroom areas in the immediate vicinity (usually about 10 feet) of all bedrooms; (c) on every level in the home, including basements; and (d) within 3 feet horizontally from the door of a bathroom containing a tub or a shower.

2. Locate a smoke alarm in a hallway and in a room that is open to a hallway if the height of the ceiling in the room exceeds the ceiling height of the hallway by 24 inches or more. These smoke alarms are required only if the hallway serves a bedroom.

3. Do not install an ionization smoke alarm closer than 20 feet horizontally from a permanently installed cooking appliance. Do not install a photoelectric smoke alarm closer than 6 feet horizontally from a permanently installed cooking appliance. Do not install a smoke alarm that is labeled "Helps Reduce Nuisance Cooking Alarms" (including similar wording) closer than 6 feet horizontally from a permanently installed cooking appliance.

4. You may substitute a security system that includes smoke alarms if it provides the same protection as hard-wired smoke alarms. The security system smoke alarms must: (a) comply with the National Fire Protection Association (NFPA) 72 standard and (b) must be a permanent fixture in the home. Security system smoke alarms installed as a substitute system cannot be leased. They must be a permanent part of the home.

5. You are not required to locate smoke alarms: (a) in crawl spaces and in uninhabitable attics, and (b) on the middle level of split-level homes if smoke alarms are installed on the upper level, if the middle level is less than one story below upper level, and if there is no door between levels. Note that some jurisdictions require smoke alarms on all levels of a split-level home.

Smoke Alarm Power Source

1. Install smoke alarms that take primary power from the building electrical wiring and that have a battery backup.

2. Connect all smoke alarms together so one alarm activates all alarms (interconnection). Physical interconnection is not required if the alarms are listed for wireless interconnection.

Do not locate a smoke alarm closer than 4" to the intersection of a wall and ceiling. The smoke alarm may not detect smoke in this dead air zone.

3. Provide arc-fault circuit-interrupter protection for the smoke alarm primary power.

Smoke Alarm Installation

1. Install smoke alarms according to manufacturer's instructions. This often includes locating the smoke alarm on the ceiling or on a wall not more than 12 inches from the ceiling. Do not locate a smoke alarm closer than 4 inches to the intersection of a wall and ceiling. The smoke alarm may not detect smoke in this dead air zone.

Smoke Alarm + CO Alarm Updates When Remodeling

1. Update the entire smoke alarm and carbon monoxide alarm system to current code requirements (including alarm interconnection and hard-wiring) when building alterations, repairs, or additions require a permit. This update requirement does not apply to: (a) exterior work such as roofing, siding, window, and door repair and replacement, (b) installation of or repairs to plumbing and HVAC systems.

Carbon Monoxide Alarm Requirements

1. Install carbon monoxide alarms in homes equipped with fuel-fired appliances, such as gas and oil-fired furnaces, and in homes with an attached garage or a fireplace. The alarms must comply with UL2034.

2. Install an alarm outside of bedroom areas in the immediate vicinity (usually about 10 feet) of all bedrooms.

3. Connect all carbon monoxide alarms together so one alarm activates all alarms (interconnection). Physical interconnection is not required if the alarms are listed for wireless interconnection.

4. Install carbon monoxide alarms in a bedroom if a fuel-fired appliance is located in the bedroom or in an attached bathroom.

Structural Components

A safe and healthy building begins with a solidly built structure. The building's foundation should rest on stable soil and should be strong enough to support the home during normal conditions as well as during disasters, such as hurricanes and earthquakes. The building's floors, walls, and roof should be secured to the foundation and to each other and should be strong enough to support the home during extreme conditions.

This chapter will help you understand basic structural requirements for building as defined by the building codes. The intent is to help you identify work that may violate building codes so that you can bring it to the attention of a contractor or other qualified professional. Except for projects such as simple decks and storage sheds, you should seek guidance from qualified professionals before using the information in this chapter to design you own buildings or to perform structural remodeling on existing buildings.

In this chapter:
- Foundations
- Crawl Spaces
- Decks
- Floor Systems
- Wall Systems
- Wall Penetration Flashing
- Roof Systems

Special Requirements for High Wind + Seismic Risk Areas

Seismic Design Areas

1. Provide increased strength and structural integrity for foundations, walls, roofs, gas pipes and appliances, and other components in seismic design areas. Refer to the IRC and consult a qualified engineer or other qualified professional when building in seismic design areas.

Hurricane ties. If building codes in your area require them, nail metal hurricane ties to the wall top plates before installing the rafters.

2. Verify the seismic design category with the local building official. The following may be in seismic design areas: large parts of Alaska, California, Hawaii, Nevada, Oregon, and Washington State; small parts of Arizona, Colorado, Idaho, Montana, New Mexico, New York, and Utah; the area near Memphis, Tennessee, and the area near Charleston, South Carolina.

High Wind Design Areas

1. Provide increased strength and structural integrity for foundations, walls, roofs, windows, and other components in high wind design areas. Refer to the IRC and consult a qualified engineer or other qualified professional when building in high wind design areas.

2. Verify the wind design category with the local building official. The following may be in high wind design areas: much of Florida and Hawaii; the areas within about 100 miles of the coastlines of Alabama, Alaska, Georgia, Louisiana, Mississippi, North and South Carolina, Texas, and Virginia; the areas within about 50 miles of the coastlines of Connecticut, Delaware, Maine, Maryland, Massachusetts, New Hampshire, New Jersey, and New York. Several "Special Wind Areas" exist in scattered areas of the country. These areas are mostly in mountainous areas and in the West.

Deflection of Structural Components

Most readers should not deal with bending of structural components, such as floors, walls, ceilings, and roofs. Leave this to qualified engineers and contractors. Because "spongy" floors and rattling walls are common complaints, this section explains some basic concepts involved in deflection and helps you understand when deflection may be excessive.

Deflection + Loads: Definitions

Deflection is when a component of a building bends under a load. It can be a single component, such as a floor joist, or it can be a system, such as a floor or a wall. Deflection causes a component to compress on one side (compression) and expand on the other side (tension).

A load is a force (weight) placed on a component of a building. Example: a building's foundation carries the load of the entire building. The dead load is the weight of the construction materials, such as drywall, shingles, siding, and floor coverings, and the weight of fixed equipment, such as a water heater. The live load is the weight of people and furnishings that occupy a building. A point load is a load in a small area. The heel of a high-heel shoe is an example of a point load. Environmental loads include wind, snow, and forces created during earthquakes.

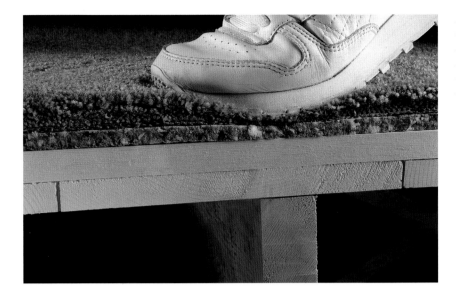

A point load is a type of live load that is concentrated in a small area, such as a footstep. Point loads are temporary, and in many cases they can exceed the deflection minimums without causing any particular problems.

Deflection Under Live Load

1. Install structural components, such as joists, studs, and rafters, so that they will not bend more than the amount shown in Table 1 under an evenly distributed live load. L is the unsupported length of the component in inches. H is the unsupported height of the component in inches. Example: for a bedroom floor, the general codes assume that a live load of at least 30 pounds of people, floor coverings, and furnishings will be placed over each square foot of the floor area. Example: the maximum deflection of bedroom floor joists with the length between supports of 180 inches would be $^{180}/_{360}$, or ½ inch.

TABLE 1: DEFLECTION UNDER LIVE LOAD

STRUCTURAL COMPONENT	MAXIMUM DEFLECTION (INCHES)
Rafters with greater than 3/12 slope + no attached ceiling finish	L/180
Interior walls	H/180
Floors + plastered ceilings	L/360
Exterior walls with plaster or stucco finish	H/360
Other structural members	L/240
Ceilings with flexible finishes, such as drywall	L/240
Exterior walls with flexible finishes, such as vinyl or fiber cement siding + drywall inside	H/180

DEFLECTION DISCUSSION

Walking on a floor or slamming a door hard does not generate the live load assumed in deflection tables. In fact, the load created by walking on a floor or slamming a door may be greater than the design live load at the point where the load is applied. Thus, even a floor that feels "spongy" or a wall that shakes often may not exceed the maximum deflection allowed. If a "spongy" floor or a shaky wall is not causing other problems, such as cracking drywall or plaster, then it is probably not exceeding the maximum allowed deflection and should be of little concern.

Note that the maximum deflection allowed by general codes does not apply to some rigid floor coverings, such as tile. Refer to the manufacturer's design and installation instructions when installing stiff finish materials. The manufacturer may stipulate a maximum deflection that's below the amount allowed by codes.

Foundations

Soil Load-Bearing Capacities

1. Place structural footings on undisturbed soil of known bearing capacity or on a bed of fill material approved by an engineer.

2. Have a geotechnical engineer evaluate the soil in areas known to have expansive or other unfavorable soils or if the soil-bearing capacity is unknown. Beware of clay soils. Some clay soils are unstable and can cause serious foundation problems.

3. Use the following table to estimate soil-bearing capacity if the soil type is known and if the local building official approves.

TABLE 2: SOIL LOAD-BEARING CAPACITIES

SOIL TYPE	PRESUMED SOIL BEARING CAPACITY
Bedrock (e.g., granite)	12,000 psi
Sedimentary-type rock	4,000 psi
Gravel + sandy gravel	3,000 psi
Sand, silty sand, clayey sand, silty gravel, clayey gravel	2,000 psi
Clay, sandy clay, silty clay, clayey silt, silt, sandy silt	1,500 psi

Common Soil Types

Gravel and sandy gravel soils have a presumed 3,000 psi load-bearing capacity.

Sandy soils have a presumed 2,000 psi load-bearing capacity.

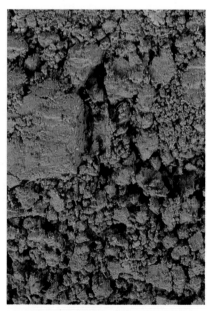

Clay and silt soils have a presumed 1,500 psi load-bearing capacity.

Footing Width + Depth

Footing Width

1. Use the tables in general codes to determine the minimum footing width and depth required to support load-bearing walls. You may also use material found in The American Concrete Institute document ACI 332 (see Resources, page 234).

2. Refer to general codes for special footing and footing reinforcement requirements in seismic design areas.

Footing Thickness + Slope

1. Make spread footings at least 6 inches thick.

2. Project spread footings at least 2 inches beyond the foundation wall. Do not project the footing beyond the foundation wall more than the thickness of the footing. Example: if the footing is 6 inches thick, then the edge of the footing should be not more than 6 inches beyond the edge of the foundation wall.

3. Locate the bottom of footings at least 12 inches below finish grade or below the local frost line, whichever is deeper. This does not apply to accessory buildings with an area 600 square feet or less and an eave height of 10 feet or less, and this does not apply to decks not supported by the home.

4. Do not place footings on frozen ground unless the frozen condition is permanent (permafrost).

5. Make the top surface of footings level.

6. You may slope the bottom of footings not more than 10 percent, without reducing the minimum thickness.

7. Make step footing thickness at least 6 inches. Make step footing height not more than the length of the footing above the step.

Leveling footing forms is very important. Measure footing depth and width at the top of the forms. Here, batterboards and strings are used to level footing forms.

Spread footing for basement or crawl space (A), interior load-bearing wall footing (B), or step footing (C).

Specifications for Foundation Concrete

Concrete in Basement Slabs + Interior Slabs-on-Grade (Not Garage Floors)

1. Use at least 2,500 psi concrete in all weathering potential environments.

2. Use air-entrained concrete (between 5 and 7 percent total air content) in severe weathering potential environments if the concrete may be subject to freezing and thawing during construction.

Concrete in Foundation Walls, Exterior Walls + Other Vertical Concrete Exposed to Weather

1. Use at least 2,500 psi concrete in environments with negligible weathering potential.

2. Use at least 3,000 psi air-entrained concrete (between 5 and 7 percent total air content) in moderate and severe weathering potential environments.

Concrete in Porches, Garage + Carport Floors + Other Horizontal Concrete Exposed to Weather

1. Use at least 2,500 psi concrete in environments with negligible weathering potential.

2. Use at least 3,000 psi air-entrained concrete (between 5 and 7 percent total air content) in moderate weathering potential environments.

3. Use at least 3,500 psi air-entrained concrete (between 5 and 7 percent total air content) in severe weathering potential environments.

4. You may use at least 4,000 psi air-entrained concrete with at least 3 percent total air content in steel-troweled garage floors in moderate and severe weathering potential environments.

Confirm with the concrete provider that the product you've ordered meets specs for your area, and be sure to have your forms inspected and approved well in advance of the delivery.

Foundation Anchors

1. Install at least ½-inch-diameter bolts in exterior footings, stem walls, basement walls, interior braced walls, monolithic slabs, and other places to which sill or sole plates for load-bearing and braced walls will be attached.

2. Install and tighten a nut and washer on each bolt. Verify washer size with your local building official.

3. Locate the bolts at least seven bolt diameters and not more than 12 inches from the ends of each plate and not more than every 6 feet on center in between.

4. Locate bolts in the middle third of the plate.

5. Install at least two bolts per plate section.

6. Embed the bolts at least 7 inches into the foundation.

7. Use approved fasteners to anchor the sole plates of interior load-bearing walls that are not braced walls.

8. You may substitute anchor straps for bolts if they provide equal anchorage. Place straps in the same locations as bolts, or per strap manufacturer's instructions.

9. Refer to general codes for foundation anchor exceptions involving braced walls 24 inches long and shorter. These walls may require specific placement of foundation anchors.

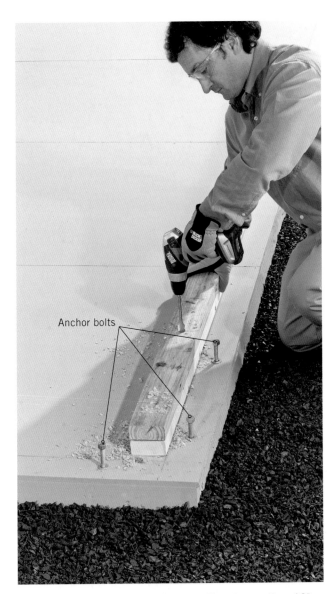

Anchor bolts

Install ½"-diameter anchor bolts every 6', not more than 12" from the end of each bottom plate, and in the middle ⅓ of the plate.

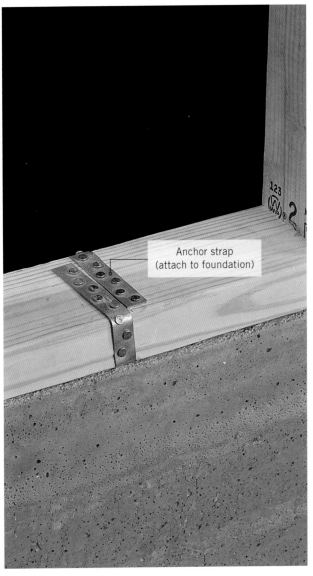

Anchor strap (attach to foundation)

You may be allowed to substitute straps for bolts. Install straps according to manufacturer's instructions. The strap in this picture is improperly installed.

Crawl Spaces

Crawl Space Ventilated to Exterior

1. Provide at least 1 square foot of net free ventilation area for every 150 square feet of crawl space floor in a ventilated crawl space. You may reduce the net free ventilation area to at least 1 square foot for every 1,500 square feet of crawl space floor if you cover the floor with a vapor retarder, such as 6-mil polyethylene sheeting.

2. Install covers in the ventilation openings. Use screens, grates, grills, or plates with openings at least ⅛ inch and not more than ¼ inch.

3. Subtract the space used by opening covers from the net free ventilation area of a ventilation opening. Example: a 1-square-foot opening may be reduced to an effective ⅔-square-foot opening when covered by a cast iron grill or grate. The cover manufacturer's instructions should indicate the cover's opening reduction amount.

4. Locate a ventilation opening not more than 3 feet from every corner of the crawl space wall. This is not required if the crawl space floor is covered with an approved vapor retarder and if the ventilation openings are located to provide cross-ventilation.

5. Install a Class I or Class II vapor retarder on the face of air-permeable insulation installed between floor joists in a ventilated crawl space. Be careful to install the vapor retarder so that crawl space air cannot leak around openings in the vapor retarder. Moisture in the air can condense into liquid water and damage the insulation and wood framing.

   Polyethylene is a common Class I vapor retarder. Kraft paper is a common Class II vapor retarder. Fiberglass batts are a common type of air-permeable insulation. This provision applies only in warm/humid climate zones, such as the southeastern United States.

6. There is considerable controversy about the effectiveness of crawl space ventilation, particularly in warm, humid climates. Check with a qualified energy efficiency professional before adding insulation between floor joists in crawl spaces. Check the condition of existing floor joist insulation in crawl spaces at least annually.

Unventilated Crawl Space

1. You may eliminate crawl space ventilation openings by insulating the crawl space walls or floor system as required by general codes and by installing all the following moisture control and ventilation components:

   (a) Cover all exposed soil in the crawl space floor with an approved vapor retarder, such as 6-mil, preferably thicker, polyethylene sheeting.

Unventilated crawl spaces are recommended by experts for most crawl spaces.

(b) Lap all vapor retarder seams by at least 6 inches, and seal or tape the seams.

(c) Extend the vapor retarder at least 6 inches up the crawl space wall, and attach and seal the vapor retarder to the wall.

(d) Provide one of the following ventilation methods:

- continuous mechanical exhaust ventilation

- a conditioned air supply at a rate of 1 cfm for every 50 square feet of crawl space floor area and provide a return air opening to the building interior

- dehumidification designed to provide at least 70 pints of moisture removal per day for every 1,000 square feet of crawl space floor area

2. Do not connect the return air opening for the building interior to a forced-air return duct. Use an opening in the floor or use an unpressurized duct between the crawl space and the building interior.

3. There is some controversy about providing conditioned air to a crawl space. Do not exceed the 1 cfm conditioned air ventilation rate.

Ventilation Opening Locations

3' min.

3'

Provide 1 sq. ft. of ventilation for every 150 sq. ft. of crawl space soil floor area or 1 sq. ft. for every 1,500 sq. ft. of vapor-retarder-covered floor area.

Min. 16 × 24" access

Unventilated and insulated crawl spaces often perform better than ventilated crawl spaces.

Decks

Most decks are relatively simple structures, but even a basic deck project must conform to the requirements of building codes in your area. In fact, virtually every aspect of your deck—from its location on your property to the design you choose and the materials you buy to build it—must meet stringent guidelines for safety. Codes vary, sometimes significantly, among jurisdictions. Your local building inspector can provide you with a list of the relevant deck codes and help you interpret them so you can create code-compliant plans for your deck project. You may also want to download a free PDF copy of the "DCA6-15 Prescriptive Residential Deck Construction Guide" (see Resources, page 234).

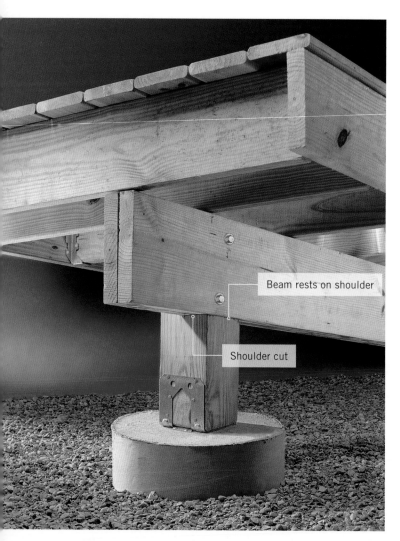

Meet or exceed all lumber size code requirements. Lumber sizes are contained in tables in general codes.

General Deck Building Guidelines

1. Use hot-dipped zinc-coated galvanized steel for all fasteners (nails and screws) and hardware (joist hangers and support post caps and bases). Stainless-steel fasteners and hardware are recommended when building decks near water, and are required for decks located within 300 feet from saltwater.

2. Drill holes for bolts at least $\frac{1}{32}$ inch and not more than $\frac{1}{16}$ inch larger than the bolt. Predrill holes for $\frac{1}{2}$-inch-diameter and larger lag screws.

3. Use hot-dipped zinc-coated galvanized steel or flexible flashing material when installing flashing at the deck ledger. Be sure that the flexible flashing is approved for exposure to sunlight. Do not use aluminum flashing.

4. Use at least #2 grade preservative-treated lumber or #2 grade naturally durable lumber for deck structural members. Lumber for deck structural components must be rated for ground contact, UC4A or better. You may use approved composite materials for components, such as deck flooring and railings. Read and follow manufacturer's instructions when using composite materials.

5. Field-treat cuts, holes, and notches in preservative-treated wood with an approved preservative, such as copper napthenate.

6. Consult with the building inspector or a qualified engineer when building decks in seismic and high wind zones, in areas with heavy snowfall, and when building complex decks, such as multi-level decks.

Deck Ledger Attachment to the Home

1. Install a preservative-treated #2 grade or better Southern Pine or Hem Fir deck ledger board that's at least a 2 × 8 in size.

2. Secure the deck ledger to one of the following band or rim joists: (a) 2-inch-thick (1½-inch actual thickness) SPF sawn lumber, (b) 1 inch minimum thickness by 9½ inches deep Douglas fir

laminated veneer lumber, or (c) another approved engineered material.

3. Secure the band or rim joist to sawn lumber joists or wood I-joists that are perpendicular to the band or rim joist.

4. Use hold-down tension devices to provide lateral load connections, or have an engineer approve the lateral load connections. You may use one of the following methods.

    (a) Install two 1,500 pound hold-down tension devices according to the device manufacturer's instructions.

    (b) Install four 750 pound hold-down tension devices according to the device manufacturer's instructions.

5. Support the band or rim joist directly on the foundation or on a wall supported directly on the foundation. Do not support the band or rim joist using a cantilevered structure, such as a bay window or a framed chimney. Do not support the band or rim joist on veneer, such as masonry and stone.

6. You may use other methods and materials when the details are designed by a qualified structural engineer.

7. You may make a deck entirely self-supporting as an alternative to attaching the deck to the home.

Hang a double joist between joists to support the deck in areas where obstructions won't allow a ledger.

Do not attach the ledger through siding or other wall coverings. Remove all wall coverings in the installation area so you can attach the ledger to the wall framing members. Cut the siding with a circular saw, and finish the corners with a chisel. Do not attach the ledger to brick or stone wall coverings. A self-supporting deck may be necessary.

Lateral load connector hardware should be attached to the deck joists and house rim joist to minimize lateral movement. A Simpson Strong-Tie DTT1 connector is seen here. *Photo courtesy Simpson Strong-Tie*

Deck Ledger Attachment
Using Screws or Bolts

1. Install the screws or bolts in the deck ledger board and in the band joist or rim board. Stagger the screws or bolts vertically along the length of the deck ledger board.

2. Install at least ½-inch hot-dipped galvanized lag screws or machine bolts (not carriage bolts).

NOTE: there are proprietary screws that are thinner than ½ inch and are approved for attaching deck ledgers to the home. Read and follow the manufacturer's instructions if you use these screws.

3. Install a washer on each end of the machine bolts and a washer on the head end of the lag screws.

4. Make the distance between the interior face of the ledger board and the exterior face of the band board (rim joist) not more than 1 inch.

5. Use lag screws that are long enough to penetrate the band or rim board but not long enough to penetrate through the interior wall.

Deck Footings

1. Place the bottom of footings for deck support posts below the local frost line. You do not need to place deck footings below the frost line if the deck is not attached to the home (but it is best practice to do so anyway).

2. Place the bottom of footings for deck support posts that are within 5 feet from the house at the same level as the house footings.

3. Refer to DCA-6 or local codes for footing size and thickness.

4. Slope the top of footings to drain water if the top of the footings are above the ground.

5. Space footings as required for beam support. See the DECK BEAMS section on page 56.

Install **staggered fasteners** on the ledger board.

6. You are not required to install deck footings if the deck is not attached to the home and if the joists are supported on the ground over their entire length. Note that while this is allowed, it is not recommended because the joists are more likely to deteriorate.

7. You are not required to install deck footings if the deck satisfies all of these conditions: (a) all deck joists are supported on precast concrete piers without posts or beams, (b) the deck area is not more than 200 sq. ft., and (c) the deck walking surface is not more than 20 inches above grade at any point within 36 inches measured horizontally.

Deck Joists

1. Use the correct size joist hanger to attach joists to the sides of ledgers and beams. Do not support joists using wood ledger strips, such as 2 × 2s. You may support joists on the top of a beam.

2. Fasten joist hangers using the size and type of fastener specified by the joist hanger manufacturer. In general, place a fastener in every round and oblong hole.

3. Support joists on a joist hanger (the joist should be fully seated in the hanger), on at least 1½ inches of wood, or on at least 3 inches of concrete or masonry.

4. You may use three 8d nails to fasten joists that bear on top of a beam to the beam if the deck is supported by the house. Best practice is to use hurricane clips to fasten all joists to a beam.

5. Secure the rim joist to the deck floor joists using at least three 10d nails or three #10 × 3-inch wood screws.

6. Use local codes to determine the correct joist span and on center spacing. Use local codes to determine the maximum amount of cantilever past the beam.

Measuring Deck Joist Span

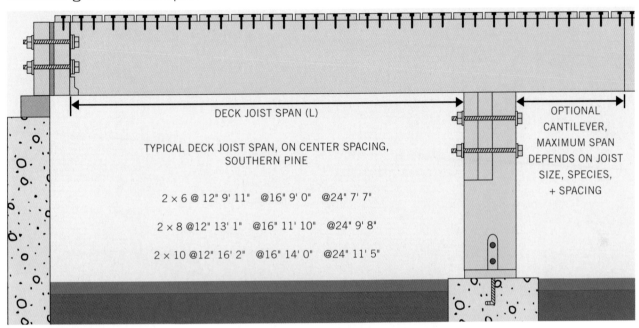

DECK JOIST SPAN (L)

TYPICAL DECK JOIST SPAN, ON CENTER SPACING, SOUTHERN PINE

2 × 6 @ 12" 9' 11"   @16" 9' 0"   @24" 7' 7"

2 × 8 @12" 13' 1"   @16" 11' 10"   @24" 9' 8"

2 × 10 @12" 16' 2"   @16" 14' 0"   @24" 11' 5"

OPTIONAL CANTILEVER, MAXIMUM SPAN DEPENDS ON JOIST SIZE, SPECIES, + SPACING

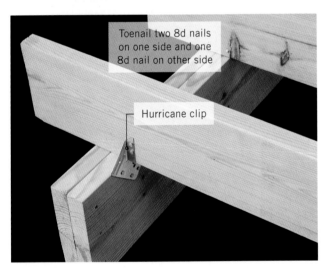

Toenail two 8d nails on one side and one 8d nail on other side

Hurricane clip

You may toenail joists to a beam only if the deck is attached to the house. Best practice is to secure joists to the beam using a hurricane clip.

Epoxy

Rim joist

Ledger

Concrete or grout

Ledgers and block walls. When fastening ledgers to hollow concrete block walls, the block cells in the ledger attachment areas must be filled with concrete or grout. Secure the attachment bolts to the wall with approved epoxy anchors with washers.

TABLE 3A: DECK FLOOR JOIST ON CENTER SPACING

SPECIES#2 GRADE	JOIST SIZE	DECK JOIST SPACING, NO CANTILEVER (INCHES)		
		12	16	24
Southern Pine	2 × 6	9-11	9-0	7-7
	2 × 8	13-1	11-10	9-8
	2 × 10	16-2	14-0	11-5

TABLE 3B: DECK BEAM SPAN (MAXIMUM DISTANCE BETWEEN SUPPORT POSTS)

SPECIES #2 GRADE	BEAM SIZE	DECK JOIST SPAN LESS THAN OR EQUAL TO (FEET)					
		6	8	10	12	14	16
Southern Pine	2-2 × 8	8-9	7-7	6-9	6-2	5-9	5-4
	2-2 × 10	10-4	9-0	8-0	7-4	6-9	6-4
	2-2 × 12	12-2	10-7	9-5	8-7	8-0	7-6
	3-2 × 8	10-11	9-6	8-6	7-9	7-2	6-8
	3-2 × 10	13-0	11-2	10-0	9-2	8-6	7-11
	3-2 × 12	15-3	13-3	11-10	10-9	10-0	9-4

Deck Beams

1. Fasten beam members to each other using two staggered rows of at least 10d nails spaced not more than 16 inches on center.

2. Support beams on at least 1½ inches of wood or on at least 3 inches of concrete or masonry. This includes the bearing points where a splice in a multiple-member beam is supported on a post.

3. You may extend (cantilever) the ends of a beam past the support not more than one-quarter of the span of the beam between the support posts.

4. Place splices between beam members above deck posts.

5. Use local codes to determine the correct beam span and on-center post spacing.

Fasten beam members using two staggered rows of 10d nails at 16" on center. Fasten 3-member beams from both sides of the beam.

Deck Posts

1. You may install 6 × 6 and larger Southern Pine deck posts up to 14 feet tall, in most cases. Measure post height from the top of the footing to the bottom of the beam.

2. Use tables in local codes to determine the maximum height of support posts that are: (a) smaller than 6 × 6, (b) made from wood other than Southern Pine, or (c) located in climates where snow loads are an issue.

3. Consult an engineer when using steel support posts.

4. Place the post in the center one-third of the footing.

5. Secure the post to the footing. Best practice is to use a post base and extend the footing above the soil as shown in the photo.

6. You may embed the post in the footing. Place the footing on at least 4 inches of gravel. Install ½-inch diameter through bolts (not screws) on each side of the post and embed the post in at least 12 inches of concrete.

7. You are not required to secure the post to the footing if you embed the post in at least 12 inches of stable and compacted soil.

8. Embedding the post in the footing or in the soil is not recommended because the post is likely to deteriorate over time.

9. Secure the post to the beam using an approved method. Approved methods include using a manufactured post cap or bolting the beam into a notch at the top of the beam.

Deck Flashing

1. Install flashing between the deck ledger and the house when the deck is attached to the house. Proper flashing is essential. A common cause of deck collapse is the deck pulling away from rotted wood caused by improper flashing.

Beams may not be attached to the side of a post with through bolts, even when mortises are cut into the posts to partially support the beam.

Best Practice for Installing Deck Flashing

WATER-RESISTIVE BARRIER

SHEATHING

WALL COVERING

DECKING

L FLASHING

WASHERS FOR < ½" DRAINAGE SPACE (OPTIONAL)

WATER-RESISTIVE MEMBRANE FLASHING

HOUSE RIM JOIST

DECK LEDGER

WATER-RESISTIVE BARRIER

Deck flooring made from composite materials may last longer and require less maintenance than wood flooring. Install composite materials according to the manufacturer's instructions.

Deck Flooring

1. You may use 2-inch-thick (nominal) wood, 1¼-inch-thick wood (5/4 board), or other listed deck flooring (wood composites, metal) material as deck flooring.

2. Do not install 2-inch-thick flooring across joists that are more than 24 inches on center when the flooring is perpendicular to the joist or more than 16 inches on center when the flooring is diagonal (maximum 45 degrees) to the joist.

3. Do not install 1¼-inch-thick flooring across joists that are more than 16 inches on center when the flooring is perpendicular to the joist or more than 12 inches on center when the flooring is diagonal (maximum 45 degrees) to the joist.

4. Install two 8d threaded nails or two #8 × 3-inch wood screws per floorboard in each joist.

5. Install flooring across at least 4 joists (best practice).

6. Leave about ⅛ inch between flooring boards, including at the ends, to allow for drainage and for expansion (best practice).

7. Install other listed deck flooring material according to manufacturer's instructions.

Deck Stairs Recommendations

1. Use 2 × 12 #2 or better Southern Pine or equivalent lumber for deck stair stringers.

2. Leave at least 5 inches of uncut wood when cutting the stair risers and treads into the stringers. Do not cut the stringer past the riser and tread.

3. Do not exceed 6 feet of unsupported length for deck stair stringers where the risers and treads are cut into the stringer (cut stringers).

4. Do not exceed 13 feet, 3 inches of unsupported length for deck stair stringers where the risers and treads are not cut into the stringer (solid stringers).

5. Measure stringer length horizontally. You may support long stringers near the center to reduce the unsupported length.

6. Provide a solid landing, such as concrete, at the bottom of deck stairs. Support the stringers on the landing or by appropriate footings.

7. Support the entire stringer plumb cut at the top landing on the deck rim board or by other approved means.

8. Attach the stringers to the top landing support using hangers or brackets. Do not rely only on nails or screws to attach stringers to supports.

9. Do not exceed 18 inches of unsupported length for deck stair treads using 2 × 4 or 5/4 Southern Pine. Refer to DCA-6-15 for maximum stair tread lengths for other lumber sizes and species. Install treads made from composite materials according to manufacturer's instructions.

Deck Guards + Handrails

1. Refer to the guards and handrails section of this book for general guidelines about installing guards and handrails for decks. The guidelines for interior guards and handrails apply to exterior guards and handrails too (see page 25).

2. Space deck guard 4 × 4 support posts at least every 6 feet. This also applies to stair guards and handrails (best practice).

3. Secure the deck guard support posts to deck floor joists using at least ½-inch-diameter bolts and attachment hardware (best practice). Do not rely only on the deck band and rim boards to secure deck guard support posts (required).

4. Refer to DCA-6 or attachment hardware manufacturer's instructions for information about attaching deck guard support posts if the posts do not line up with deck floor joists (best practice).

Cut stringers (top) should be supported every 6'. Solid stringers (bottom) should be supported every 13' to 3".

Attach stringers to support using a hanger, not just nails.

5. Install guards, such as wire cables and composite materials, according to manufacturer's instructions.

Deck Bracing Recommendations

1. Install bracing between the deck support posts and the deck beam on all decks that are more than 2 feet above the ground.

2. Install bracing between the deck support posts and a deck rim board, floor joist, or blocking on free-standing decks that are more than 2 feet aboveground.

3. Use 2 × 4 or larger lumber for the brace.

4. Secure the braces using at least ⅜-inch-diameter bolts with washers on both ends.

5. Secure the brace at least 2 feet away from the support post.

Deck guard support posts should be secured using attachment hardware for long-term strength.

Bracing is recommended to reduce movement that can weaken the deck and cause it to collapse.

Floor Systems

Floor Joist Span Tables (Selected)

1. Use 30 psf live load and 10 psf dead load for joists under bedrooms and in attics with access by permanent stairs, in most cases. Permanent stairs do not include pull-down folding attic ladders.

2. Use 40 psf live load and 10 psf dead load for joists under living areas, other than bedrooms, and under decks, and balconies, in most cases.

3. Use L/360 deflection (length of joist span in inches divided by 360) for all floor joists.

4. Refer to the IRC or to the AF+PA Span Tables for Joists and Rafters to find joist spans not contained in the following tables.

5. Apply the following tables to floor systems framed with nominal 2-inch-wide dimensional lumber, such as 2 × 10. **An engineer must design floor truss and I-Joist systems.**

Floor joists must conform to minimum span rating codes according to how long they are, how far apart they are spaced, and the type and grade of wood from which they are made.

TABLE 4: BEDROOM FLOOR JOIST SPANS AT 16" ON CENTER

SPECIES	GRADE	2 × 8 FEET-INCHES	2 × 10 FEET-INCHES	2 × 12 FEET-INCHES
Douglas fir	2	14-2	17-5	20-3
Hem fir	2	13-2	16-10	19-8
Southern pine	2	13-3	15-8	18-6
Spruce-pine-fir	2	13-6	17-2	19-11

Double headers

Bridging

Double trimmers

Central beam

Rim joist

Install floor system framing members according to this illustration. The provisions in this section refer to floor system framing using nominal 2"-thick dimensional lumber. Follow engineering instructions when using floor truss and I-joist systems.

TABLE 5: BEDROOM FLOOR JOIST SPANS AT 24" ON CENTER

SPECIES	GRADE	2 × 8 FEET-INCHES	2 × 10 FEET-INCHES	2 × 12 FEET-INCHES
Douglas fir	2	11-8	14-3	16-6
Hem fir	2	11-4	13-10	16-1
Southern pine	2	10-10	12-10	15-1
Spruce-pine-fir	2	11-6	14-1	16-3

TABLE 6: LIVING AREA FLOOR JOIST SPANS AT 16" ON CENTER

SPECIES	GRADE	2 × 8 FEET-INCHES	2 × 10 FEET-INCHES	2 × 12 FEET-INCHES
Douglas fir	2	12-9	15-7	18-1
Hem fir	2	12-0	15-2	17-7
Southern pine	2	11-10	14-0	16-6
Spruce-pine-fir	2	12-3	15-5	17-10

TABLE 7: LIVING AREA FLOOR JOIST SPANS AT 24" ON CENTER

SPECIES	GRADE	2 × 8 FEET-INCHES	2 × 10 FEET-INCHES	2 × 12 FEET-INCHES
Douglas fir	2	10-5	12-9	14-9
Hem fir	2	10-2	12-5	14-4
Southern pine	2	9-8	11-5	13-6
Spruce-pine-fir	2	10-3	12-7	14-7

Floor Joists Under Load-Bearing Walls

1. Install additional floor joists under load-bearing walls that run parallel with the floor joists. Ensure that the number of joists is sufficient to support the load imposed by the wall and the loads supported by the wall. Parallel floor joists run the same direction as the wall being supported. Example: install at least two floor joists under a wall supporting a roof and at least three floor joists under a wall supporting a full story and a roof.

2. You may separate the additional joists under a load-bearing wall, if necessary, to fit pipes, vents, or ducts. Install solid 2-inch-thick blocking at least every 4 feet along the full depth of the separated joists.

3. Place load-bearing walls that run perpendicular to the floor joists not more than one joist depth from the supporting wall or beam below unless the joists are sized to carry the load. Perpendicular joists run at a 90-degree angle to the wall being supported. Example: place a load-bearing wall that runs perpendicular to 2 × 10 floor joists not more than 10 inches from the supporting wall or beam below.

Header, Girder + Floor Joist Bearing on Supports

1. Place at least 1½ inches of a floor joist, header, girder, or beam on the supporting wood or metal wall. Supporting wood includes a sill plate bearing on a masonry or concrete wall.

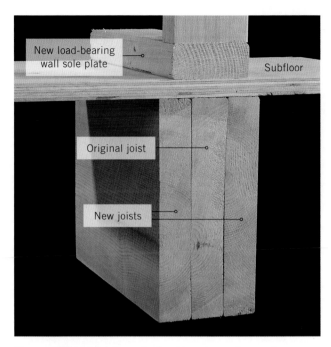

Place additional joists under load-bearing walls running parallel to the joists.

2. Place at least 3 inches of a floor joist, header, girder, or beam on the supporting masonry or concrete wall. Comply with this requirement when the member bears directly on the masonry or concrete wall, not on a sill plate that bears on the wall. This requirement usually applies to beams and girders.

3. You may support floor joists on at least a 1 × 4 ledger if the ledger is attached to each stud and if the joist is attached to a stud.

Place load-bearing walls running perpendicular to the joists not more than one joist depth away from the supporting wall or beam.

Place at least 1½" of wood on the supporting wood.

Place at least 3" of wood on supporting concrete or masonry.

Lap joints that meet over supports with at least 3" overlap. Reinforce the lap joint with at least three 10d nails.

Attaching the ends of the floor joists to a band board is a common way to keep joists from twisting.

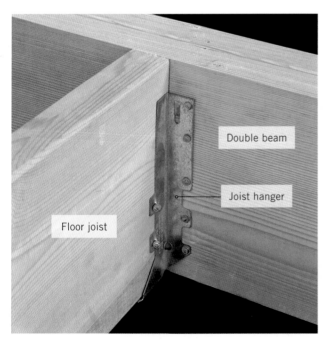

Attach floor joists to beams using metal joist hanger hardware.

Floor Joist Lap at Supports

1. Lap floor joists from opposite sides that meet over a bearing support at least 3 inches at the support, and nail the joists at the lap using at least three 10d nails. You may substitute a wood or metal splice of equal or greater strength for the nailed lap.

Floor Joist Attachment to Beams

1. Use an approved joist hanger or at least a 2 × 2 wood ledger to support floor joists that connect to a beam or girder.

Floor Joist Blocking

1. Install full-depth solid blocking that's at least 2 inches thick at both ends of floor joists. Or, attach the joists to a header, band, or rim joist or to an adjoining stud. This helps reduce joist twisting.

2. Install blocking at all intermediate load-bearing supports in seismic design areas.

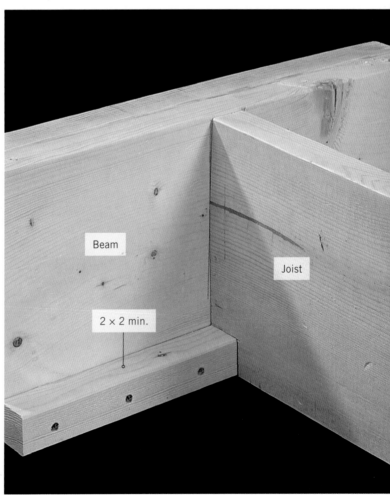

You may attach floor joists to beams using a 2 × 2 ledger, but this is no longer considered best practice.

Floor Joist Bridging

1. Install bridging at intervals not more than every 8 feet of floor joist length on floor joists deeper than 2 × 12.

2. You may use solid, full-depth blocking, wood or metal diagonal bridging, or other means to provide required floor joist bridging. Some code officials require bridging on all floor joists regardless of what the code stipulates.

Options for floor bridging include: Full depth lumber bridging (A); metal X bridging (B); wood X bridging (C).

BRIDGING

Metal bridging (left) can be secured with joist hanger nails. For wood X-bridging, drive 10d common nails to secure the board ends to the floor joists.

FLOOR JOIST OPENINGS

Framed openings in floor joists are used mostly for stairways between floors and for chimneys. The header joists distribute the load of the tail joists to the trimmer joists.

Floor Joist Openings
Not More than 4 Feet Wide

1. Install double trimmer joists on both sides of header joists. You may use a single trimmer joist on both sides of the header joists if the header is not more than 3 feet from the trimmer bearing point.

2. You may use a single header joist if the header joist span is not more than 4 feet wide.

3. Install approved joist hangers or a 2 × 2 ledger strip to connect tail joists to header joists and header joists to trimmer joists.

Use double trimmer joists at most openings. Use double header joists if the opening is more than 4' wide.

Floor Joist Openings
More than 4 Feet Wide

1. Install double trimmer joists and double header joists if the header joist span is more than 4 feet wide.

2. Install approved joist hangers to connect header joists to trimmer joists if the header joist span is more than 6 feet wide.

3. Install approved joist hangers or a 2 × 2 ledger strip to connect tail joists to header joists if the tail joists are more than 12 feet long.

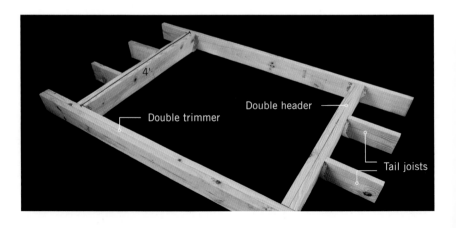

Double header

Double trimmer

Tail joists

Floor Sheathing

1. Install wood floor sheathing panels: (a) so that they continuously span at least two framing members, (b) with the long dimension perpendicular (90-degree angle) to supports, and (c) that are at least 24 inches wide. Panels less than 24 inches wide can deflect or fail under load.

2. Support wood floor sheathing panel edges with solid blocking, tongue-and-groove edges, or other approved means. An additional underlayment layer that is at least ¼ inch or ¾-inch wood floor covering can substitute for edge support in some cases.

3. You may use wood floor sheathing panels (such as ²³⁄₃₂-inch and ¾-inch nominal thickness plywood or OSB and ¾-inch sanded plywood) as a combination subfloor and underlayment. Install combination subflooring as described in #1 above. Be aware that while combination subflooring panels comply with the IRC, they may not comply with manufacturer's installation for some floor coverings, such as tile.

Support edges of floor sheathing with tongue-and-groove edges.

Support edges of floor sheathing with solid blocking.

HOW TO READ THE LABEL ON PLYWOOD AND OSB

A plywood or OSB panel label contains much information. Here is the most important information you need to know when buying these products.

- **Exposure 1 (A):** Exposure 1 means the panel can withstand some exposure to weather during construction but is not designed for long-term weather exposure; Exterior means the panel is designed for long-term weather exposure.

- **Number before slash (B):** maximum on-center support span when used as roof sheathing; edge support may be required to achieve the rated span.

- **Number after slash (C):** maximum on-center support span when used as floor sheathing; on panels with one number, the number is the floor sheathing span.

- **Performance category (D):** use this when referencing the panel's thickness in the IRC.

Draftstopping

Draftstopping helps limit the spread of fires in floor framing and in floor/ceiling assemblies. It is most often required when using open web floor trusses and when a ceiling is suspended under a floor. Do not confuse draftstopping with fireblocking. Fireblocking occurs in wall assemblies.

Installing Draftstopping

1. Install draftstopping when usable space exists both above and below the floor/ceiling assembly and when the open area within the concealed floor/ceiling assembly exceeds 1,000 square feet.

2. Use at least ½-inch drywall, ⅜-inch wood structural panels (plywood or OSB), or other approved material.

3. Divide the space to be draftstopped into areas that are approximately equal.

4. Install the draftstopping material parallel with the framing.

5. Repair draftstopping that is damaged or penetrated by pipes, ducts, or other materials.

Fire Protection of Floor Framing

1. Install at least ½-inch-thick drywall or ⅝-inch-thick wood structural panels on the bottom side of floor systems in basements and

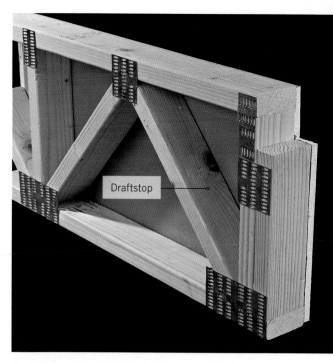

Some floor trusses require draftstopping to prevent horizontal air movement that can conduct fire. Solid wood floor joist systems typically do not, because they are naturally closed off. Install a draftstop in web floor trusses when there is usable space above and below and when the concealed area is more than 1,000 sq. ft. Drywall and wood structural panels may be used for draftstops.

in crawl spaces containing fuel-fired or electric-powered heating appliances. This provision does not apply if the floor system is built using 2 × 10 or larger dimensional lumber; it will usually apply only to floor systems built using wood I-joists.

NOTCHES + HOLES IN I-JOISTS AND TRUSSES

Notch, bore, splice, or alter wood I-joists, trusses, or engineered wood members only according to manufacturer's instructions.

Altering the top and bottom flange of I-joists is usually not allowed. Hole boring is usually allowed in the middle third of the span and is restricted near the I-joist ends.

Cutting the ends of engineered wood beams and I-joists to length is usually permitted.

Common types of engineered wood: laminated beam (A); web-type truss, metal plate connected truss (B); I-joist (C).

Notches + Holes in Joists + Rafters

Boring + Notching Definitions

A bore is a hole drilled in a stud or joist. Use the actual dimensions to determine the depth of framing lumber and when calculating the maximum hole diameter.

A notch is a piece cut from the smaller dimension of framing lumber, such as a stud or joist. Use the actual dimensions to determine the depth of framing lumber and when calculating the maximum notch depth. Actual dimensions are the dimensions of framing lumber after finishing at the mill. Example: the nominal dimensions of a 2 × 6 are 2 inches by 6 inches, and the actual dimensions, after finishing, are about 1½ inches by 5½ inches.

Wood Joist Notching + Boring

1. You may notch solid lumber rafters, floor and ceiling joists, and beams not deeper than ⅙ the depth of the member. You may notch the ends of the member not deeper than one fourth the depth of the member. Example: notch a 2 × 10 joist not deeper than 1½ inches, except at the ends, where you may notch not deeper than 2⁵⁄₁₆ inches.

2. You may notch solid lumber rafters, floor and ceiling joists, and beams not longer than one-third the depth of the member. Example: notch the top or bottom of a 2 × 10 joist not longer than 3¹⁄₁₆ inches.

3. You may notch solid lumber rafters, floor and ceiling joists, and beams only within the outer one-third of the span. Example: notch a 10-foot-long joist only within 40 inches from each end.

4. You may notch the tension side (bottom) of solid lumber rafters, floor and ceiling joists, and beams more than 4 inches thick only at the ends.

5. You may drill holes in solid lumber rafters, floor and ceiling joists, and beams with a diameter not more than ⅓ of the depth of the member. Example: drill a hole with a diameter not more than 3⅛ inches in a 2 × 10 joist.

6. Locate holes at least 2 inches from the edge of the member and at least 2 inches from any other hole or notch.

7. Use actual joist depths, not nominal joist depths. Example: use 9¼ inches for a 2 × 10 joist, not the nominal depth of 10 inches.

Drill holes not more than ⅓ of the member depth and cut member notches not deeper than ⅙ of the member depth.

Notch wood joists and rafters not longer than ⅓ of the depth and only in the outer ⅓ of the member.

Drill holes in wood joists and rafters not larger than ⅓ the depth and at least 2" from the edge of the member.

Wall Systems

Whether they are interior or exterior, load-bearing or nonload-bearing, made from wood studs or metal, walls must meet very specific construction standards to ensure that they do not impede the structural integrity of a house and do their part to prevent fires from spreading within wall cavities. Nevertheless, be aware that designing and building load-bearing walls is a closely regulated process. **In most cases, you would be well advised to consult a structural engineer to make sure that the lumber sizes and spacing conform to code standards and that any beams are appropriately sized, properly supported, and made from qualifying materials.**

Even nonload-bearing walls must conform to construction codes.

WOOD NAILING DEFINITIONS

Using the proper size and type of nail and installing the nail where required is critical to the structural integrity of a building. Analysis of building failures frequently shows that failures result from improper nailing. The following are definitions of nailing methods and installation requirements contained in the IRC.

Edge spacing: Edge spacing means installing a nail every indicated number of inches around the perimeter of a wood structural panel. If blocking is required by the IRC, then edge spacing includes nailing the panel to the blocking.

Endnailing: An endnail is driven straight into the end of the member. An example of endnailing is attaching studs to sill plates through the sill plate before the sill plate is attached to the foundation or subfloor.

Facenailing: A facenail is driven straight into the member, often into the long dimension of the member. Examples of facenailing include ceiling and floor joist laps over supports and attaching wood panels to studs and joists.

Intermediate spacing: Intermediate spacing means installing a nail every indicated number of inches at studs or joists in the interior area of a wood structural panel.

O.C. means "on center." Install nails every indicated number of inches.

Toenailing: A toenail is driven at an angle through the edge of the member. Toenailing usually occurs when one member is already attached in place, such as when a stud is toenailed to a sill plate that is already attached.

Endnailing (A), toenailing (B), facenailing (C).

Wood Nailing Requirements

Wood Nailing General Installation Requirements

1. Use nails that are at least as thick and long as indicated in the following tables. Common nails and box nails are thicker and longer than hand-driven sinker nails and pneumatic-driven nails commonly used in residential construction. You cannot directly substitute sinker and gun nails for common, box, or deformed shank nails. Substitution of sinker and gun nails should be based on engineering analysis.

Wood Nailing to Framing Materials

1. Use Tables 8, 9, and 10 to determine the type of nail and nail spacing for attaching wood framing materials to other wood framing materials in other than high wind and seismic design areas. Refer to the general codes for fastener type, quantity, and spacing in high wind and seismic design areas.

Install nails around the edge of wood panels and at intermediate supports at the required on-center spacing.

TABLE 8: NAILING OSB + PLYWOOD SHEATHING TO FRAMING

PANEL THICKNESS	NAIL TYPE	EDGE SPACING	INTERMEDIATE SPACING
3/8 to 1/2"	6d common or deformed (2" or 2⅜" × 0.113") for subfloor and wall and 8d common (2½" × 0.131") or RSRS-01 for roof	6" o.c.	6" o.c.
19/32 to 3/4"	8d common (2½ × 0.131") for subfloor and wall	6" o.c.	12" o.c.
	8d common (2 ½" × 0.131") or RSRS-01 for roof	6" o.c.	6" o.c.
	Deformed 2⅜" × 0.113" for subfloor and wall	6" o.c.	6" o.c.
7/8 to 1¼"	10d common (3 × 0.148") or 8d deformed (2½ × 0.120")	6" o.c.	12" o.c.

TABLE 9: NAILING ONE-PIECE SUBFLOOR TO FRAMING

PANEL THICKNESS	NAIL TYPE	EDGE SPACING	INTERMEDIATE SPACING
3/4" + less	Deformed 2" × 0.113" or 2" × 0.120" or 8d common (2½ × 0.131")	6" o.c.	12" o.c.
7/8 to 1"	8d common (2½ × 0.131") or deformed 2" × 0.113" or 2½" × 0.120"	6" o.c.	12" o.c.
1⅛ to 1¼"	10d common (3 × 0.148") or deformed 2" × 0.113" or 2½" × 0.120"	6" o.c.	12" o.c.

TABLE 10: NAILING STRUCTURAL LUMBER

LUMBER DESCRIPTION, NAILING METHOD	NUMBER/TYPE OF FASTENERS	FASTENER SPACING
FLOOR NAILING		
Joist to sill, girder, plate, toenail	3-8d common (2½" × 0.131") OR 3-3" × 0.131"	--
Rim joist, band joist, or blocking to sill or to top plate, toenail	8d common (2½" × 0.131") OR 3-3" × 0.131"	6" o.c.
Ledger supporting joists	3-16d common (3½" × 0.162") OR 4-3" × 0.131"	under each joist
Built-up beams, using 2"-thick lumber	10d box (3" × 0.128") OR 3" × 0.131" AND 3-10d box (3" × 0.128") OR 3-3" × 0.131"	24" o.c. face nail stagger at top + bottom on opposite sides face nail at ends + at splices
Band or rim joist to joist, end nail	3-16d common (3½" × 0.162") OR 4-3" × 0.131"	--
Bridging or blocking to joist	2-8d common (2½" × 0.131") OR 2-3" × 0.131"	Toenail each end
WALL NAILING		
Sill or sole plate to joist, rim joist, or blocking (not a braced wall)	16d common (3½" × 0.162") OR 3" × 0.131"	16" o.c. face nail 12" o.c. face nail
Sill or sole plate to joist, rim joist, or blocking (at a braced wall)	2-16d common (3½" × 0.162") OR 4-3" × 0.131"	2 each 16" o.c. face nail 4 each 12" o.c. face nail
Adjacent full-height stud to end of header	4-16d box (3½" × 0.135"); or 3-16d common (3½" × 0.162"); or 4-10d box (3" × 0.128"); or 4-3" × 0.131"	end nail end nail end nail end nail
Stud to top or bottom plate, toenail	4-8d common (2½" × 0.131") OR 4-3" × 0.131"	--
Stud to top or bottom plate, end nail	2-16d common (3½" × 0.162") OR 3-3" × 0.131"	--
Double top plate, face nail	16d common (3½" × 0.162") OR 3" × 0.131"	16" o.c., 12" o.c.
Double top plate splice	8-16d common (3½" × 0.162") OR 12-3" × 0.131"	Face nail on each side of end joint (min. 24" lap splice length on each side of end joint)
Top plates, laps at corners + intersections	2-16d common (3½" × 0.162") OR 3-3" × 0.131"	--
Stud to stud + studs connecting at intersecting walls (at a braced wall panel)	16d common (3½" × 0.162") OR 3" × 0.131"	16" o.c. 12" o.c.
Header to stud, toenail	5-8d box (2½" × 0.113") OR 4-8d common 2½" × 0.131"	--
ROOF NAILING		
Blocking between ceiling joists, rafters, or trusses to top plate or other framing below	4-8d box (2½" × 0.113"); or 3-8d common (2½" × 0.131"); or 3-10d box (3" × 0.128"); or 3-3" × 0.131" nails	end nail end nail end nail end nail
Blocking between rafters or trusses not at the wall top plates, to rafter or truss	2-8d common (2½" × 0.131"); or 2-3" × 0.131" nail 2-16d common (3½" × 0.162"); or 3-3" × 0.131" nails	each end, toe nail each end, toe nail end nail end nail
Flat blocking to truss and web filler	16d common (3½" × 0.162"); or 3" × 0.131" nails	6" o.c. face nail 6" o.c. face nail
Ceiling joist to plate, toenail	3-8d common (2½" × 0.131") OR 3-3" × 0.131"	--
Collar tie to rafter	4-10d box (3" × 0.128"); or 3-10d common (3" × 0.148"); or 4-3" × 0.131"	face nail each rafter
Rafter or truss to plate, toenail	3-16d box (3½" × 0.135") OR 4-3" × 0.131"	2 toenails on one side and other nails on other side of rafter or truss
Rafters to ridge, valley, or hip rafters, toenail	4-16d (3½" × 0.135") OR 4-3" × 0.131"	--
Rafters to ridge, valley, or hip rafters, end nail	3-16d (3½" × 0.135") OR 3-3" × 0.131"	--

Wall Stud Size + Spacing

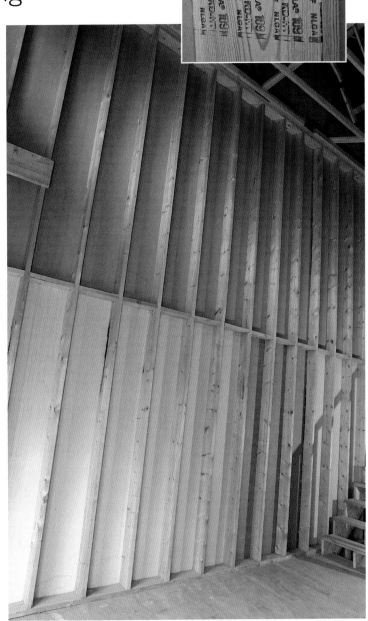

Wood Grades
Used in Wall Construction

1. Use Number 3, standard, or stud grade wood for most load-bearing walls not more than 10 feet tall. Do not use this wood for load-bearing walls more than 10 feet tall. Use Number 2 grade or better lumber for walls more than 10 feet tall.

2. You may use utility grade wood for nonload-bearing walls.

3. Refer to general codes for more information about other wall height and stud spacing combinations.

4. Refer to general codes for wall height and stud spacing requirements in high wind, heavy snow load, and seismic design areas.

Stud Size + Spacing
for Load-Bearing Walls
Not More than 10 Feet Tall

1. Use Table 11 to determine stud size and spacing when the unsupported vertical height of an exterior load-bearing wall is not more than 10 feet. Measure vertical height between points of horizontal (lateral) support between studs. Vertical wall height is usually measured between the bottom of the sole or sill plate and the bottom of the floor or ceiling. Consult a qualified engineer before measuring unsupported vertical wall height between points other than at floor levels.

Wall studs taller than 10' require No. 2 or better grade construction lumber. Shorter walls may be built with cheaper No. 3 grade in most cases.

TABLE 11: STUD SIZE + SPACING FOR LOAD-BEARING WALLS

STUD SIZE (INCHES)	MAXIMUM STUD SPACING SUPPORTING ONLY ONE FLOOR, OR SUPPORTING A CEILING + ROOF WITH OR WITHOUT A HABITABLE ATTIC	MAXIMUM STUD SPACING SUPPORTING ONE FLOOR + A CEILING + ROOF WITH OR WITHOUT A HABITABLE ATTIC	MAXIMUM STUD SPACING SUPPORTING TWO FLOORS + A CEILING + ROOF WITH OR WITHOUT A HABITABLE ATTIC
2 × 4	24"	16"	Not allowed
2 × 6	24"	24"	16"

Walls supporting roof only

Walls supporting two floors + roof

Walls supporting one floor + roof

Stud size and spacing depends on what the studs are supporting.

TABLE 12: STUD SIZE + SPACING FOR NONLOAD-BEARING WALLS

STUD SIZE	MAXIMUM STUD HEIGHT	MAXIMUM STUD SPACING
2 × 4	14'	24"
2 × 6	20'	24"

Stud Size + Spacing for Nonload-Bearing Walls

1. Use Table 12 to determine stud size and spacing for nonload-bearing walls. Measure vertical height between points of horizontal (lateral) support between studs. Vertical wall height is usually measured between the bottom of the sole or sill plate and the bottom of the floor or ceiling. Consult a qualified engineer before measuring unsupported vertical wall height between points other than at floor levels.

Top + Bottom Plate Construction

1. Use at least two 2-inch-deep (nominal) top plates that are at least as wide as the studs at the top of load-bearing walls. Examples: use two 2 × 4 top plates on top of a 2 × 4 wall, and use 2 × 6 top plates on top of 2 × 6 walls.

2. Offset joints where two pieces of top plate meet by at least 24 inches. You do not need to place a stud under a joint in a top plate unless the stud would be placed there for other reasons.

3. Lap one top plate from one wall over the top plate of an intersecting wall at the wall corners and at the intersection with load-bearing walls.

4. You may use a single top plate at the top of nonload-bearing walls.

5. Install one galvanized metal strap at least 0.054 inch thick (16 gauge) and 1½ inches wide on a top plate if it is cut more than 50 percent of its actual depth. These metal straps are sometimes called FHA straps. It is not necessary to install a strap on both top plates for purposes of this section. You may need to install shield plate to protect plumbing pipes and electrical wires.

6. Extend the strap at least 6 inches beyond each side of the cut opening. Secure the strap with at least eight 16d nails on each side of the strap.

7. Apply this strap requirement to top plates in exterior and interior load-bearing walls.

8. You do not need to install the strap if wood structural panel sheathing covers the entire side of the wall with the notched or cut top plates.

9. Use at least one 2-inch-deep (nominal) bottom plate that is at least as wide as the studs. Note that some jurisdictions allow treated plywood to serve as the bottom plate for curved walls. Verify this local exception with the building official.

24" min.

Offset joints where two top plates meet by at least 24". Nail the top plate on each side of the splice as described in Table 10.

Deep notch

Shield plate — Strap

Install a strap across one top plate when it is notched more than half its width. Install another strap or a shield plate when required to protect pipes and electrical wires.

Notches + Holes in Wall Studs

Boring + Notching Definitions

A bore is a hole drilled in a stud or joist. Use the actual dimensions to determine the depth of framing lumber and when calculating the maximum hole diameter.

A notch is a piece cut from the smaller dimension of framing lumber, such as a stud or joist. Use the actual dimensions to determine the depth of framing lumber and when calculating the maximum notch depth. Actual dimensions are the dimensions of framing lumber after finishing at the mill. Example: the nominal dimensions of a 2 × 6 are 2 inches by 6 inches, and the actual dimensions, after finishing, are about 1½ inches by 5½ inches.

You may repair overnotched and overbored studs by installing an approved stud shoe. Install the stud shoe according to manufacturer's instructions.

Wood Stud Notching

1. Notch a load-bearing stud not more than 25 percent of its actual depth. Example: notch a 2 × 6 load-bearing stud not more than 1⅜ inches.

2. Notch a nonload-bearing stud not more than 40 percent of its actual depth. Example: notch a 2 × 6 nonload-bearing stud not more than 2¼ inches.

Wood Stud Boring

1. Bore a hole in a single load-bearing stud not more than 40 percent of its actual depth. Example: bore a 2 × 6 load-bearing stud not more than 2¼ inches in diameter.

2. You may bore holes in load-bearing studs not more than 60 percent of their actual depth if you install a double stud and do not bore more than two successive studs.

3. Bore a hole in a nonload-bearing stud not more than 60 percent of its actual depth. Example: bore a 2 × 6 nonload-bearing stud not more than 3¼ inches in diameter.

4. Leave at least ⅝ inch of undisturbed wood between the hole and the stud edge.

5. Do not place a hole and a notch in the same horizontal section of the stud.

Notch a load-bearing stud not more than 25 percent of its actual depth.

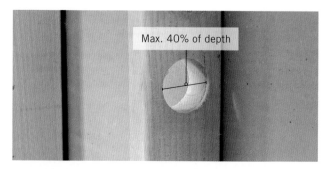

Drill a hole in a load-bearing stud not more than 40 percent of its actual depth.

Double two load-bearing studs if the holes are not more than 60 percent of their actual depth.

VIOLATION! Do not locate a notch and a hole in the same part of the stud.

Cripple Wall Framing

Cripple Wall Requirements

1. Install cripple walls using studs that are at least the same width as the wall studs above.

2. Frame cripple walls more than 4 feet tall as though they are full height walls. This means using the stud sizes and framing requirements previously described. Example: if full height wall studs on the same floor level as the cripple wall are 2 × 6, use 2 × 6 studs for the cripple wall.

3. Brace cripple walls using the same bracing method and length as the wall above, except multiply the cripple wall brace length by 1.15. Example: if the cripple wall is a 2-foot-tall basement wall and the wall brace length for the first story wall above is 3 feet, brace at least 3.45 feet (3 × 1.15) of the cripple wall.

4. Install sheathing that covers at least one full side of an exterior cripple wall less than 14 inches tall. Fasten the sheathing to both the top and bottom plates.

5. Support cripple walls on a continuous foundation.

6. You may substitute solid blocking for a framed and sheathed cripple wall less than 14 inches tall.

CRIPPLE WALL DEFINITION

A cripple wall is a framed wall that is less than one story tall. Cripple walls often occur with basement foundations that are stepped down to follow finished grade, and they may occur in split-level homes.

Cripple walls may be load-bearing or nonload-bearing. This bearing version is used to bridge a gap between the foundation wall and the first floor framing members. Anchor cripple walls to the foundation, and brace as required.

7. Anchor cripple walls to the foundation like other framed walls.

8. Refer to the IRC for additional bracing requirements in seismic design areas.

Cripple walls are often combined with egress window framing. The cap plate on the block wall supports the floor trusses for this addition. The 2 × 6 construction allows the project to meet minimum wall insulation codes.

Wall Bracing

General codes present many methods and rules for framed wall bracing. This section discusses some general rules about how to install wall bracing. Wall bracing is very complicated. The intent of this section is to introduce you to the concepts. Refer to general codes and consult with qualified professionals for more information about wall bracing, particularly when dealing with wall bracing in high wind, seismic design, and heavy snow load areas.

Wall Brace + Braced Wall Definitions

Braced wall (braced wall line). A braced wall is a mostly straight interior or exterior wall that contains the required length of approved wall braces (braced wall panels). Most exterior walls and some interior walls are braced walls. The illustration shows examples of where wall braces might be installed in braced walls. Offsets from a straight wall are allowed if the offset is not more than 4 feet. Angled walls are allowed if the angled wall is not more than 8 feet long.

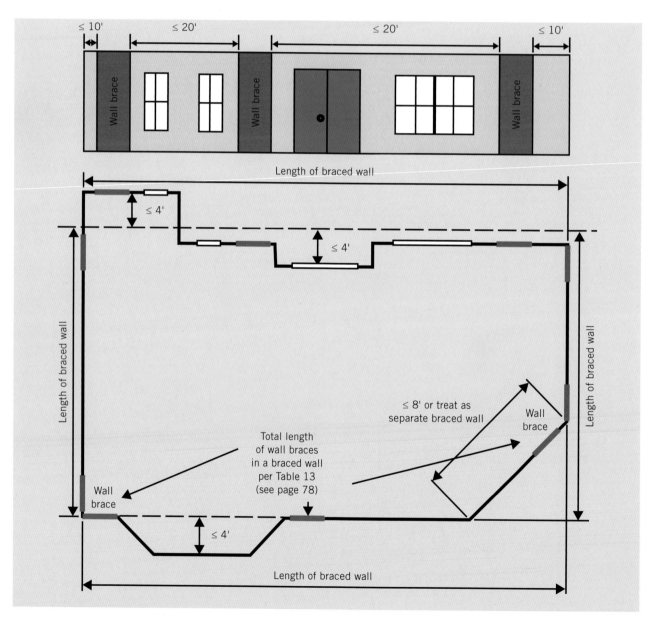

Structural panel wall bracing. To prevent framed walls from racking or leaning, bracing is required. In most cases, bracing can be accomplished by fastening full-height structural panels to the wall framing at defined intervals, near corners and around wall openings.

Wall brace (braced wall panel). A wall brace is a full height wall with no vertical or horizontal offsets that has approved wall bracing material attached. A wood structural panel (such as OSB) and panel-type siding are common examples of approved wall bracing materials. Each braced wall must have an approved total length of wall braces. The total length of wall braces depends on: (a) the criteria described in the next section; (b) the type of bracing material, such as wood structural panels and panel siding bracing; (c) the story being braced; (d) the design wind speed; and (e) the seismic design category.

Wall Bracing Methods

1. Use one of the approved wall bracing methods. Common wall bracing methods include wood structural panel sheathing that is at least ⅜ inch thick, hardboard panel siding that is at least ⁷⁄₁₆ inch thick, let-in bracing, and portal frame braces that provide shorter length bracing near large openings and garage doors. Each of these methods is an intermittent bracing method. This means that individual wall braces are installed near the ends of each braced wall.

2. You may use a continuous sheathing wall bracing method. This means that all braced walls have sheathing, such as wood structural panels applied continuously to the walls, including above and below openings and on gable end walls. Refer to the IRC for requirements regarding panel lengths near openings and for panel installation and hold-down straps at the ends of continuously sheathed braced walls.

3. Refer to the IRC for information about other wall bracing materials and methods. Refer to manufacturer's instructions for information about manufactured wall braces.

4. You may use different wall bracing methods within the same braced wall, and you may use different bracing methods on different stories. Example: you may use let-in bracing at one end of a braced wall and structural panel bracing on the other end. Use the highest required bracing length in the table when using different bracing methods in the same braced wall. Refer to the IRC for some restrictions when mixing wall bracing methods.

Wall Bracing General Installation Requirements

1. Install a wall brace near the end of each braced wall.

2. Begin the wall brace not more than 10 feet from the end of a braced wall.

3. Begin a wall brace not less than 20 feet from the closest edge of the next wall brace in the braced wall.

4. Do not exceed 60 feet between braced walls. Smaller distances between braced walls are required in the D series seismic design areas. Refer to the IRC.

Wall Brace Length

1. Install at least two 48-inch-long wall braces in braced walls longer than 16 feet. Install at least one 48-inch-long wall brace or two smaller wall braces in braced walls 16 feet long or less.

Fastening Wall Braces

1. Fasten wall bracing material to framing according to the fastening schedules in the Wood Nailing Requirements section of the IRC or according to the brace manufacturer's instructions.

2. Fasten vertical joints at panel sheathing edges to studs. Fasten horizontal joints to at least (≥) 1½-inch-thick blocking.

3. Use fasteners and uplift connectors as required by good engineering practices to connect rafters and trusses to wall braces and to connect the wall braces to framing in stories below.

4. Install at least (≥) ½-inch drywall on the interior side of wall braces. You will need to multiply the wall brace length by 1.40 if drywall is omitted. Space drywall fasteners not more than (≤) 8 inches on center at panel edges when using let-in wall braces.

Example of continuous wood structural panel wall sheathing. These walls in a crawl space are cripple walls.

TABLE 13: SIMPLE WALL BRACING MINIMUM NUMBER OF BRACING UNITS (WIND SPEED NOT MORE THAN 115 MPH, URBAN + SUBURBAN AREA)

STORIES ABOVE	EAVE TO RIDGE HEIGHT (FEET)	LONG SIDE (FEET)						SHORT SIDE (FEET)					
		10	20	30	40	50	60	10	20	30	40	50	60
0	10	1	2	2	2	3	3	1	2	2	2	3	3
1	10	2	3	3	4	5	6	2	3	3	4	5	6
0	15	1	2	3	3	4	4	1	2	3	3	4	4
1	15	2	3	4	5	6	7	2	3	4	5	6	7

Simple Wall Bracing

1. You may use a less complex wall bracing method for certain homes that are basically rectangles with insets and pop-outs. The home must comply with all of the following to qualify for this less complex method: (a) wind speed area not more than 130 miles per hour; (b) wind exposure category is B or C; (c) wall height not more than 10 feet; (d) seismic design category A, B, or C for one- and two-family homes; (e) not more than three stories above a concrete or masonry foundation or basement wall; (f) cantilevered floors extend not more than 24 inches beyond the bearing point; (g) roof eave to ridge height not more than 15 feet; (h) at least (≥) ½-inch drywall installed on the interior side of all exterior walls; and (i) no cripple walls allowed in three-story homes.

2. Use wood structural panels that are at least ⅜ inch thick as the wall bracing material. Fasten ⅜-inch-thick wood structural panels using 6d common nails. Fasten ⁷⁄₁₆-inch-thick wood structural panels using 8d common nails. Space the nails 6 inches on center at the edges and 12 inches on center at intermediate supports.

3. Build bracing units as full height walls with no openings and no vertical or horizontal offsets. A bracing unit must be one fully sheathed vertical wall segment.

4. Use bracing units that are at least 3 feet long when the walls are continuously sheathed with the wall bracing material. Continuously sheathed means all wall areas have structural sheathing

applied, including above and below openings and at gable wall ends. Use bracing units that are at least 4 feet long when the walls are not continuously sheathed.

5. Begin a bracing unit not more than 12 feet from a wall corner. Make the distance between adjacent bracing units in the same wall not more than 20 feet. Place at least one bracing unit in any wall more than 8 feet long.

6. Determine the length of exterior walls as shown in the illustration on page 76. Do not include open structures, such as porches, decks, and carports. Interior walls do not count as braced walls.

7. You may count bracing units that are wider than the minimum width as multiple bracing units. Divide the width of the bracing unit by the minimum bracing unit width to determine the number of bracing units. Example: a bracing unit is 7 feet wide. The wall is not continuously sheathed, so the minimum bracing unit width is 4 feet. The 7-foot-wide bracing unit counts as 1¾ bracing units (7/4 = 1.75).

8. Do not count sheathed wall segments that are narrower than the 3- or 4-foot minimum lengths as bracing units. Refer to the IRC for exceptions involving certain continuous sheathing methods at garage doors and large openings.

FIRST STORY PLAN

SECOND STORY PLAN

Wood Structural Panel Wall Bracing

1. Install wood structural panel wall bracing using 4 × 8 or 4 × 9 panels at least ⅜ inch thick (span rating 24/0).

2. Install panels that are at least 48 inches wide and cover at least three stud bays for studs spaced 16 inches on center.

3. Secure wood structural panel bracing to studs as presented in Table 10.

4. Install solid blocking where panel joints occur between studs to maintain fastener spacing. Use at least 1½-inch-thick wood for blocking. The

Wood structural panel wall bracing may be used on all stories and in all seismic and wind design areas.

blocking is usually the same dimensions as the studs. Example: 2 × 6 blocking is normally used with 2 × 6 studs, although 2 × 4 blocking is acceptable.

5. You may use wood structural panel wall bracing on all stories and in all wind speed and seismic design areas.

Fireblocking

Fireblocking (also called firestopping) limits the spread of fires vertically between stories in concealed wood-framed walls and horizontally in long concealed areas, such as double walls, framed openings, and drop soffits above cabinets. Concealed vertical spaces in wood-framed walls can act like a chimney, providing fire an easy and rapid path between stories. Lack of fireblocking increases the chance of property damage and loss of life during a fire. Lack of fireblocking is a common reason for failing government inspections.

Do not confuse fireblocking with draftstopping (see page 66). Draftstopping limits the horizontal movement of air in concealed floor/ceiling assemblies.

Where Fireblocking Is Required

1. Install fireblocking in any concealed wall space if an opening exists that would allow fire to spread from one story to another or from a lower story into the attic. Examples of such openings include: openings for plumbing pipes, openings for electrical wires and conduit, HVAC duct chases between stories, laundry chutes, and openings at the tops of framed columns, niches, and arches.

2. Install fireblocking in concealed wall spaces at every ceiling and floor level. An intact top and

bottom plate usually provides fireblocking in platform framing.

3. Install fireblocking where concealed vertical and horizontal wall spaces intersect. Examples of concealed horizontal spaces include soffits for kitchen cabinets and recessed vanity lights, and drop ceilings.

4. Install fireblocking between stair stringers at the top and bottom of each flight of stairs. Also install drywall (at least ½ inch thick) on all walls and soffits if the area under the stairs is accessible by a door or access panel.

5. Install fireblocking around chimneys and flues where they intersect framing at floor and ceiling levels.

6. Install fireblocking in concealed wall spaces if the concealed space is open for more than 10 feet horizontally. A common example of a long concealed horizontal wall space is a double wall built using two rows of staggered studs. Another example is a large arched opening between rooms.

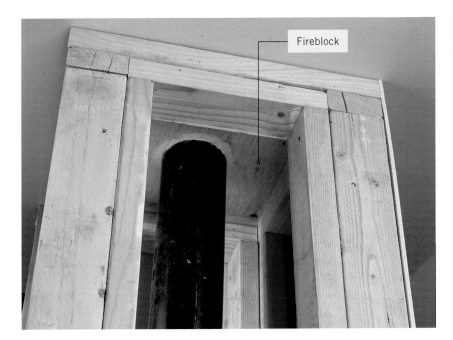

Fireblock

Install fireblocking in framed columns, framed arches, and similar openings between stories.

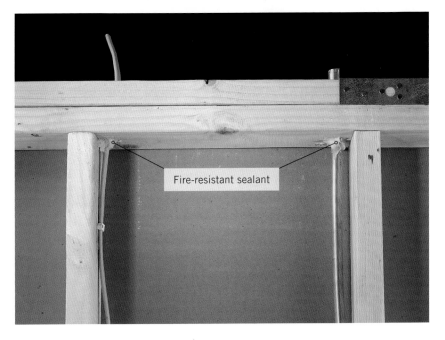

Fire-resistant sealant

Install listed fire-resistant caulk or foam sealant at penetrations for wires, pipes, and ducts. This helps reduce the spread of fires and helps limit air and moisture flow.

Fireblocking Materials + Installation

1. You may use any of the following fireblocking materials: (a) 2-inch-thick lumber (example: a 2 × 4), (b) two pieces of 1-inch-thick lumber with staggered joints (example: two 1 × 4), (c) at least $\frac{23}{32}$-inch-thick wood structural panels, (d) at least ¾-inch-thick particleboard, (e) at least ½-inch-thick drywall, (f) at least ¼-inch-thick cement-based millboard, or (g) unfaced batts or blankets of mineral wool or fiberglass insulation if it is secured in place.

2. Install backing at any joints in fireblocking material when using wood structural panels or particleboard. Use the same fireblocking material for the backing. Example: if a joint exists in OSB fireblocking material, place another piece of the same OSB material over the joint. Most general codes do not state how far to extend the backing.

3. Do not use loose fill insulation as a fireblocking material unless it is specifically tested and approved for the intended location and installation method.

4. Repair fireblocking that is damaged or penetrated by pipes, ducts, or other materials.

Wall Penetration Flashing

Kick-out flashing is inserted between the underside of the roof-covering layer and a sidewall to redirect water away from the sidewall. Flashing should be at least 4" tall and 4" wide.

It is not possible to overstate the importance of flashing to the long-term integrity and health of your home. Sealants, such as caulk, degrade over time and require maintenance. Exterior wall coverings move and crack, creating gaps into which moisture can flow. People often do not maintain caulking and sealants as they should. The best long-term solution to avoiding moisture intrusion is a combination of a water-resistant barrier and flashing integrated to form a drainage plane that prevents moisture from reaching vulnerable wood framing materials and drains the moisture away from the structure.

Flashing General Requirements

1. Use only corrosion-resistant flashing material, such as galvanized steel and peel-and-stick material. Corrosion resistance includes fasteners or other materials used to secure the flashing.

2. Use flashing, fasteners, and other materials that are compatible with each other and with surrounding materials. Incompatible materials will react with each other and degrade over time. Example: do not use galvanized material with aluminum or with copper.

3. Flash and seal all wall penetrations and other vulnerable areas so that moisture will not enter the structure. Flash and seal any point where moisture could enter the structure, regardless of whether it is mentioned in the list of areas where flashing is specifically required.

4. Install flashing "shingle fashion" so that upper flashing laps over lower flashing, resulting in a drainage plane that will drain water toward a designated discharge point. This includes integrating flashing with the water-resistant barrier.

5. Extend flashing to the surface of the exterior wall finish material if necessary to assure that water is drained. This may be necessary with brick veneer, at horizontal joints in panel siding, with Z flashing at window and door headers, and at other drainage points.

Flashing Required Locations

1. Install flashing at all window and door openings. Refer to the window and door manufacturer's installation instructions and to the instructions for any weather-resistive material (such as house wrap) or flashing material.

2. Install an air-sealing material (such as spray foam) between the window/door and the framing.

3. Install pan flashing at the window and door sills unless the window or door manufacturer's instructions state otherwise. Slope the pan flashing so that water drains toward the exterior. Integrate the pan flashing with jamb (side) flashing, header (top), and the weather-resistant barrier. Install all window and door flashing so that water drains away from the opening and out from the structure.

4. Install sidewall flashing where chimneys or other masonry construction intersect with walls.

5. Install projecting lips (sometimes called kick-out flashing) at chimneys and other sidewalls where a roof extends past a vertical sidewall. Kick-out flashing helps divert water away from this vulnerable intersection.

6. Install header/sidewall flashing under and at the ends of all copings and sills, including masonry, metal, and wood.

7. Install header/sidewall flashing above all wood trim that projects from the adjoining wall and forms a shelf where water can collect.

8. Install flashing at the attachment point of exterior porches, decks, balconies, stairs, or floor assemblies to wood-framed construction.

9. Install sidewall flashing at all roof and wall intersections.

How to Flash a Window + a Door

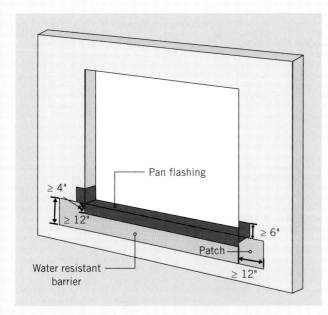

Install a water-resistant barrier, such as flexible flashing, to the sheathing beneath the window opening. Attach the barrier at the top only so material may be slipped underneath later. Install a metal or peel-and-stick window pan in the opening. Cut small patches of adhesive membrane to cover the corners where the pan climbs up the side jambs.

***

NOTE: If building wrap has already been installed, remove just enough to expose the exterior wall sheathing around the window opening.

Cut strips of self-adhesive flashing membrane and apply them to the wall at each side of the window opening. The flashing should extend into the window opening an amount roughly equal to the thickness of the wall. Make slits in the flashing at the top and bottom and fold over to cover the side jambs and the vertical portion of the pan. Apply a bead of adhesive caulk around the sides and top of the opening.

Install the window according to the manufacturer's directions. Apply a strip of self-adhesive flashing membrane across the top of the opening, covering the top window nailing flange.

Install building wrap according to the manufacturer's instructions. The edges of the wrap at the window opening should be secured to the flanges with building wrap tape supplied by the building wrap manufacturer. At the bottom of the window, slide the top edge of the building wrap behind the moisture barrier that was left unfastened at the bottom.

Roof Systems

This section addresses the roof structural system. Refer to other sections of this book, general codes, and manufacturer's instructions for information about installing roof coverings. The number and size of the rafters or trusses is a vital element of home design, as are the methods for fastening these elements to the house structure. If you live in a coastal area or any region that is prone to earthquakes or hurricanes, a separate set of codes exists for your roof system. Be sure to enforce its more rigorous standards when you build.

Ridge, Valley + Hip Rafter Framing

1. Install at least a 1-inch (nominal thickness) ridgeboard at roof ridges in houses built with rafters (truss-built roofs do not have ridgeboards). Install a ridgeboard that is at least as deep as the (plumb) cut end of the rafter. Install rafters across from each other (within 1½ inch) at the ridgeboard. You may omit the ridgeboard if you secure the rafters to each other with a gusset plate.

2. Install at least a 2-inch (nominal thickness) hip rafter and valley rafter at all hips and valleys, including valleys formed when one roof is framed on top of another, collar tie, or ridge strap.

3. Support hip and valley rafters at the ridge with a brace to a load-bearing wall, or design the hip and valley rafters to bear the load at the ridge.

4. Design and support ridge, hip, and valley rafters as beams when the roof pitch is less than $\frac{3}{12}$.

5. Design and support the ridge as a beam and design the walls supporting the ridge to bear the ridge load when framing cathedral and vaulted ceilings without ceiling joists and rafter ties.

A roof system comprises rafters or trusses that support roof sheathing. The sheathing is covered with an underlayment and roofing materials. Soffits, flashing, and ventilation are also important parts of the roof system.

Rafters have specific names that are assigned according to their function in the roof system.

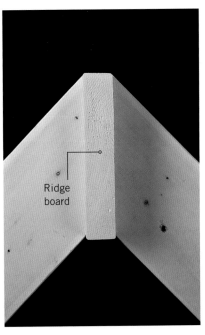

Position rafters across from each other on a ridgeboard or beam that is at least as deep as the rafter plumb cut.

Purlins

1. You may use purlins to support rafters that would otherwise span a greater distance than allowed. Example: a properly installed purlin at the center of an 18-foot-long rafter would allow you to use 9 feet as the rafter span distance.

2. Install purlins that are at least the same depth as the rafters they support. Example: use a 2 × 6 purlin to support a 2 × 6 rafter.

3. Use at least one 2 × 4 brace to carry the purlin load to a load-bearing wall. The purlin brace length should not exceed 8 feet without additional bracing (usually an additional 2 × 4 nailed to the brace). Purlin braces should bear on a load-bearing wall and may not slope at less than a 45-degree angle from horizontal. Space the purlin braces not more than 4 feet apart.

Use purlins to support rafters if the rafter span is longer than allowed.

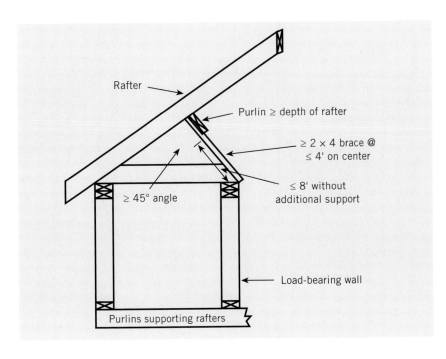

Purlins supporting rafters

Collar Ties

1. Install a collar tie or a ridge strap between every pair of rafters when using a ridge board. Use collar ties that are at least 1 × 4. Collar ties and ridge straps are not required when connecting rafters using a gusset plate.

2. Use ridge straps that are at least 1¼ inches wide 20 gauge steel. Fasten ridge straps using at least three 10d nails with the nails at least 2⅜ inches from the end of the rafter.

3. Locate collar ties in the upper one-third of the attic space.

4. Connect collar ties and rafters as specified in Table 10 (see page 70).

Rafter + Ceiling Joist Bearing on Support

1. Install rafters and ceiling joists with at least 1½ inches of the rafter or joist bearing on supporting wood members (such as a top plate or a valley rafter) and at least 3 inches of the rafter or joist bearing on masonry or concrete.

2. Toenail rafters to the top plate as specified in Table 10 (see page 70).

3. Install plates with a bearing area of at least 48 square inches when the plate bears on concrete or masonry. This means that the plate should have at least 48 square inches of surface area in contact with the masonry or concrete.

Rafter + Ceiling Joist Bridging + Lateral Support

1. Install bridging on rafters and ceiling joists deeper than 2 × 12 (six-to-one depth-to-thickness ratio). Space bridging not more than every 8 feet. Bridging should consist of solid, full-depth blocking, wood or metal diagonal bridging or by nailing at least a 1 × 3 wood strip to each rafter or ceiling joist. Bridging is required by some building officials on ceiling joists smaller than 2 × 12.

2. Install lateral support at bearing points on rafters and ceiling joists deeper than 2 × 10 (five-to-one depth-to-thickness ratio).

Ceiling Joist + Rafter Notching + Boring

1. Notch and bore dimensional lumber ceiling joists and rafters using the same rules as for floor joists, except as indicated below.

Connect one ceiling joist to one rafter when the ceiling joists and rafters are parallel.

FASTEN RAFTERS TO RIDGE AND TO PLATE PER TABLES

FASTEN RAFTER TIES TO RAFTER PER TABLE

Install rafter ties not more than 48 inches apart.

2. Leave at least 3½ inches of wood above the notch (bird mouth cut) where the rafter bears on the exterior wall, and do not cantilever the rafter past the wall more than 24 inches.

3. Do not taper a ceiling joist more than the actual depth of the ceiling joist divided by 4 if notching the ceiling joist where it bears on the wall. Example: do not cut more than 1⅞ inch of a 2 × 8 ceiling joist where it bears on the wall.

Ceiling Joist Nailing to Rafter

1. Toenail all rafters to the top plate as specified in Table 10 (see page 70).

2. Install a method to prevent rafter thrust from pushing on supporting walls. You may use ceiling joists, rafter ties, or kickers to comply with this requirement.

3. Connect one rafter to one ceiling joist when the ceiling joists are parallel to the rafters. Locate the ceiling joists in the lower third of the attic area, if possible. Facenail these ceiling joists to rafters using 16d common nails or 40d box nails. (See Table 14, page 88.)

4. Connect a rafter tie to the corresponding rafter on the other side of the roof when the ceiling joists are not parallel to the rafters. Locate the rafter ties in the bottom one-third of the rafter height,

if possible. Install rafter ties not more than 48 inches apart. Facenail rafters ties to rafters using the quantity of 16d common nails or 40d box nails indicated in Table 14. Use 2 × 4 or larger lumber for rafter ties.

5. Lap ceiling joists that meet over interior walls or beams at least 3 inches, and facenail using the same quantity and type of nails indicated in Table 14. Apply this requirement when the ceiling joists are designed to resist rafter lateral thrust. This requirement usually applies when the ceiling joists are attached to the rafters.

6. You may butt the ends of ceiling joists together over interior walls or beams. Fasten the ceiling joists as specified in Table 10 (see page 70) if the ceiling joists are not designed to resist rafter lateral thrust. This exception usually applies when the ceiling joists are not attached to the rafters.

Ceiling Joist Nailing to Rafter Exceptions

1. Note the following exceptions to the quantity of nails required by codes:

   (a) You may reduce the required quantity of nails by 25 percent if the nails are clinched (the pointed ends sticking out from the wood are bent over).

   (b) You may use fewer fasteners if you support the ridge board on load-bearing walls or if you design and support the ridge as a beam.

   (c) You may use a smaller roof span column if you install purlins to support the rafters. Example: if you install purlins at the center of rafters with a roof span of 24 feet, you may reduce the roof span by 50 percent and use the 12-foot roof span column.

   (d) You may reduce the actual rafter slope by one-third if you substitute rafter ties for ceiling joists, Example: if the actual rafter slope is 9/12, use 6/12 as the adjusted rafter slope, but because there is no 6/12 slope row, use the nearest more conservative 5/12 row.

   (e) Increase the quantity of nails in the table if the ceiling joists or rafter ties are not located at the bottom of the attic space.

TABLE 14: NAIL QUANTITIES CEILING JOISTS + RAFTER TIES TO RAFTERS

Rafter Slope	Rafter Spacing (inches)	GROUND SNOW LOAD (PSF)											
		20			30			50			70		
		Roof Span (feet)											
		12	24	36	12	24	36	12	24	36	12	24	36
3:12	12	3	5	8	3	6	9	5	9	13	6	12	17
	16	4	7	10	4	8	12	6	12	17	8	15	23
	24	5	10	15	6	12	18	9	17	26	12	23	34
4:12	12	3	4	6	3	5	7	4	7	10	5	9	13
	16	3	5	8	3	6	9	5	9	13	6	12	17
	24	4	8	11	5	9	13	7	13	19	9	17	26
5:12	12	3	3	5	3	4	6	3	6	8	4	7	11
	16	3	4	6	3	5	7	4	7	11	5	9	14
	24	3	6	9	4	7	11	6	11	16	7	14	21
7:12	12	3	3	4	3	3	4	3	4	6	3	5	8
	16	3	3	5	3	4	5	3	5	8	4	7	10
	24	3	5	7	3	5	8	4	8	11	5	10	15
9:12	12	3	3	3	3	3	3	3	3	5	3	4	6
	16	3	3	4	3	3	4	3	4	6	3	5	8
	24	3	4	5	3	4	6	3	6	9	4	8	12
12:12	12	3	3	3	3	3	3	3	3	4	3	3	5
	16	3	3	3	3	3	3	3	3	5	3	4	6
	24	3	3	4	3	3	5	3	5	7	3	6	9

Rafter + Truss Connection to Walls

1. Attach trusses and rafters to the supporting walls as specified in Table 10 (see page 70). The truss design drawings supersede this requirement.

2. Refer to the IRC or engineered plans for wall attachment requirements. Some building inspectors require hurricane ties on all trusses and rafters.

Hurricane ties (also called clips) are recommended for all rafter or truss connections to walls. In some areas, they are required.

Selecting the correct size and type of ceiling joist requires that you know whether the attic may be used for storage. Selecting the correct size and type of rafter requires that you know the loads imposed by roof covering materials and loads imposed by snow accumulation on the roof.

Use these attic storage definitions to help you determine the correct ceiling joist span table. Access to attics with limited storage may be through a scuttle hole or by pull-down stairs. If attic access is by a permanent stairway, then consider the attic to be habitable space, and use the bedroom floor joist span tables instead of the ceiling joist span tables.

These attic storage definitions do not affect the requirements for access to attics. Refer to the Attic Access section (page 93) for attic access requirements.

An attic without storage, built with joists and rafters, has less than 42" between the top of the ceiling joists and the bottom of the rafters. An attic without storage, built with trusses, has fewer than three adjacent trusses with the same web configuration that could contain a cube not more than 42" wide and 24" tall located in the same plane (area) of the truss.

An attic with limited storage, built with joists and rafters, has at least 42" between the top of the ceiling joists and the bottom of the rafters. An attic with limited storage, built with trusses, has three or more adjacent trusses with the same web configuration that could contain a cube more than 42" wide and 24" tall located in the same plane (area) of the truss. An attic with limited storage is designed with an additional 10 psf live load compared to an attic without storage. Verify the storage capacity of truss-built attics with the truss engineer before using the attic for storage.

Roof live and snow load. Use the roof live load 20 psf tables in areas where the design ground snow load is less than (<) 30 psf. Use the rafter snow load tables in areas of the country with ground snow loads of 30 psf or more. Verify the design ground snow load with the local building official.

Rafter dead loads. Use the 10 psf rafter dead load columns when using one layer of roof coverings such as fiberglass shingles and wood. Use the 20 psf rafter dead load columns when using roof coverings such as tile and slate.

"Limited storage" in an attic with joists and rafters requires a clear span of 42" tall. In an attic built with trusses, you must have at least three consecutive bays where a 24"-high by 42"-wide cube can pass through without changing direction.

"Limited storage" in attic with rafters

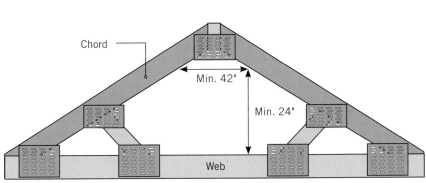

"Limited storage" in attic with trusses

Ceiling Joist + Rafter Deflection

1. All ceiling joist spans in the tables below use L/240 deflection, where L is the length of the joist or rafter in inches divided by 240.

2. All rafter spans in the tables below use L/180 deflection.

Ceiling Joist + Rafter Span Tables

1. Use the following tables to determine the maximum unsupported horizontal distance that ceiling joists and rafters can span.

2. Refer to the IRC or to the AF+PA Span Tables for Joists and Rafters to determine spans for lumber widths, species, grades, and snow load factors not in these tables.

3. These tables apply to roof systems framed using standard 2-inch (nominal thickness) dimensional lumber. An engineer must design roof truss systems.

TABLE 15: CEILING JOIST SPANS 16" ON CENTER UNINHABITABLE ATTICS, NO STORAGE

SPECIES	GRADE	2 × 6 FT.-IN.	2 × 8 FT.-IN.	2 × 10 FT.-IN.
Douglas fir	2	17-8	23-4	>26-0
Hem fir	2	16-6	21-9	>26-0
Southern pine	2	16-11	21-7	>25-7
Spruce-pine-fir	2	16-11	22-4	>26-0

TABLE 16: CEILING JOIST SPANS 24" ON CENTER UNINHABITABLE ATTICS, NO STORAGE

SPECIES	GRADE	2 × 6 FT.-IN.	2 × 8 FT.-IN.	2 × 10 FT.-IN.
Douglas fir	2	15-0	19-1	23-3
Hem fir	2	14-5	18-6	22-7
Southern pine	2	13-11	17-7	20-11
Spruce-pine-fir	2	14-9	18-9	22-11

TABLE 17: CEILING JOIST SPANS 16" ON CENTER UNINHABITABLE ATTICS WITH LIMITED STORAGE

SPECIES	GRADE	2 × 6 FT.-IN.	2 × 8 FT.-IN.	2 × 10 FT.-IN.
Douglas fir	2	13-9	17-5	21-3
Hem fir	2	12-8	16-0	19-7
Southern pine	2	12-0	15-3	18-1
Spruce-pine-fir	2	12-10	16-3	19-10

TABLE 18: CEILING JOIST SPANS 24" ON CENTER UNINHABITABLE ATTICS WITH LIMITED STORAGE

SPECIES	GRADE	2 × 6 FT.-IN.	2 × 8 FT.-IN.	2 × 10 FT.-IN.
Douglas fir	2	10-8	13-6	16-5
Hem fir	2	10-4	13-1	16-0
Southern pine	2	9-10	12-6	14-9
Spruce-pine-fir	2	10-6	13-3	16-3

TABLE 19: RAFTER SPANS 16" ON CENTER, ROOF LIVE LOAD 20 PSF, CEILING NOT ATTACHED

DEAD LOAD	10 PSF	10 PSF	10 PSF	20 PSF	20 PSF	20 PSF
	2 × 6	2 × 8	2 × 10	2 × 6	2 × 8	2 × 10
SPECIES-GRADE	FT.-IN.	FT.-IN.	FT.-IN.	FT.-IN.	FT.-IN.	FT.-IN.
Douglas fir - 2	14-4	18-2	22-3	12-5	15-9	19-6
Hem fir - 2	14-2	17-11	21-11	12-3	15-6	18-11
Southern pine - 2	13-6	17-1	20-3	11-8	14-9	17-6
Spruce pine fir - 2	14-4	18-2	22-3	12-5	15-9	19-3

TABLE 20: RAFTER SPANS 24" ON CENTER, ROOF LIVE LOAD 20 PSF, CEILING NOT ATTACHED

DEAD LOAD	10 PSF	10 PSF	10 PSF	20 PSF	20 PSF	20 PSF
	2 × 6	2 × 8	2 × 10	2 × 6	2 × 8	2 × 10
SPECIES-GRADE	FT.-IN.	FT.-IN.	FT.-IN.	FT.-IN.	FT.-IN.	FT.-IN.
Douglas fir - 2	11-11	15-1	18-5	10-4	13-0	15-11
Hem fir - 2	11-7	14-8	17-10	10-0	12-8	15-6
Southern pine - 2	11-0	10-11	16-6	9-6	12-1	14-4
Spruce pine fir - 2	11-9	14-10	18-2	10-2	12-10	15-8

TABLE 21: RAFTER SPANS 16" ON CENTER, GROUND SNOW LOAD 30 PSF, CEILING NOT ATTACHED

DEAD LOAD	10 PSF	10 PSF	10 PSF	20 PSF	20 PSF	20 PSF
	2 × 6	2 × 8	2 × 10	2 × 6	2 × 8	2 × 10
SPECIES-GRADE	FT.-IN.	FT.-IN.	FT.-IN.	FT.-IN.	FT.-IN.	FT.-IN.
Douglas fir - 2	12-1	15-4	18-9	10-10	13-8	16-9
Hem fir - 2	11-9	14-11	18-2	10-6	13-4	16-3
Southern pine - 2	11-2	14-2	16-10	10-0	12-8	15-1
Spruce pine fir - 2	11-11	15-1	18-5	10-8	13-6	16-6

TABLE 22: RAFTER SPANS 24" ON CENTER, GROUND SNOW LOAD 30 PSF, CEILING NOT ATTACHED

DEAD LOAD	10 PSF	10 PSF	10 PSF	20 PSF	20 PSF	20 PSF
	2 × 6	2 × 8	2 × 10	2 × 6	2 × 8	2 × 10
SPECIES-GRADE	FT.-IN.	FT.-IN.	FT.-IN.	FT.-IN.	FT.-IN.	FT.-IN.
Douglas fir - 2	9-10	12-6	15-3	8-10	11-2	13-8
Hem fir - 2	9-7	12-2	14-10	8-7	10-10	13-3
Southern pine - 2	9-2	11-7	13-9	8-2	10-4	12-3
Spruce pine fir - 2	9-9	12-4	15-1	8-8	11-0	13-6

Roof Truss Installation

Truss Design + Bracing Written Specifications Requirements

1. Use a qualified engineer to design all wood trusses, such as roof and floor trusses. The engineer and/or truss manufacturer should provide written truss design and installation specifications and deliver them to the job site with the trusses. These specifications should include engineering information, such as chord live and dead loads; assembly information, such as the size, species, and grade of each truss member; and installation instructions, such as where each truss should be located on the structure and how the trusses should be permanently braced.

Truss Installation Tolerance Recommendations

1. Install trusses according to the installation tolerances contained in the written truss specifications. Use the following installation tolerances from the booklet *Guide to Good Practice for Handling, Installation + Bracing of Metal Plate Connected Wood Trusses* only if the engineer and/or truss manufacturer does not provide installation instructions. The IRC does not specifically require installation to these tolerances; however, installation to these tolerances is implied by the general IRC requirement that components be installed according to manufacturer's installation instructions.

2. Install trusses so that a bow in either the top or bottom chord is not more than L/200 or 2 inches, whichever is less. L is the length of the truss chord in inches.

3. Install trusses that are out-of-plumb (vertical) by not more than D/50 or 2 inches, whichever is less. D is the depth of the truss in inches at the point of measurement.

4. Install trusses at load-bearing points not more than ¼ inch from the location on the plans.

5. Install trusses that use the top chord as the weight-bearing point with a gap of not more than ½ inch between the inside of the load-bearing support and the first diagonal or vertical truss web.

Alteration + Repair of Trusses

1. Do not alter trusses in any way, including cutting, notching, boring, and splicing, without written instructions from a qualified engineer.

2. Do not use trusses to carry the weight of equipment (such as furnaces or water heaters), use the attic area for storage, or hang storage units from trusses unless the trusses have been designed to carry the additional weight.

3. Do not repair damaged trusses without written instructions from a qualified engineer.

A = Truss bearing on top chord; B = Truss not plumb; C = Truss parts; D = Bowed truss chords

Truss Details

Truss bearing point

Top chords

Bearing wall

≤ ½"

A

First web

Depth of truss

Max. out of plumb

B

Length of truss chord

Max. bow

D

Webs

C

Gusset

Bottom chord

Truss chord

Bearing point

Attic Access

General Attic Access Requirements

1. Provide an access opening to every attic with at least 30 square feet of attic area and a vertical height of at least 30 inches at some point in the 30 square feet. Measure the vertical height from the top of the ceiling joists (or truss bottom chord) to the bottom of the rafters (or truss top chord).

2. Provide a rough opening (size before finishing) for a ceiling attic access of at least 22 inches by 30 inches. Locate the opening in a hallway or other readily accessible location. Locate the opening so that at least 30 inches of unobstructed headroom exists at some point above the opening.

3. Provide a rough opening (size before finishing) for a wall attic access of at least 22 inches wide by 30 inches high.

4. You do not need to provide attic access if the ceiling and roof systems are built using non-combustible materials. This is rare in residential construction.

5. Refer to the IRC for additional access requirements if appliances are located in the attic.

Insulation Clearance to Heat-Producing Devices

1. Provide at least 3 inches clearance between combustible insulation and heat-producing devices, such as recessed lighting fixtures and fan motors. Most insulation used in modern homes is considered combustible.

2. You may reduce the 3-inch clearance requirement if the device is listed for a lesser clearance and is installed according to manufacturer's instructions.

3. Install an insulation shield around any gas or oil vent that passes through an attic or other insulated area (such as a floor/ceiling assembly).

4. Use at least 26-gauge sheet metal for the insulation shield.

5. Extend the shield at least 2 inches above attic insulation material.

6. Secure the insulation shield to prevent movement of the shield.

Shield

CAUTION. RISK OF FIRE. DO NOT INSTALL. REMOVE THIS INSULATION IN ATTIC SPACE TO ENCLOSING CHIMNEY IN ATTIC SPACE

Install an insulation shield around equipment vents that pass through insulation.

Exterior Components

The primary function of the exterior components of a building is to keep the elements out. Of these elements, the most destructive is water. Water causes more damage than almost any other natural source, including fire and termites. Water can destroy most building materials, and it is an essential ingredient for mold growth.

In this chapter you will learn about three common water control issues. Shingle roof coverings are the most common type of material for keeping water that falls on the roof out of the home. You will learn about the code requirements for shingle installation and about where to install flashing that keeps water away from vulnerable areas, such as where roofs intersect with walls and chimneys. You will also learn about code requirements for water control around your home so that water stays out of basements and crawl spaces.

This chapter also contains information about fireplaces and chimneys. Water infiltration is common around these components, and fire safety is an additional important consideration.

In this chapter:
- Shingle Roof-Covering Installation
- Fireplaces + Chimneys

Shingle Roof-Covering Installation

When it comes to installing roof coverings, it can be a little hard to define where enforceable codes end and ordinary best practices begin. But it is safe to say that most codes contain guidelines for installing roof coverings that, if followed, will ensure a long-lasting roof that keeps moisture from penetrating your house. The following information applies to asphalt shingles.

"Asphalt shingles" is a fairly general description that includes three-tab, dimensional, and laminated shingles.

Roof slope is measured by the number of inches the roof increases in height (rise) in 12" horizontally (run).

It does not include asphalt-based roll roofing. This section applies to shingle roof-covering installation in almost all areas. Consult your local building inspector for additional requirements if you live in a very high wind speed design area, such as near the ocean.

Always read and follow the shingle manufacturer's instructions. They are printed on every package of shingles. Details that seem minor, such as failing to install the starter course or incorrectly installing nails, can make a big difference in how the shingles perform under stress. Failing to follow instructions can void the shingle warranty. This section applies to shingle roof-covering installation in almost all areas. Consult your local building inspector for additional requirements if you live in a very high wind speed design area, such as near the ocean.

Roof Slope + Sheathing

Roof Slope Restriction

1. Do not install shingles on roofs with a slope less than 2/12. Low slope and flat roofs require a roof covering designed for a low slope roof. Membranes, such as modified bitumen and EPDM, and standing seam metal are examples of low slope roof coverings.

2. Install a double underlayment layer under shingles on roofs with a slope between 2/12 and 4/12.

3. Verify shingle manufacturer's instructions about minimum roof slope. Some do not allow installation on slopes less than 2½/12.

Roof Deck Type Restriction

1. Install shingle roof covering only on solid sheathed roofs. In residential construction this means roofs covered by OSB or plywood, which includes virtually all houses built in the last generation or two.

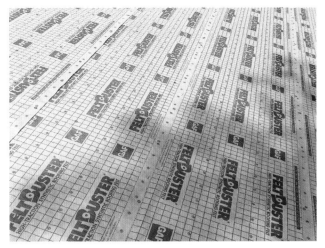

Underlayment for new and replacement shingle roofs is often a synthetic material recommended by the shingle manufacturer instead of the roofing felt used in older installations.

Underlayment Specifications

1. Underlayment for shingles is usually a proprietary product recommended by the shingle manufacturer. Other materials may include #15 roofing felt and modified bitumen sheets. Refer to general codes and manufacturer's instructions for other acceptable underlayment materials.

Underlayment Application for Roof Slopes 4-in-12 + Greater

1. Begin at the eaves and apply at least a 36-inch-wide strip of underlayment parallel to the eaves.

2. Lap horizontal joints at least 2 inches with the upper strip over the lower strip.

3. Lap end joints as specified by the shingle manufacturer. End joint laps are usually between 4 and 6 inches.

4. Offset end joints by at least 6 feet.

5. Use sufficient fasteners to hold underlayment in place. The IRC does not specify fastener type and quantity.

6. Minimize wrinkles and distortions in the underlayment. Wrinkles should not interfere with the ability of the shingle's sealing strips to seal. Underlayment wrinkles and distortions can appear through the shingles, creating a cosmetic issue.

Drip Edge

1. Install drip edge flashing at eaves and at gable rakes.

2. Use drip edge flashing that extends at least ¼ inch below the roof sheathing and extends at least 2 inches up the roof deck.

3. Lap adjacent drip edge pieces at least 2 inches.

4. Attach drip edge using roofing nails spaced not more than 12 inches on center.

5. Install underlayment under the drip edge at rakes.

6. Install underlayment over the drip edge at eaves.

Proper installation of underlayment is important for reducing roof leaks. The underlayment should overlap the top of the drip edge at the eave, with the drip edge along the rake edges installed after the underlayment so it overlaps and directs runoff onto the underlayment.

Underlayment Application for Roof Slopes Between 2-in-12 + 4-in-12

1. Begin at the eaves and apply at least a 19-inch-wide strip of underlayment parallel to the eaves.

2. Begin again at the eaves and apply at least a 36-inch-wide strip of underlayment.

3. Lap each successive layer at least 19 inches over the previous layer, with the upper layer lapping over the lower layer.

4. Lap end joints at least 6 inches.

5. Use sufficient fasteners to hold underlayment in place. Most codes do not specify fastener type and quantity.

6. Install drip edge as previously described.

Underlayment Application in Ice Dam Areas

1. Install ice dam underlayment where there is a history of water backup at the eaves caused by ice. Verify ice dam requirements with the local building official. You do not need to install ice dam underlayment on unconditioned detached accessory structures, such as an unheated garage.

2. Install either a sheet of self-adhering, polymer-modified bitumen roofing or at least two layers of roofing felt, or other approved material, bonded together with roofing cement. Begin the ice dam underlayment at the lowest edge of all roof surfaces, and extend it at least 24 inches beyond the exterior wall of the building.

3. Measure distances horizontally, not up the roof sheathing. Begin the 24-inch measurement from the interior side of the wall. Example: if the eaves extend 12 inches horizontally from the exterior wall of the building, extend the ice dam underlayment at least 39 inches horizontally from the edge of the eaves (assuming a 2 × 4 wall).

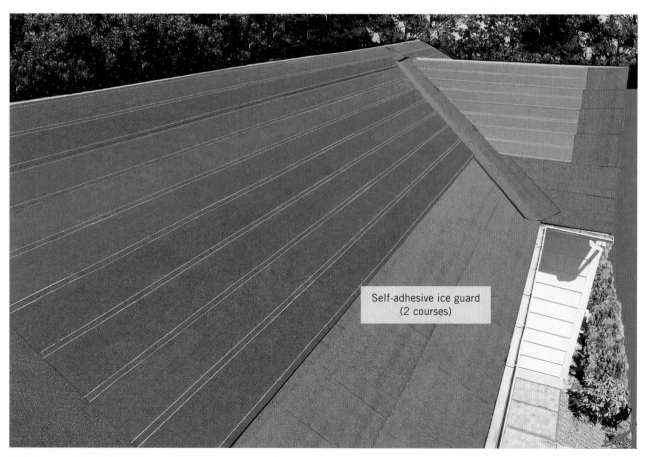

Self-adhesive ice guard
(2 courses)

Install one or two courses (depending on local codes) of fully-bonded, self-adhesive ice dam underlayment in cold-weather climates. Ice dam underlayment helps prevent liquid water from running under the shingles and leaking into your home.

Roof Flashing

Roof flashing used with asphalt shingles is typically made of metal: primarily galvanized steel, aluminum, or copper. The timing for installing it depends on the type of flashing. Some, such as valley flashing, is installed prior to the finished roof covering (shingles). Other types, such as step-flashing, is interwoven with the shingles during the installation process. In some cases, formable, self-adhesive flashings can be used instead of metal. In some code areas, roll roofing may be used as valley flashing—check with your building inspector.

Closed-Cut Valley Flashing

1. Before installing the shingles, install valley flashing material according to the shingle manufacturer's instructions. You may use at least a 36-inch-wide strip of smooth roll roofing material as valley flashing material with at least 18 inches on each side of the valley; or you may use any open valley lining material.

2. Place nails at least 6 inches away from the valley centerline, unless other spacing is approved by the shingle manufacturer.

3. Apply the shingles across one side of the valley at least 12 inches, or as recommended by the shingle manufacturer.

4. Apply shingles from the other direction to before the valley centerline, and trim the edges as recommended by the shingle manufacturer. Seal the cut shingles in a closed-cut valley, as recommend by the manufacturer. Sealing the cut shingles is frequently omitted.

Woven valleys are a common shingle valley treatment. Some manufacturers do not allow these valleys when using laminated shingles.

Closed-cut valley shingles are cut in a straight line about 2" from the valley center line. The cut should be on the side where the least amount of water is likely to flow.

Chimney Crickets

1. Install a cricket (also called a saddle) on chimneys that are more than 30 inches wide in the dimension parallel to the roof ridgeline. A cricket is not required if the chimney intersects the roof ridgeline. This also applies to factory-built chimneys that are installed inside a wood chimney chase.

2. Flash the cricket at the chimney wall using step and counter flashing that is compatible with the roof covering material.

3. Install the cricket with a vertical height at the chimney based on Table 23. W is the width of the chimney. Leave at least a 1-inch air space between a wood-framed cricket and a masonry chimney wall.

Step Flashing

1. Install step flashing at the intersections of a sloped roof and a vertical side wall. Use flashing that is at least 4 inches wide by 4 inches high. Install kick-out flashing at the end of the wall to direct water away from the side wall.

2. Flash the intersection of a sloped roof and a chimney according to the shingle manufacturer's instructions. This typically includes step flashing covered with counter flashing.

3. Flash other roof penetrations, such as plumbing and gas vents, according to the shingle manufacturer's instructions.

4. Flash skylights according to the skylight manufacturer's instructions.

⟋ TABLE 23: CHIMNEY CRICKET HEIGHT

ROOF SLOPE	CRICKET HEIGHT
12/12	1/2 W
8/12	1/3 W
6/12	1/4 W
4/12	1/6 W
3/12	1/8 W

Flash roof and sidewall intersections using step and counter flashing.

Flash all penetrations, such as plumbing vents and equipment vents, with preformed flashing, often called boots. Make sure the flashing conforms to your roof slope.

Most skylights for residential installation come with a flashing kit. Improper installation and flashing of skylights is a common cause of roof leaks.

Integrate kickout flashing with sidewall flashing and the water-resistive material.

Flash brick veneer using base and counterflashing that is integrated with the water-resistant material.

A properly flashed roof/sidewall intersection includes roof covering underlayment, base and counterflashing, water-resistive material, and kickout flashing.

A headwall is where a roof rises to meet a sidewall. Flash headwalls using base and counterflashing integrated with water-resistive material.

Roofing Fasteners

Fastener Type + Quantity in Standard Shingling Conditions

1. Use the type and quantity of fasteners recommended by the shingle manufacturer. Locate nails on the shingle strip precisely as recommended by the shingle manufacturer. Some manufacturers recommend installing nails below the black adhesive seal strip. Other manufacturers leave a gap in the seal strip for installing nails. Do not install nails above the seal strip unless allowed by the manufacturer. Failure to comply with manufacturer's installation instructions is a code violation and may void the manufacturer's warranty.

2. Use corrosion-resistant roofing nails (usually galvanized steel) with at least a 12-gauge shank and a ⅜-inch-diameter head. Use nails long enough to penetrate into the roof sheathing at least ¾ inch and completely through any sheathing that is less than ¾ inch thick. Install at least four nails per shingle strip, with a nail at 1 inch from each end and two nails equally spaced in the center of the strip.

STAPLES AS SHINGLE FASTENERS

Staples are not endorsed in general codes as an approved shingle fastener. Some shingle manufacturers allow staples, but few recommend them. Avoid using staples as shingle fasteners in both new construction and when replacing an existing shingle roof.

Fireplaces + Chimneys

Installing a factory-built or gas fireplace is a do-it-yourself project because you can design and build the fireplace frame to suit your needs and add your own finish treatments. It all starts with some careful planning. Once you decide on the fireplace model and determine where to place it, order all of the vent pipes and fittings needed to complete the vent run.

NOTE: Consult the manufacturer's instructions for the specifications regarding placement, clearances, and venting methods for your fireplace.

Start your planning by determining the best location for the fireplace. Placing the unit next to an exterior wall simplifies the venting required. One important specification for a direct-vented gas fireplace located in a basement is that the termination cap (on the outside end of the vent) must be 12 inches above the ground and away from openings, such as windows and doors.

For help with any of these planning issues, talk with knowledgeable dealers in your area. They can help you choose the best fireplace model for your situation and help you with venting and other

Provide a hearth extension (the area of the floor adjoining the fireplace) that meets minimum size standards based on the square footage of the fireplace opening.

considerations. Remember that all installation specifications are governed by local building codes and that a building permit will be required. Check with the building department to make sure your plans conform to regulations.

NOTE: The information on pages 102 to 103 apply specifically to masonry fireplaces, but many are useful guidelines for gas fireplaces as well.

Masonry Fireplace Clearance to Combustible Materials

Masonry Fireplace Hearth Extension Clearance to Combustible Materials

1. The hearth extension is the area in front of the firebox. It must be made of non-combustible material upon which sparks and hot materials from the firebox may land without starting a fire. Tile and masonry units are typical.

2. Build a hearth extension for a masonry fireplace at least 16 inches in front of the firebox opening and at least 8 inches to the sides of the firebox opening, if the firebox opening is less than 6 square feet.

3. Build a hearth extension for a masonry fireplace at least 20 inches in front of the firebox opening and at least 12 inches to the side of the firebox opening, if the firebox opening is 6 square feet or more.

4. Build a hearth extension for a factory-built fireplace according to the fireplace manufacturer's

instructions. The hearth extension size is often the same as for a masonry fireplace.

Masonry Fireplace Clearance to Mantels + Trim

1. Locate all combustible mantels and wood trim at least 6 inches from a masonry fireplace opening.

2. Provide at least 1 inch of clearance to the masonry firebox opening for every ⅛ inch that combustible material projects from the fireplace surround. This applies to materials within 12 inches of the fireplace opening. Example: locate 1-inch-thick fireplace mantel legs at least 8 inches from the fireplace opening. Example: locate greater than 12 inches from the fireplace opening any part of a fireplace mantel or mantel leg that is more than 1½ inches thick.

3. Provide clearance to combustible materials for a factory-built fireplace according to the fireplace

manufacturer's instructions. The clearance is often the same as for a masonry fireplace.

Spark Arrestor + Rain Cap

1. You are not required to install a spark arrestor or a rain cap on a masonry chimney, unless the local building official requires one. They are, however, recommended to protect the home and surrounding area from fire and to protect the chimney and home interior from water damage.

2. Comply with all of the following requirements for installed spark arrestors: (a) make the unobstructed arrestor area at least four times the area of the flue it serves; (b) make the arrestor screen using heat- and corrosion-resistant material equal to 19-gauge galvanized steel or 24-gauge stainless steel; (c) build the arrestor screen so it does not pass ½-inch-diameter spheres and does not obstruct ⅜-inch-diameter spheres; (d) make the arrestor accessible for cleaning and make the cap removable to allow for flue cleaning.

Chimney Used as Appliance Vent

1. Have a qualified contractor evaluate a chimney before using it to vent an appliance, such as a gas furnace or water heater, an oil-fired furnace, or a pellet stove. Chimneys that are too small may allow unsafe backdrafting of carbon monoxide into your home. Chimneys that are too large may allow water to condense in the chimney and cause considerable damage to the chimney.

2. Do not use a chimney as a gas appliance vent if any side of the chimney is exposed to the outdoors below the roofline. This means that a chimney must be completely enclosed within the house walls until it reaches the attic.

3. You may use a chimney as a vent for one draft hood-equipped gas water heater if the area of the chimney flue as at least as large as the area of the draft hood outlet and not more than seven times the area of the draft hood outlet.

Locate wood trim far enough from the firebox to avoid fires.

4. Do not use a chimney as a vent for one fan-assisted, medium efficiency gas furnace.

5. Do not connect an appliance vent to a masonry chimney flue if the area of the appliance connector is larger than the area of the chimney flue.

6. Install a permanent label in a conspicuous location warning occupants if a chimney has been relined and warning them what types of appliances may be connected to the chimney.

7. Have gas appliance vents connected to masonry chimney flues according to the provisions for gas appliance vents in IRC Chapter 24.

Wood-Burning Fireplace Energy Efficiency Requirements

1. Install an air barrier on fireplace walls.

2. Install doors with gaskets at fireplace openings.

3. Install a tight-fitting flue damper.

Combustion Air For Fireplaces

1. Provide combustion air from outside for solid fuel-burning masonry and factory-built fireplaces. Install combustion air ducts for factory-built fireplaces according to manufacturer's instructions.

2. Provide combustion air from the outside for vented gas and oil fireplaces according to manufacturer's instructions.

3. Locate the outside combustion air inlet at or below the firebox level. Cover the inlet with a screen having ¼-inch mesh.

4. Install combustion air openings and ducts that have an area of at least 6 square inches and not more than 55 square inches. Use a combustion air duct that is designed for that purpose, or keep the duct at least 1 inch away from combustible materials within 5 feet from the firebox.

5. Locate the inside combustion air outlet in the back or side of the firebox or at hearth level and not more than 24 inches from the firebox opening.

6. Install a closure mechanism at the combustion air outlet.

Factory-Built Fireplaces

Factory-built fireplaces and chimneys include components tested, listed, and labeled to be installed together as a system. Such fireplaces are usually designed to burn solid fuels, such as wood, though they may be converted to use gas if approved by the fireplace manufacturer. Do not mix components from different manufacturers unless approved by the fireplace manufacturer.

Fireplaces designed to burn only gas are not really fireplaces. They are decorative gas appliances. Vented decorative gas appliances are more like a water heater than like a fireplace. Unvented decorative gas appliances are more like a gas range than like a fireplace. Install and use decorative gas appliances according to manufacturer's instructions and IRC Chapter 24. Note that some jurisdictions do not allow unvented decorative gas appliances. Also note that manufacturers of unvented decorative gas appliances recommend limits on the duration of use.

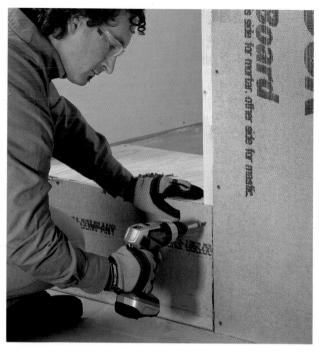

Create wall surrounds for fireplaces with cementboard, which has some heat-resistant qualities and also makes a good backer for ceramic tile—a popular choice for finished fireplace surrounds.

GAS FIREPLACES

Direct vent gas fireplace
- Vent pipe
- Elbow
- Blocking for top plates
- Cripple studs
- ½" clearance at back of unit
- Header
- Standoffs (¼" clearance)
- ½" clearance at sides of unit

Vent-free gas fireplace
- Chase framework (optional)
- Framework for fireplace surround
- Platform

A gas fireplace behaves more like a water heater than like a fireplace, but these appliances do produce dangerous gases and are by their very nature a fire hazard. The two most common types are direct-vent gas fireplaces, which produce heat that can contribute to your home heat plan and are vented to the exterior, and vent-free gas fireplaces (not allowed in some states) that are purely decorative. Because the amount of gas they consume is so small (comparable to a gas range with all burners on), they do not require venting.

Factory-Built Fireplace + Chimney Installation

Install factory-built chimneys and fireplaces according to the manufacturer's instructions. These instructions include requirements for hearth extensions, clearances to combustible materials, and installation of combustion air ducts.

Decorative Chimney Covers

Do not install decorative chimney covers, shrouds, or similar components at the chimney termination unless the component is listed and labeled for use with your particular fireplace system.

Structural Support for Factory-Built Fireplaces

Provide adequate structural support for factory-built fireplaces and chimneys according to manufacturer's recommendations.

Direct-vent gas fireplaces may be vented through a sidewall. Chimneys for wood-burning fireplaces are vertical.

Vents for gas fireplaces must have a protective termination cap (supplied by manufacturer). Note the black stain on the termination. This stain may indicate that the gas fireplace is not functioning properly.

Factory-built fireplaces (including direct-vent and vent-free gas fireplaces) typically require structural support. If the fireplace is recessed into a wall, structural support is in the form of a mounting platform located on the other side.

Heating + Air Conditioning

In this chapter you will learn about how improper installation of heating/air conditioning appliances can create risks including fire, carbon monoxide poisoning, energy inefficiency, and increased operating costs. You should comply with building code provisions, and with manufacturer's installation instructions, to avoid these and other risks. You should install fuel-burning appliances and their vents so that they do not ignite combustible materials, and so that combustion products are safely directed outside the building.

Energy efficiency and air quality are increasingly important elements of building codes. The heating/air-conditioning system is usually the most significant consumer of energy in a home. The system can also have a significant impact on maintaining indoor air quality. Building codes, therefore, have several requirements relating to these areas. Requirements include: programmable (setback) thermostats, duct insulation, air-sealing ducts and furnaces/air handlers, and ventilation air from outdoors. Inspection and testing to demonstrate that these requirements are met is often required. Check with your local building official about interpretation and enforcement of energy efficiency and ventilation air requirements. These requirements apply to new construction, and may apply to replacement of heating/air-conditioning appliances and duct/piping systems.

In this chapter:
- HVAC Appliances
- HVAC Duct Installation
- Combustion Air for Fuel-Burning Appliances
- Vents for Fuel-Burning Appliances

HVAC Appliances

Heating, ventilation, and air conditioning systems are often referred to as a group by the term HVAC. This is because they share a common purpose: to keep the air in your home comfortable. All HVAC systems—even hot-water-based systems—rely on the flow of air to heat, cool, and ventilate your home.

Most homes today include two separate major appliances in the HVAC system: a furnace and a central air conditioning unit. In most cases, even when the AC has been retrofitted, the appliances share ductwork.

The information in this chapter is intended mostly for general education purposes and to assist with diagnosing system problems. **Unless you are a very experienced DIYer, installing and servicing HVAC equipment is a job best left to professionals.**

Central air conditioner parts include: (A) Power shutoff for service personnel, (B) Condenser unit, (C) Fan, (D) Condenser coil, (E) Compressor, (F) Plenum, (G) Evaporator coil, (H) Blower motor, (I) Filter, (J) Air return.

Gas furnace parts include: (A) Inshot burners, (B) Draft inducer fan, (C) Combustion air pipe, (D) Vent, (E) Heat exchanger, (F) Filter, (G) Blower motor.

Prohibited Locations for Appliance Installation

1. Do not locate gas or other fuel-burning appliances in bedrooms, bathrooms, toilet rooms, or storage closets. Do not draw combustion air for any fuel-burning appliance from these rooms regardless of where the appliance is located.

2. Do not locate appliances anywhere that is not approved by the manufacturer's instructions.

3. Do not apply this provision to appliances powered only by electricity, such as heat pump air handlers and electric water heaters.

Exceptions: Prohibited Locations for Appliance Installation

1. You may install direct-vent appliances in prohibited locations if the appliance draws all combustion air directly from the outdoors.

2. You may install vented room heaters, vented wall furnaces, vented decorative appliances, and decorative appliances listed for installation in vented, solid fuel-burning fireplaces (such as gas logs) in prohibited locations if the room satisfies combustion air volume requirements.

3. You may install one listed, wall-mounted, unvented room heater in a bathroom if the appliance has an oxygen depletion safety shutoff system, the appliance input rating is not more than 6,000 BTU/hour, and the bathroom satisfies combustion air volume requirements.

4. You may install one listed, wall-mounted, unvented room heater in a bedroom if the appliance has an oxygen depletion safety shutoff system, the appliance input rating is not more than 10,000 BTU/hour, and the bedroom satisfies combustion air volume requirements.

5. You may install appliances in an enclosure accessible from the prohibited locations if all combustion air is drawn directly from the outdoors and the enclosure is equipped with a self-closing door that is weather-stripped.

6. The standard combustion air volume requirement is at least 50 cubic feet per 1,000 BTU/hour appliance input rating. This standard volume requirement does not apply if the home is tightly sealed with a known air infiltration rate of less than 0.40 air changes per hour. Tightly sealed homes are rare.

A typical forced air heating system delivers heated air to a room through registers while drawing cool air through return ducts. The cool air is reheated in the furnace and recirculated for maximum efficiency. A fresh air intake provides a constant supply of combustion air.

A direct-vented appliance may be installed in a prohibited location because it draws all combustion air from the outdoors. One pipe is the combustion air intake. The other is the appliance vent.

Electric Radiant (Baseboard) Heating Systems

Electric radiant heating systems provide heat to a single room. They usually have no fan and provide heat by natural movement of the heated air and by thermal radiation. They are common in small, seasonally occupied buildings, some rural homes, and in buildings without ducts for forced-air heating and cooling. These elements become very hot, and proper installation is important to prevent fires and electrical problems.

Installation Requirements

1. Install electric radiant heating panels according to manufacturer's installation instructions and applicable provisions of general and local codes.

2. Install radiant panels parallel to wood framing members, and fasten the panels to the surface of the framing members or mount the panels between framing members.

3. Install fasteners only in areas of the appliance's radiant panel designed for fasteners. Install fasteners at least ¼ inch away from a heating element.

4. Install radiant panels as complete units, unless listed and labeled for field modifications.

5. Do not install radiant panels on drywall unless the panel's maximum operating temperature is not more than 125 degrees Fahrenheit.

A bollard, like this steel pole, is one way to protect appliances from vehicle impact.

Appliances Installed in Garages

In warmer areas of the country some major household appliances are routinely located in garages to conserve interior floorspace. Water heaters are code-regulated to be installed in garages. Others, such as central vacuum units, should be installed following the manufacturer's instructions and best practices, but typically they are not subject to specific codes beyond applicable wiring, plumbing, and fire safety codes.

Elevated Appliances in Garages

1. Elevate the appliance ignition source at least 18 inches above the floor when the appliance is located in a garage or in an unconditioned room that opens directly into the garage. Appliances with a potential ignition source include gas and electric water heaters, gas and electric clothes dryers, gas and electric furnaces, and heat pumps with auxiliary resistance-heating elements. Rooms that open directly into the garage include storage and utility rooms that are not part of the conditioned living space. These rooms include rooms separated from the garage by a door opening into the garage.

2. Measure the elevation distance to the ignition source in the equipment, not to the bottom of the equipment (unless the ignition source is at the bottom of the equipment).

3. You may install appliances on the floor in rooms that are adjacent to a garage but do not have an opening into the garage.

4. You are not required to elevate the ignition source of flammable vapor ignition resistant (FVIR) gas water heaters. All new gas water heaters are FVIR (and have been for many years).

Protection of Appliances from Vehicles

1. Protect HVAC appliances and water heaters from vehicle impact. The appliance or water heater does not need to be located in a garage or carport to qualify for protection from vehicle impact. General codes do not specify how to provide this protection. Common protection methods include steel poles called bollards, vehicle tire stops, and encasing the equipment in substantial framing.

Appliances, such as water heaters, that are installed in a garage must have the ignition source elevated at least 18" off the floor.

HVAC Appliance + Duct Sizing

Appliance Sizing

1. Size heating and cooling appliances according to The Air Conditioning Contractors of America (ACCA) Manual S or a similar approved method. Manual S and Manual J account for conditions such as the direction the structure faces, the size and type of windows and doors, local temperature conditions, and insulation. Contractors should provide a copy of the sizing calculations for all new construction and when replacing existing appliances. Improper appliance sizing may cause inefficient appliance operation or may allow excessive moisture to remain in the home. Excessive moisture can damage the home and provide moisture for mold growth.

Duct Design

1. Design duct systems according to ACCA Manual D or a similar approved method. Contractors should provide a copy of the duct design calculations for all new construction. Improper duct sizing and installation can cause inefficient appliance operation and can cause uneven temperatures in the home.

Air Conditioner Condensate Disposal

The process of removing heat from the air is often called air conditioning. Water is a byproduct of air conditioning, because water vapor condenses out from the air when the air temperature is reduced. In areas with high humidity, air conditioning can produce significant amounts of water. The water removed from the air during air conditioning is called condensate.

Condensate Disposal Location Requirements

1. Do not discharge condensate onto a street, alley, or any other place that would create a nuisance. Some jurisdictions, particularly in warm, moist areas, require that you discharge condensate away from the foundation. Verify discharge location requirements with the local building official.

Condensate Discharge Pipe Requirements

1. Use at least ¾-inch-diameter pipe for primary and auxiliary condensate discharge pipes. Do not decrease pipe size between the collection and discharge point.

2. Install horizontal pipe sections with a uniform slope in the direction of the discharge point of at least ⅛ inch in 12 inches.

3. Use fittings, primers, cements, hangers, and other components that are compatible with the pipe material. Install the pipe according to the provisions in general codes.

4. Use pipe material use a pipe size that will accommodate the condensate temperature,

Condensate from air conditioner units should be directed to a drain through discharge pipes. NOTE: Due to acidity, avoid draining condensate to floor drain in older homes with cast iron sewer lines.

pressure, and flow rate produced by the air conditioning system.

5. Install a trap in the primary condensate discharge pipe according to the appliance manufacturer's instructions. The minimum trap depth is often about 2 inches.

6. You may use most water supply and drain pipes for condensate discharge pipes. The most common condensate discharge pipes are PVC, CPVC, and ABS.

7. Connect a condensate pump to the appliance it serves so that the appliance will not operate if the pump will not operate. This applies to pumps located in spaces such as attics and crawl spaces.

Condensate Auxiliary (Backup) System Requirements

1. Install an auxiliary condensate system when the air conditioner evaporator coil is located where building damaage may occur if the primary condensate discharge system malfunctions. This usually applies to evaporator coils installed in or above finished space. Many jurisdictions require auxiliary condensate systems for all air conditioning systems, unless all of the equipment is located outside the building.

2. Install one of the following auxiliary condensate systems when an auxiliary condensate system is required: (a) **Install an auxiliary drain pan** under the evaporator coil. Use a pan that is at least 1½ inches deep and at least 3 inches larger than the evaporator coil in both length and width. Construct the pan using either at least 0.0276-inch galvanized sheet metal or at least a 0.0625-inch, nonmetallic pan. Slope the pan toward the discharge pipe connection. Install the auxiliary discharge pipe using the same materials and methods as the primary discharge pipe. Terminate the auxiliary discharge pipe at a conspicuous point so that the occupants can see when the primary condensate discharge system is not functioning properly (a conspicuous point often means above a window). (b) **Install a water level cutoff switch** above the primary condensate discharge pipe where it connects to the evaporator coil and below the evaporator coil interior condensate pan overflow rim. Or, you may install the switch in the primary or secondary discharge pipes. The switch location should allow the switch to shut off the air conditioner before water overflows into the building.

MAINTENANCE TIP: KEEP DISCHARGE TUBES CLEAR

Condensate discharge tubes that run from your air conditioner evaporator have a strong tendency to become clogged with mildew, algae, bacteria, and other unappealing nuisances. To prevent clogging, flush the discharge tube every couple of months with a solution of 2 tablespoons household chlorine bleach dissolved into a cup of water.

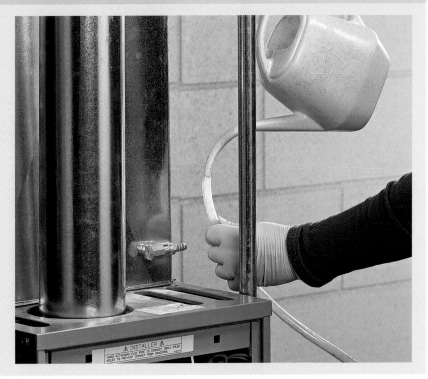

HVAC Duct Installation

Improper duct installation and duct damage are common problems. Ducts that leak, have sharp bends, or sag reduce the volume of air that moves through the duct and increase the friction between the air and the duct walls. This causes the HVAC system to work harder and longer than necessary, wasting energy and money and causing comfort problems with different temperatures in different rooms.

Flexible HVAC Duct Installation

General Installation Requirements

1. Install flexible ducts according to manufacturer's installation instructions. The installation instructions that follow are based on material from the Air Diffusion Council. The full, original version may be downloaded from their website (see Resources, page 234).

2. Use flexible ducts that are labeled at least every 36 inches with information, such as the manufacturer's name and the R-value of the duct insulation.

3. Do not expose flexible ducts to direct sunlight, such as may occur under roof vents. Direct sunlight can damage the duct outer cover.

4. Extend flexible duct to its full length. Do not leave excess duct material in a duct run, and do not compress the duct.

Duct Support

1. Support flexible ducts using material at least 1½ inches wide. You may support flexible ducts on 1½-inch-wide framing.

2. Support flexible ducts at not more than 4-foot intervals. You may use a fitting or distribution plenum to provide initial flexible duct support.

3. Do not allow flexible duct to sag between supports more than ½ inch per foot.

4. Support bends in long horizontal runs of flexible duct at not more than one duct diameter on both sides of the bend.

5. Support bends in flexible duct that occur near the plenum connection. Allow flexible ducts to run at least several inches beyond a plenum connection before making a bend.

6. Provide independent support for duct fittings and distribution plenums. Support duct fittings at not more than 1 foot from the fitting.

7. Support vertical runs of flexible duct at more than 6-foot intervals.

Flexible ductwork may not be bent at an overly tight angle. The radius of any curved bend should be no less than the diameter of the duct.

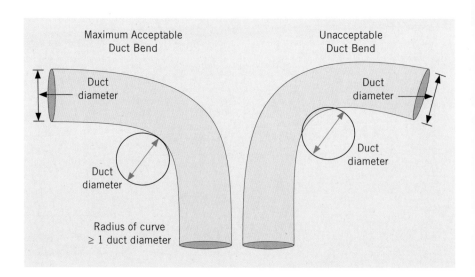

Maximum Acceptable Duct Bend — Duct diameter — Duct diameter — Radius of curve ≥ 1 duct diameter

Unacceptable Duct Bend — Duct diameter — Duct diameter

Duct Bends

1. Do not bend flexible ducts at sharp angles across obstructions, such as framing lumber and pipes. Such bends reduce the duct area and restrict air flow.

2. Do not bend flexible ducts so that the bend radius at the centerline is less than one duct diameter.

3. Avoid changing the shape of the duct. The area of a round duct is greater than the area of the same duct compressed into an ellipse.

Duct Connections + Splices

1. Connect and splice ducts according to manufacturer's instructions.

2. Connect flexible ducts to metal collars that are at least 2 inches long.

3. Splice two ducts together using a metal sleeve at least 4 inches long.

4. Use approved clamps and tape to secure nonmetallic flexible ducts to metal collars and sleeves.

5. Use approved tape and mastic to seal duct collars, plenums, and other fittings to ensure minimum air leakage.

Duct Insulation + Sealing

1. Insulate HVAC supply ducts located in unconditioned areas, such as attics and crawl spaces, to at least R-8. Insulate most other ducts to at least R-6. Verify duct insulation with your local building official or with a qualified HVAC contractor.

2. You are not required to insulate ducts that are completely within conditioned space.

3. Seal ducts, furnaces, air handler, filter boxes, junction boxes, and fittings.

4. Verify duct and air handler sealing with a duct pressure test. You may perform this test during rough-in or after final installation of the HVAC system. Refer to the IRC for test requirements.

5. Do not use framing cavities, such as stud walls and floor framing, as HVAC ducts or plenums.

Prohibited Sources for Return + Outdoor Air

Prohibited Sources of Return Air

1. Do not locate a return air register in a closet, bathroom, toilet room, kitchen, garage, mechanical room, furnace room, or an unconditioned attic.

2. Do not locate a return register closer than 10 feet in any direction to an open combustion chamber or to a draft hood-equipped appliance. Common examples of these prohibited sources include a fireplace and a water heater.

3. Do not take more return air from a room or a space than is supplied to that room or space.

Prohibited Sources of Outdoor Air

1. Locate outdoor air intake openings connected to forced-air heating and cooling systems at least 10 feet horizontally from contaminant sources, including gas equipment vents, chimneys, plumbing vents, or the discharge outlet of an exhaust fan.

2. You may locate outdoor air intake openings closer than 10 feet horizontally to a contaminant source if the outdoor air intake opening is at least 3 feet below the contaminant source.

3. Do not locate outdoor air intake openings where objectionable odors, fumes, or flammable vapors may be present.

4. Locate outdoor air intake openings at least 10 feet above a public walkway or driveway.

5. Do not locate outdoor air intake openings at grade level next to a sidewalk, street, alley, or driveway.

6. Provide an automatic or gravity-operated damper for air intake systems that will close the damper when the system is not operating.

Combustion Air for Fuel-Burning Appliances

Fuel-burning appliances, such as gas furnaces, boilers, and water heaters, need air to support the fuel-burning (combustion) process. These appliances also need air for cooling, ventilation of the appliance, and for proper operation of the vent system that expels combustion byproducts outside. The air required to support operation of fuel-burning appliances is called combustion air.

Without adequate combustion air, incomplete fuel combustion may occur. Byproducts of incomplete fuel combustion can include carbon monoxide and soot that can damage the appliance and its vent. This

Fuel for appliances (natural gas, propane, fuel oil) requires an adequate supply of fresh combustion air for efficient burning, as well as a means of effective venting.

is a health and safety hazard. Appliances operating without adequate combustion air can cost more to operate and maintain.

Do not confuse combustion air with the similar term "makeup air." Makeup air replaces air that is exhausted by clothes dryers, exhaust fans, fireplaces, and similar devices.

Appliances Needing Combustion Air

1. Provide combustion air for Category I gas appliances and for liquid fuel-burning (oil) appliances according to the appliance manufacturer's recommendations and to code requirements. Category I gas appliances include the gas furnaces and water heaters found in most homes.

2. Provide combustion air for direct vent and for Category II, III, and IV gas appliances according to the appliance manufacturer's instructions. Do not apply combustion air requirements to these appliances. Category II appliances do not currently exist. Category III and IV appliances include medium and high-efficiency gas appliances that operate with positive vent pressure.

3. Do not apply combustion air requirements to fireplaces and fireplace stoves. Refer to other general codes for fireplace combustion air requirements.

COMBUSTION AIR DEPLETION BY OTHER SYSTEMS

Other appliances compete with gas- and oil-burning appliances for combustion air. This can create negative pressure that can interfere with operation of the gas- and oil-burning appliances and their vents. General codes do not define how to account for air exhausted by other appliances. Gas- and oil-burning appliances located in or near rooms containing clothes dryers, exhaust fans, and fireplaces require special attention to ensure that combustion air and venting needs are satisfied.

Account for air exhausted by appliances (such as clothes dryers, bathroom and kitchen exhaust fans, fireplaces), and account for combustion air used by other fuel-burning appliances when determining combustion air requirements. This is important when drawing all combustion air from inside the home.

Combustion Air Duct Materials + Construction

1. Use galvanized steel to construct combustion air ducts. Refer to other general codes for duct material specifications.

2. You may use unobstructed stud and joist spaces as combustion air ducts if only one required fireblock is removed.

3. Terminate combustion air ducts in unobstructed space that allows free air movement.

4. Do not open combustion air ducts into more than one room or enclosure.

5. Do not use the same combustion air duct for both the upper and lower duct openings.

6. Do not install a screen on any combustion air duct opening in the attic.

7. Do not slope horizontal combustion air ducts downward toward the source of combustion air. Make the duct level or slope it toward the appliance.

8. Do not use the space in a masonry, metal, or factory-built chimney that surrounds a chimney liner, gas vent, plastic piping, or other devices as a combustion air duct.

9. Locate the lowest point of an exterior combustion air opening at least 12 inches above exterior grade.

AIRTIGHT CONSTRUCTION

Homes built using airtight construction techniques do not allow enough air infiltration into the home to safely support fuel combustion. The lack of adequate combustion air can cause many problems, including the production of carbon monoxide and soot that can be a health hazard and can damage appliances and vents. Do not draw combustion air from inside the home if it is built using airtight construction techniques. You'll need to bring it in from outdoors. Even when drawing combustion air from inside is allowed, it is not considered best practice. You should consider direct-vented appliances that draw combustion air from outdoors when replacing existing appliances.

To be considered airtight, a home must have measured air changes that are less than 0.4 per hour. You'll need to contact a qualified building energy analyst to determine whether your home meets this standard, but here are some hints:

- If your home is airtight, the thermal envelope walls have a continuous air barrier and any openings in the air barrier are sealed.

- Doors and operable windows meet air leakage requirements of the International Energy Conservation Code.

- Gaps and spaces are sealed—including gaps and spaces between windows and doors and the surrounding framing, between sill plates and floors, between wall and ceiling joints, between wall panels, and at wall penetrations for utilities, such as plumbing, electrical, and gas.

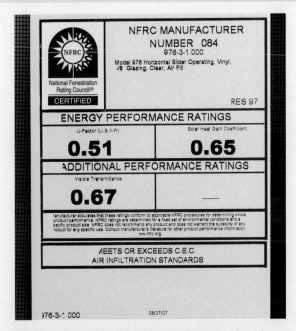

Windows that meet air leakage requirements should come with a rating label from a sanctioned source. Among these sources are the International Energy Conservation Code and the National Fenestration Rating Council, which employs the California Energy Commission standards for air infiltration.

Older homes rarely satisfy these requirements, unless they have been retrofitted for improved energy efficiency by air-sealing. Existing fuel-burning equipment is usually acceptable in older homes, although this is not considered best practice. Consider direct-vented equipment when replacing fuel-burning appliances.

Newer homes should satisfy these requirements; therefore, drawing combustion air from inside the home is suspect. You may wish to have a combustion safety test conducted on a newer home where combustion air is drawn from inside the home.

Combustion Air from Within a Room

Combustion air may be drawn from the room where the appliance is located if the room is large enough. Consult with an engineer or inspector to help you determine if the room meets the minimum size requirement for your appliance.

Required room volume is at least 50 cu. ft. per 1,000 BTU input for all appliances in the room.

Combustion Air Using One Permanent Opening to Outdoors

Import combustion air by creating one permanent opening to the outdoors. To do this, draw air in from an opening in an exterior wall or from an opening in the roof.

A - Attic
B - Exterior through roof
C - Exterior through wall

One air intake opening of at least 1 sq. in. per 3,000 BTU input for all appliances in the room. Terminate the opening within 12" from the ceiling.

Vents for Fuel-Burning Appliances

A vent is generally a vertical component, such as a metal pipe, that conducts combustion products from a gas- or oil-burning appliance to the outdoors. A vent for a single appliance begins at the fitting where the vent connector, if any, connects to the vent. A common vent for multiple appliances begins at the highest connector fitting. If a vent is located directly over the appliance draft hood or flue collar, or if the vent connects directly to the appliance, then the vent begins at the appliance and there is no vent connector.

A vent connector is a pipe that connects an appliance to its vent or flue. A vent connector is required if the appliance is not located directly under its vent. A vent connector for a Category I gas appliance may be a listed vent material, such as a Type B vent; a listed flexible vent connector; or a field-constructed, single-wall metal pipe made of at least 28-gauge galvanized steel. While a vent connector is part of the venting system, it is not the vent itself.

Common types of vents and vent connectors include the Type B vent used with most gas appliances, Type L vents used with oil-burning appliances, flexible connectors used with gas appliances, and single-wall connectors that may be used with either gas or oil-burning appliances.

The material in this section deals with vents for low- and medium-efficiency appliances. Fewer of these appliances are being installed in favor of high-efficiency appliances and appliances with special venting requirements. Examples of special-vented appliances include high-efficiency gas furnaces (vented with plastic pipe), sidewall-vented appliances, and appliances using positive pressure vent systems. Do not apply the material in this section to special-vented appliances.

Venting of special-vented appliances is governed by the appliance manufacturer's instructions. These instructions will vary by manufacturer and by appliance model. Thus, the only way to determine if a special-vented appliance vent is installed properly is to compare the appliance vent installation to the instructions for the appliance in question.

Vents for special-vented appliances are frequently improperly installed. Proper vent (and combustion air) installation is important for proper and safe appliance operation. It is a good idea to evaluate and confirm vent installation for special-vented appliances.

Vent connectors and fittings include: (A) Single wall-vent connector; (B) Type B elbow; (C) Type B vent; (D) Type L vent; (E, F) vent caps.

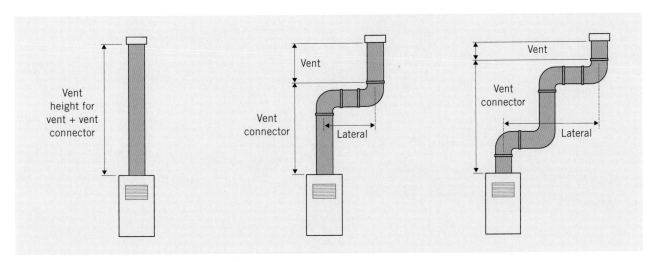

Vents and vent connectors often look the same, but they have different installation requirements.

Vent Clearance to Combustible Materials

1. Provide the distance between a vent or a vent connector and combustible materials based on the vent or vent connector manufacturer's installation instructions and based on the appliance manufacturer's installation instructions. Table 24 contains typical clearance distances for common types of vents and vent connectors. Confirm the distances in Table 24 with the appliance manufacturer's instructions and the vent manufacturer's instructions.

Vent Clearance to Roof + Obstructions

1. Terminate a Type L vent at least 2 feet above the roof and at least 2 feet above any part of the home within 10 feet of the vent. Measure termination height above the roof from the highest point where the vent penetrates the roof to the bottom of the vent cap.

2. Terminate a masonry chimney at least 3 feet above the roof and at least 2 feet above any part of the building within 10 feet of the chimney. Measure termination height above the roof from the highest point where the chimney penetrates the roof to where the flue exits the chimney. This provision also applies to many factory-built chimneys. Confirm factory-built chimney termination height using the manufacturer's installation instructions.

3. Use Table 25 to determine the minimum height above the roof of a Type B gas vent not more than 12 inches in diameter. Measure termination height above the roof from the highest point where the vent penetrates the roof to the bottom of the listed cap. For thick roof-covering materials, such as tile, measure from the tile to the bottom of the listed cap.

4. Do not use Table 25 if a Type B vent is closer than 8 feet to a vertical side wall, gable end, or similar

Avoid fires by maintaining distance between vents and combustible materials.

vertical obstruction. Terminate these vents at least 2 feet higher than the highest point where the vent penetrates the roof and at least 2 feet higher than any part of the roof or building within 10 feet horizontally.

5. Terminate all vents and chimneys at least 8 feet horizontally from operable windows unless the vent is at least 3 feet above the window.

6. Do not install a vent terminal where a door can swing within 12 inches horizontally from the vent terminal. This will apply mostly to direct vent terminals.

7. Do not install a decorative shroud or surround at a vent termination unless the shroud or surround is listed for use with the specific venting system and unless the shroud or surround is installed according to manufacturer's instructions. This prevents an unlisted shroud from interfering with the drafting characteristics of the vent system.

TABLE 24: TYPICAL CLEARANCE DISTANCES TO COMBUSTIBLE MATERIALS FOR COMMON TYPES OF VENTS + VENT CONNECTORS

VENT OR CONNECTOR TYPE	APPLICATION	TYPICAL CLEARANCE DISTANCE
Type B vent + vent connector	Category I gas appliance	1"
Type L vent + vent connector	Oil-burning + Category I gas appliance	3"
Single-wall vent + vent connector	Category I gas appliance	6"
Single-wall vent + vent connector	Oil-burning appliance listed for Type L vent	9"

Joints Between Vents + Vent Connector Sections

1. Secure joints between the vent or vent connector and the flue collar or draft hood, vent or vent connector sections, and vent connector and the vent using (a) sheet metal screws (usually three); (b) listed, interlocking vent material (such as Type B vent) connected according to the vent manufacturer's instructions; or (c) other approved means.

Slope of Vents + Vent Connectors

1. Slope vents and vent connectors up toward the roof termination at least ¼ inch per foot. Do not allow any dips or sags in the vent or vent connector.

Appliances Not Requiring a Vent

1. You are not required to vent the following gas appliances: (a) ranges and other domestic cooking appliances listed and labeled for optional venting; (b) domestic (Type 1) clothes dryers; (c) portable, countertop, and similar small kitchen and laundry appliances; (d) gas-fueled refrigerators; (e) listed, unvented room heaters; and (f) listed, unvented decorative gas appliances (unvented gas fireplaces).

TABLE 25: TYPE B GAS VENT HEIGHT ABOVE ROOF

ROOF PITCH	MIN. VENT HEIGHT
Flat to 6/12	12"
Over 6/12 to 7/12	15"
Over 7/12 to 8/12	18"
Over 8/12 to 9/12	24"
Over 9/12 to 10/12	30"
Over 10/12 to 11/12	39"
Over 11/12 to 12/12	48"
Over 12/12 to 14/12	60"
Over 14/12 to 16/12	72"
Over 16/12 to 18/12	84"
Over 18/12 to 20/12	90"

2. Verify venting requirements using manufacturer's instructions. Some manufacturers of appliances such as unvented gas fireplaces recommend limiting the duration of use and/or opening a window while the appliance is operating.

A gas vent roof terminator cap protects the vent from moisture and pests. These caps are designed so they do not impede or restrict air flow.

SAFETY TIP

Always have combustion vent installations diagnosed and inspected by a qualified professional.

Plumbing System

Plumbing projects are popular among do-it-yourselfers, so naturally there's a strong demand for information on home plumbing subjects to make sure home projects are accomplished correctly. Water supply pipes must be properly sized, supported, and connected to avoid water leaks and low water flow at fixtures.

Wastewater drain pipes must be properly installed to avoid water leaks and sewage backups. Traps and vents must be correctly hooked up in drain lines.

Finally, in this chapter you'll learn basic requirements for installing water supply pipes and water drain and vent pipes, as well as for installing common plumbing fixtures, such as water heaters, faucets, tubs, and showers.

The domestic hot water system is usually a significant consumer of energy in a home. Building codes, therefore, have several requirements relating to these areas. Requirements include insulating some hot water pipes and pipes used by hot water recirculating systems. Check with your local building official about interpretation and enforcement of energy efficiency requirements. These requirements apply to new construction and may apply to replacement of piping systems.

In this chapter:
- The Home Plumbing System
- Water Supply Piping
- Drain, Waste + Vent Piping (DWV)
- Plumbing Vents
- Plumbing Traps
- Plumbing Appliances + Fixtures

DEFINITIONS OF PLUMBING TERMS

Air admittance valve: An air admittance valve (AAV) is a one-way valve attached to a plumbing vent pipe. It is used when extending a vent to the roof or to another vent is impractical or not desirable. The valve allows air into the vent system when there is negative pressure in the vent pipe and closes to limit the flow of sewer gas into the home.

Branch drain: A branch drain is a drainage pipe that takes soil and waste from fixture drains to a stack or to the building drain.

Branch vent: A branch vent connects other vents, usually individual and common vents, to a vent stack or stack vent.

Braze (brazing): A method of joining metal pipe (such as copper and brass) at temperatures exceeding 1,000 degrees Fahrenheit. Brazing is sometimes called "silver soldering," because it uses a silver alloy as the brazing material. Brazed joints are stronger than soldered joints.

Building drain: The building drain is usually the lowest horizontal drainpipe in the building and collects material from branches and stacks. It extends to 30" beyond the

foundation, where it connects with the building sewer. A building with fixtures below the building drain (such as in a basement) has a building sub-drain. Material in a sub-drain must be pumped up to the building drain.

Building sewer: Building sewer usually refers to the pipes beginning at the building drain and ending at the public sewer or septic tank.

Drainpipe: Drainpipe usually refers to the pipes inside the building that take soil and waste to the building sewer pipe.

Fittings: These are devices that connect parts of the plumbing system together and allow pipes to change direction. Drainage fittings include wyes, sweeps, bends, tees, and couplings. Water supply fittings include elbows, tees, couplings, and valves.

Fixture: Any device that connects to water supply pipes and connects to plumbing waste pipes is a fixture. Fixtures include toilets (water closets), bathroom sinks (lavatories), kitchen and laundry sinks, bathtubs, and showers.

Fixture drain: This horizontal pipe between a trap outlet and the fitting connects it to another drain pipe. A fixture

The AAV has been endorsed as a substitute for exterior vent termination by most codes.

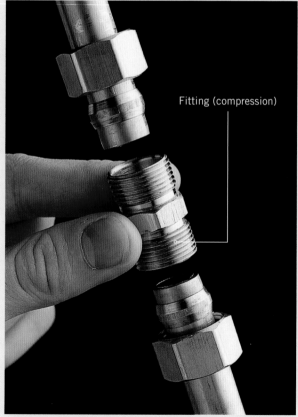

Fitting (compression)

The general term "fitting" is for any device from any material that is used to connect plumbing pipes. A brass compression fitting for copper supply pipe is shown here.

The fixture drain, or trap arm, is a piece of drain tubing that connects a fixture and its drain line to the drain stub-out in the wall or floor.

An indirect waste receptor collects drain water from a source and introduces it to the drain system, but it is not connected directly to the wastewater source. Floor drains (above) are common indirect receptors.

The hub is the enlarged fitting, usually in cast-iron drain pipe. The spigot is the end of the pipe that fits into the hub.

drain is sometimes called a "trap arm." Any pipe after the fixture drain fitting is not part of the fixture drain.

Hub: An enlarged opening molded on the end of a pipe or a fitting into which a section of pipe (the spigot) is inserted is a hub. In older plumbing, cast-iron hubs and spigots were sealed with oakum or hemp and lead. In modern plumbing, you may seal cast-iron hubs and spigots with an elastomeric O-ring gasket, or you may remove the hub and convert the pipe into a hubless pipe. Hubless pipe joints are often sealed by an elastomeric sleeve held in place by stainless steel rings (also called a banded coupling).

Laundry tray: A sink, usually located in a laundry area, used for various laundry-related and other purposes, is also known as a laundry sink or a deep sink. You may discharge a clothes washing machine into a laundry tray instead of a standpipe.

Offset: In a vertical drainpipe (drain stack), offsets change in direction in the pipe from vertical to an angle other than vertical, then back to vertical. Offsets are most often used to run a stack around an obstruction (such as a wall or beam) that cannot be drilled or notched. An offset that is not more than 45 degrees from vertical is defined to be vertical.

Receptor (indirect waste): The term receptor refers to a device such as a floor sink or a floor drain. Indirect waste receptors have a source of water that is not directly and permanently connected to the receptor. Example: a floor drain could receive condensate water from an air conditioning system. The condensate drain is not directly and permanently connected to the floor drain.

Install slip joints only on accessible traps.

Saddle fittings are prohibited on drainage pipes, but they are sometimes used in low volume applications such as this water filter discharge tube. Ask your building department if saddle fittings are allowed in your area.

Saddle fitting: A saddle fitting is a connection between pipes where a new pipe is attached to an existing pipe by puncturing the existing pipe and clamping the new pipe to the existing pipe. Saddle fittings are prohibited on water supply pipes, but are sometimes used to tap existing water supply pipes for low volume applications, such as refrigerator ice-makers and reverse osmosis water treatment systems. Saddle fittings are also prohibited in drainage pipes, but are often used in low volume applications, such as reverse osmosis water treatment system discharge tubing connection to trap arms.

Slip joint: A hand-tightened joint installed on tubular waste pipes between a fixture outlet and waste pipes. Slip joints are most common at the inlet and outlet sides of traps. Slip joints allow easy removal of the trap for cleaning. Slip joints must be accessible by an opening at least 12" in the smallest dimension.

Soil: Material in the plumbing drainage system that contains urine or fecal material.

Solder (soldering): A method of joining metal pipe (such as copper and brass) at temperatures that do not exceed 800 degrees Fahrenheit. Soldering usually uses a tin alloy as the joining material. Soldered joints are weaker than brazed joints.

Stack: A stack is a vertical plumbing drain or waste pipe that extends one or more stories. A stack collects waste material from horizontal drainage pipes and conducts it to the building drain or other horizontal drain.

Stack vent: A dry vent that connects to a soil or waste stack above the highest horizontal drainage connection and may extend through the roof to the outdoors or may terminate with a stack-type air admittance valve.

Soldering is a technique, often called "sweating," that's used to join copper and brass tubing and fittings. It is weaker than brazing, but code approved for virtually all residential plumbing joints.

Standpipe: A vertical pipe used as an indirect waste receptor. Standpipes are most often used as the receptor for a clothes washing machine.

Stop-and-waste valve: A water supply valve with an opening that allows draining of the non-pressure side. These valves are most common in cold climates and are used to protect exterior water fixtures from freeze damage.

Tailpiece: A tailpiece is a short piece of vertical pipe that runs from the plumbing fixture waste outlet (drain) to the inlet side of the fixture's trap.

Trap: A trap is a fitting, usually located either inside or under fixtures, that prevents sewer gases from escaping from the plumbing waste pipes. Traps maintain a water seal (trap seal) extending from the trap's crown weir to its dip. Vents help protect the water seal from siphoning.

Vent: Pipe or mechanical device that allows air into the plumbing drainpipes to equalize air pressure in the pipes. Plumbing vents help avoid draining (siphoning) traps and help wastewater flow freely through the system.

Plumbing vents usually terminate on the roof, although mechanical vents (called air admittance valves) are allowed in some circumstances.

Vent stack: Dry vent that connects at or near the connection of a soil or waste stack and a horizontal drain. A vent stack runs vertically and often runs parallel to the soil or waste stack that it vents.

Yard hydrant (freeze proof): A freeze proof yard hydrant is an outdoor water supply outlet that has a valve and outlet aboveground and a drain opening below the frost level. When the valve is opened, water flows. When the valve is closed, the water supply to the hydrant is shut off below the frost level and a drain hole is opened that allows the water in the yard hydrant pipe to drain into a gravel bed. This drains the yard hydrant and its riser so that the hydrant will not freeze.

Waste: Liquid material in the plumbing drainage system that does not contain urine or fecal material. Waste is sometimes referred to as gray water. Waste comes from all plumbing fixtures except toilets and urinals.

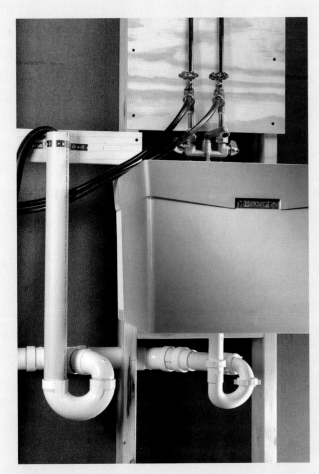

A standpipe is an open pipe mounted vertically and leading into a branch drain system. Standpipes often are installed as receptors for washing machine discharge tubes.

Traps are the S- or P-shaped pipes in a fixture drain. Their purpose is to prevent sewer gas from coming up through the drain opening.

The Home Plumbing System

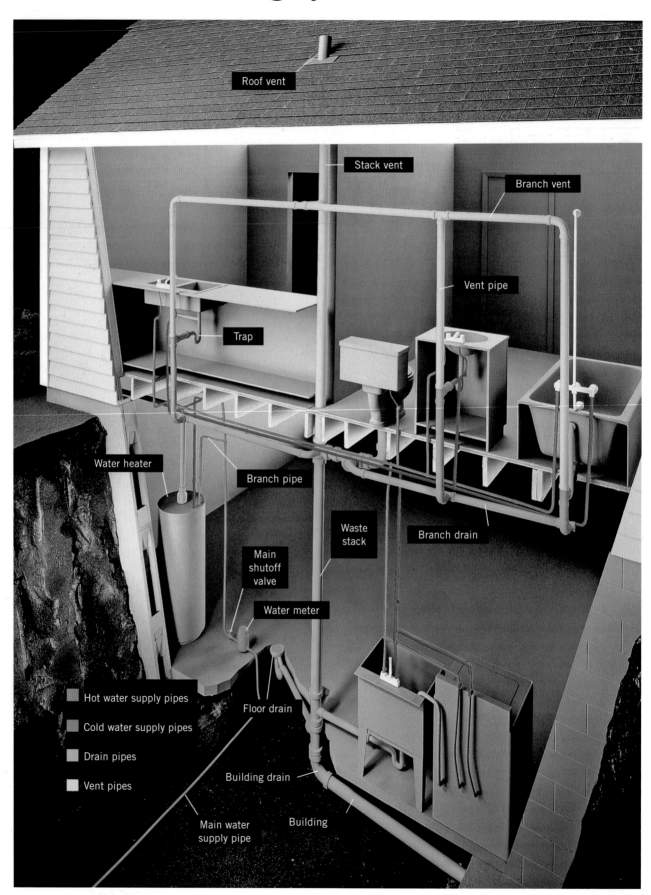

Roof vent

Stack vent

Branch vent

Vent pipe

Trap

Water heater

Branch pipe

Main
shutoff
valve

Water meter

Waste
stack

Branch drain

Hot water supply pipes

Cold water supply pipes

Drain pipes

Vent pipes

Floor drain

Building drain

Main water
supply pipe

Building

Water Supply Piping

Water supply pipes carry hot and cold water throughout a house. In homes built before 1960, the original supply pipes were usually made of galvanized steel. Newer homes have supply pipes made of copper. In most areas of the country, supply pipes made of rigid plastic or PEX are accepted by local plumbing codes.

Water supply pipes are made to withstand the high pressures of the water supply system. They have small diameters, usually ½ inch to 1 inch, and are joined with strong, watertight fittings. The hot and cold pipes run in tandem to most parts of the house. Usually, the supply pipes run inside wall cavities or are strapped to the undersides of

floor joists. They are sometimes run in the attic in warm climates.

Hot and cold water supply pipes are connected to most fixtures and appliances. Fixtures include sinks, tubs, and showers. Some fixtures, such as toilets and hose bibbs, are supplied only by cold water. Appliances include dishwashers and clothes washers. A refrigerator icemaker uses only cold water. Tradition and codes say that hot water supply pipes and faucet handles are found on the left-hand side of a fixture, with cold water on the right.

Because it is pressurized, the water supply system is prone to leaks. This is especially true of galvanized iron pipe, which has limited resistance to corrosion.

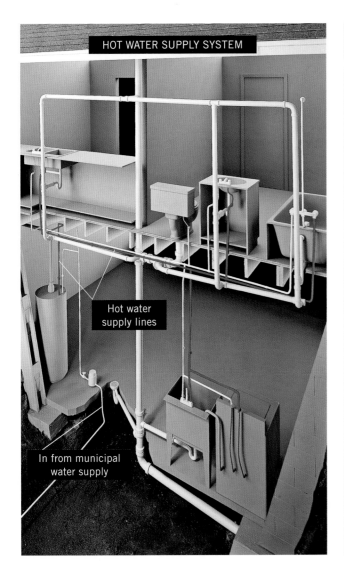

HOT WATER SUPPLY SYSTEM

Hot water supply lines

In from municipal water supply

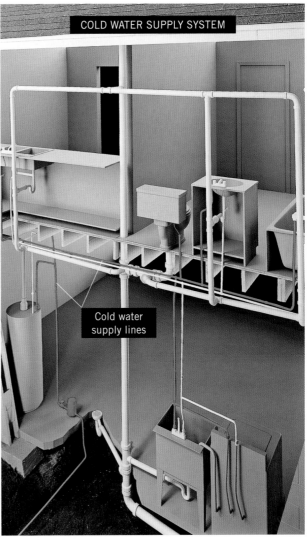

COLD WATER SUPPLY SYSTEM

Cold water supply lines

Water Pressure vs. Water Flow

Install a pressure regulator when the water pressure exceeds 80 psi.

Water flow and water pressure are often confused. Water flow is the amount of water you can get from a full water pipe. Water pressure is the amount of force that the water exerts on the walls of a full water pipe. Once a pipe is full of water, a water pressure increase will not increase the water flow in the pipe. In fact, a water pressure increase beyond a certain amount will cause the pipe to burst. The ideal water pressure is between 40 and 60 pounds per square inch (psi).

Water flow is primarily a function of the size, type, and installation of water supply pipes and supply fixtures. You can achieve more flow in a larger pipe than you can in a smaller pipe. Different pipe materials, such as PEX and copper, have different flow rates for the same size pipe. Many current water supply fixtures have flow restriction devices that limit the water flow rate to conserve water.

Water pressure is primarily a function of the force behind the water as it enters the piping system. A system with too little water pressure may not provide sufficient water flow when multiple supply fixtures are being used. Too much water pressure, exceeding 80 psi, can cause premature failure of water supply pipes and fixtures. A pressure regulator is recommended to reduce excessive water pressure.

Minimum + Maximum Water Pressure

1. Provide each dwelling with enough water pressure to provide adequate water flow at all fixtures. There is no specific minimum water pressure. This applies to both public and private (well supplied) water supplies.

2. Do not exceed 80 psi static water pressure.

3. Install an approved pressure regulator at the main water supply connection to the dwelling if the static pressure exceeds the maximum. Measure the water pressure to the point where the water supply enters the building as closely as possible.

Minimum Flow Rate at Fixtures

1. Provide at least the water flow rate in Table 26 for the indicated fixtures. Water flow rate is measured in gallons per minute (gpm). Water flow rate means the water flow from the pipe without the fixture attached. The water flow rate in the table does not mean that the water flow from the fixture must be at least the amount in the table. Some fixtures contain required flow restrictors that will limit the actual water flow from the fixture to less than the water flow rate in the table. Example: the minimum water flow rate for a shower is 3 gallons per minute, but the maximum flow-restricted rate from the showerhead is 2.5 gallons per minute.

Maximum Flow Rate at Fixtures

1. Use fixtures that allow a water flow rate that is not more than the flow rate in Table 27. Water flow rate is measured in gallons per minute (gpm). If either the water supply pressure to the building or the water pressure loss in the pipes reduces the water pressure at the fixture to less than the design pressure, the flow rate at a flow-restricted fixture may be less than the maximum.

TABLE 26: MIN. WATER FLOW RATE AT FIXTURE SUPPLY PIPE

FIXTURE	MINIMUM FLOW RATE (GPM)
Bathtub	4
Bidet	2
Dishwasher	2.75
Hose bibb	5
Laundry tub	4
Lavatory	0.8
Shower	2.5
Sink	1.75

TABLE 27: MAX. WATER FLOW RATE AT FIXTURE

FIXTURE	MAXIMUM WATER FLOW RATE AT DESIGN PRESSURE
Lavatory	2.2 gpm at 60 psi
Shower head	2.5 gpm at 80 psi
Sink	2.2 gpm at 60 psi

Common Water Distribution Pipes

1. Install water service pipe that has a working pressure rating of at least 160 psi at 73 degrees Fahrenheit or the highest available pressure, whichever is greater.

2. Common water distribution pipe materials used in modern residential construction include those in Table 28.

3. You may use other approved materials if allowed by local codes. Copper, CPVC, and PEX are the most common water distribution pipes.

TABLE 28: COMMON WATER DISTRIBUTION PIPE MATERIALS

COMMON WATER DISTRIBUTION PIPE MATERIALS	APPROVED FOR USE UNDER CONCRETE SLABS
CPVC plastic pipe	yes
Copper + copper alloy pipe + tubing	Copper tubing, minimum Type M
PEX-AL-PEX pipe	yes
PEX tubing	yes
PE-AL-PE pipe	yes

Water supply pipes include: copper, CPVC, and PEX (blue for cold, red for hot).

Fittings for water supply lines include: (A) CPVC tee, elbow and coupling; (B) copper tees and elbows; (C) brass compression fittings; (D) brass fittings, with barbs.

Water Distribution Pipe Joints + Connections

1. Use fittings made from the same material as the pipe when connecting pipes made from the same material. Example: use copper fittings to connect copper pipe and CPVC fittings to connect CPVC pipe. Use solder or brazing to connect copper pipes. Use PVC cement and primer to connect CPVC pipes.

2. You may use flared fittings to make connections between soft copper water tubing and valves and fixtures. Use approved fittings and a flaring tool to form and connect these joints.

3. Use fittings and crimping tools approved by the tubing manufacturer when connecting PEX and other water supply materials to each other. Most homeowners should not attempt to install PEX and similar materials using these fittings and tools because this requires training and experience.

4. Use push-fit fittings only with copper tubing, CPVC, and PEX. Do not use push-fit fittings with other pipe and tubing, such as polybutylene.

5. You may use mechanical fittings to connect pipes made from the same materials and pipes made from different materials. Install the fittings according to manufacturer's instructions.

Flexible Water Connectors

1. Use flexible water connectors to connect water supply pipes to appliances and fixtures. Examples of proper uses of flexible water connectors: connecting water supply pipes and a water heater, connecting valves and a clothes washing machine or a dishwashing machine, connecting a refrigerator icemaker and a valve, and connecting a valve and a faucet.

2. Use a flexible water connector that is approved for the application. Example: do not use a connector intended for a clothes washing machine to connect a water heater to the hot water supply pipe.

3. Do not run flexible water connectors through walls, ceilings, and floors or in concealed spaces.

4. Do not use flexible water connectors as a substitute for permanent water supply pipes.

Using fittings made for use with the pipe is the least expensive way to connect pipes.

Using mechanical fittings is a good (but more expensive) way for homeowners to connect different pipe types together and to connect pipes of the same type together.

Use flexible water connectors according to manufacturer's instructions. Avoid using plastic tubing. This material can burst and cause significant water damage.

TABLE 29: PLUMBING PIPE SUPPORT, WATER SUPPLY + DWV PIPES

PIPE MATERIAL	MAXIMUM HORIZONTAL SPACING	MAXIMUM VERTICAL SPACING	MID STORY GUIDE REQ'D FOR PIPE DIA. ≤ 2"
ABS pipe	48"	120"	yes
Cast-iron pipe	60"*	180"	no
Copper tubing (≤ 1¼" dia.)	72"	120"	no
Copper tubing (≥ 1½" dia.)	120"	120"	no
CPVC pipe or tubing (≤ 1" dia.)	36"	120"	yes
CPVC pipe or tubing (≥ 1¼" dia.)	48"	120"	yes
Polybutylene (PB) pipe or tubing	32"	48"	no
PEX	32"	120"	yes
PEX-AL-PEX and PE-AL-PE	32"	48"	yes
PVC pipe	48"	120"	yes
Steel pipe	144"	180"	no

* You may increase cast-iron pipe horizontal spacing to 120" when using 10' pipe lengths.

Pipe Support

1. Support pipes so they will maintain alignment and will not sag.

2. Support and install pipes so they can move with the normal expansion and contraction of the piping system without scraping or rubbing against supports or framing materials.

3. Use pipe supports that will carry the weight of the pipe and that are sufficiently wide to prevent crimping and distortion of the pipe.

4. Use pipe supports that will not cause corrosion or galvanic reaction between the pipe and the support. Example: do not use steel supports with copper pipe or copper supports with cast-iron pipe.

5. Provide rigid sway bracing at changes in pipe direction more than 45 degrees for pipe sizes at least 4 inches in diameter.

6. Provide horizontal and vertical support for pipes according to Table 30 (see page 136).

Support hangers and clamps for: CPVC and PVC (A), Copper (B), PEX (C).

Support copper tubing with compatible hangers.

Support for PEX tubing is particularly important near manifolds and fittings.

Provide vertical support for pipes running parallel to wall studs. Install supports according to Table 29.

Protect pipes 1½" from the edges of studs and joists.

Protecting Pipes from Puncture + Corrosion

1. Protect plumbing pipes (other than cast iron or galvanized steel) with shield plates, if the pipe is run through holes that are closer than 1¼ inches from the edge of studs, joists, rafters, or similar framing members. Extend the shield plate at least 2 inches below top plates and at least 2 inches above bottom plates.

2. Use shield plates at least ¹⁄₁₆-inch thick.

3. Apply these rules to pipes running through holes and notches in framing materials. While not required by most general codes, it is a best practice to protect pipes (other than cast iron or galvanized steel) that are closer than 1½ inches from the edge of framing materials. The most common example of such pipes is a pipe installed parallel to the edge of a stud or joist.

4. Protect copper plumbing pipe from corrosion where it passes through masonry or concrete. You may use pipe wrapping material designed for this purpose, or you may enclose the pipe in a sleeve.

5. Protect gas pipes, other than steel, with shield plates if the pipe is closer than 1½ inches from the edge of studs, joists, rafters, or similar framing members. Extend the shield plate at least 4 inches below top plates and at least 4 inches above bottom plates.

Protecting Pipes from Freezing

1. Do not install water supply and waste pipes outside of a building, in exterior building walls, in attics and crawl spaces, or in any other place subject to freezing temperatures, unless the pipes are protected by insulation or heat or both.

2. Install water service pipe at least 12 inches deep or at least 6 inches below the frost line.

3. Verify minimum water service and building sewer pipe depth with the local building official.

4. Apply these requirements only to areas with a winter design temperature of 32 degrees Fahrenheit or less.

Fixture Cutoff Valve (Angle Stop)

1. Provide each plumbing fixture, except for bathtubs and showers, with an accessible cutoff valve on the hot and cold water supply pipes. These valves are sometimes called "angle stop valves." You may install cutoff valves at bathtubs and showers, but these valves are not required.

Valves + Outlets Installed Below Ground

1. Do not install water supply outlets and stop-and-waste valves below ground. Example: do not install a hose bibb below ground.

2. You may install a freeze-proof yard hydrant below ground if the water supply to the hydrant is protected with a backflow preventer and the yard hydrant is permanently labeled as a "non-potable water source."

Hose Bibb Cutoff Valve

1. Provide hose bibbs that are subject to freezing with a stop-and-waste valve inside the building. This includes frost-proof hose bibbs.

2. You need not install a stop-and-waste valve on a frost-proof hose bibb if the stem extends into an open heated or semi-conditioned area of the building.

Hose bibbs that are subject to freezing require a stop-and-waste valve inside the building.

Foundation wall

Drain, Waste + Vent Piping (DWV)

Drainpipes use gravity to carry wastewater away from fixtures, appliances, and other drains. This wastewater is carried out of the house to a municipal sewer system or septic tank.

Drainpipes are usually plastic or cast iron. In some older homes, drainpipes may be made of copper, galvanized steel, or lead. Because they are not part of the supply system, lead drainpipes pose no health hazard. However, lead pipes are no longer manufactured for home plumbing systems.

Drainpipes have diameters ranging from 1¼ inches to 4 inches. These large diameters allow waste to pass through easily.

Traps are an important part of the drain system. These curved sections of drainpipe hold standing water, and they are usually found near any drain opening. The standing water of a trap prevents sewer gases from backing up into the home. Each time a drain is used, the standing trap water is flushed away and replaced by new water.

In order to work properly, the drain system requires air. Air protects trap from being drained. To allow air into the drain system, drainpipes are connected to vent pipes. All drain systems must include vents, and the entire system is called the drain-waste-vent (DWV) system. One or more vents, located on the roof, provide the air needed for the DWV system to work.

Use vent tee fittings only in vent pipes, not in drain pipes that carry wastewater. Drain pipes must maintain a minimum 2 percent slope.

Common sewer pipe materials PVC (A) or ABS (B) are allowed for use in DWV systems. Cast iron is also allowed but is rarely used in residential construction.

Drain + Sewer Pipe General Requirements

1. Install fittings that have a smooth interior surface and are compatible with the pipe to which they are attached. Example: do not use ABS fittings with PVC pipe.

2. Do not use fittings that contain ledges, shoulders, or reductions that may retard or obstruct drainage flow.

3. Install fittings that maintain a 2 percent slope and are approved for use where installed. Example: do not use a vent tee in a drainage pipe where water flows.

4. Do not use threaded connections in pipes where the threads run on the inside of the pipe and could retard or obstruct drainage flow.

5. Do not drill, tap, burn, or weld drainage, sewer, or vent pipes. Example: do not drill into a vent pipe to insert the discharge hose from a water softener.

6. Do not use the following types of joints and connections: cement or concrete, mastic or hot-pour bituminous, fittings not approved for the specific type of pipe or installation, joints between different pipe diameters made with elastomeric rolling O-rings, solvent-cement joints between different types of plastic pipe, and saddle fittings.

Common DWV Pipe Material

1. You may use any of the common drainage and sewer pipe materials listed in Table 30. You may use other materials listed if approved by your local codes.

2. Install galvanized steel drainage pipe at least 6 inches above the ground.

TABLE 30: COMMON DRAINAGE + SEWER PIPE MATERIALS

COMMON DRAINAGE + SEWER PIPE MATERIALS	USED FOR DRAINAGE	USED FOR SEWER
Cast-iron soil pipe	yes	yes
ABS-DWV pipe	yes	yes
PVC-DWV pipe	yes	yes
Steel pipe (black or galvanized)	yes	no

Water Closet Connection between Closet Flange + Pipe

1. You may use a 3-inch quarter bend to connect to a closet flange if you install a 4-inch-by-3-inch flange to receive the closet fixture horn.

2. You may use a 4-inch-by-3-inch reducing closet bend to connect to the closet flange.

Tailpieces

1. Provide sinks, dishwashers, laundry tubs, and similar fixtures with tailpieces and traps at least 1½ inches in diameter.

2. Provide vanity sinks, bidets, and similar fixtures with tailpieces and traps at least 1¼ inches.

4 × 3 reducing closet bend (horn).

Chromed P-trap with slip joints on lavatory sink.

Slip Joints

1. Use slip joints only between the fixture outlet and the connection with the drainage pipe.

2. Provide slip joints with access of at least 12 by 12 inches.

Drain tailpieces must match the diameter of the other pipes in the drain kit: 1¼ or 1½" depending on the type of fixture being drained.

VIOLATION! Flexible, ribbed material may be used only in a vertical direction as a sink tailpiece. This material may not be accepted in all areas and is not recommended because it is more likely to become clogged.

Bend (Elbow): A bend is a drainage fitting used to change the direction of flow. A bend is often called an elbow. Bends are available as a single fitting with two openings, and some are available as a double fitting with three or more openings. Some bends have inlets in addition to the openings. Use vent bends only in the dry vent sections of vent pipes. Quarter bends are sometimes called short sweeps in plastic pipes. See the definition of sweep. Quarter bends with a longer turn radius are sometimes called long turn quarter bends or long sweeps. Bends are made with the angles shown in Table 31.

Closet bend: A fitting used to connect a closet flange (a part of your toilet drain system) to other plumbing pipes. Closet bends often reduce the pipe size from the 4" of the closet flange to 3".

Closet flange: The fitting upon which a toilet (water closet) sits. Many different closet flanges are available to accommodate different fitting and pipe configurations. One type of closet flange allows you to offset the closet flange around a floor joist.

Coupling: A fitting used to join two lengths of pipe in a straight line. It has two female openings, one on each end.

Inlet: An additional opening in a fitting. A low-heel-inlet is located in a straight line with one opening of the fitting. A high-heel-inlet is located above the curved portion of the fitting. A side-inlet occurs on one side of the fitting.

TABLE 31: BEND DIRECTION CHANGE

BEND NAME	DIRECTION CHANGE
¼ bend	90°
⅙ bend	60°
⅛ bend	45°
¹⁄₁₆ bend	22½°

Bend pipes for DWV systems include: ¼ street bend (A), ¼ bend (B), ¼ vent bend (C), and ¼ bend with side inlet (D).

Parts of a toilet drain system include: closet bend (A), closet flange (B), and offset closet flange (C).

Sanitary tee: A sanitary tee is a tee fitting combined with a ¼-bend fitting.

Street fitting: A street fitting has a female opening (hub) on one end and a male opening (spigot) on the other end. Most drainage fittings have female openings on both ends.

Sweep: A sweep is a drainage fitting used to make a 90-degree change in the direction of flow. A short sweep is the same as a quarter bend in plastic pipes. Short sweeps and quarter bends are different fittings in cast iron pipes. A quarter bend with a longer radius bend is sometimes called a long sweep or a long turn quarter bend.

Tee: A fitting with three openings. Two openings are in a straight line, and one opening is at an approximate 90-degree angle to the others. Double tees, with four openings, are also available. Use vent tees only in the dry vent sections of vent pipes.

Wye: A fitting with three openings. Two openings are in a straight line and one opening is at an approximate 45-degree angle to the others. Wye fittings can be made with other fittings to make combination fittings, such as a tee-wye and a combination wye and ⅛ bend. Double wye and double tee-wye fittings are also available.

Inlet fittings include: bend with low-heel inlet (A) and bend with side inlet (B).

Tees for use in DWV systems include: Double sanitary tee (A), vent tee (B), and test tee (C).

Two types of sanitary tees include: Single sanitary tee (A) and double sanitary tee (B).

Wye fittings for DWV use include: Wye (A), double wye (B), and tee-wye (C).

TABLE 32: APPROVED DRAINAGE FITTINGS FOR CHANGING FLOW DIRECTION

TYPE OF FITTING	HORIZ. TO VERT.	VERT. TO HORIZ.	HORIZ. TO HORIZ.
22½° elbow (1/16 bend)	yes	yes	yes
45° elbow (⅛ bend)	yes	yes	yes
60° elbow (⅙ bend)	yes	yes	yes
90° elbow (¼ bend) (cast-iron pipes only)	yes	YES for fixture drains ≤ 2" NO for other pipes + sizes	YES for fixture drains ≤ 2" NO for other pipes + sizes
90° elbow (¼ bend + short sweep) (plastic pipes)	yes	YES for fixture drains ≤ 2" + all pipes ≥ 3"	YES for fixture drains ≤ 2" NO for other pipes + sizes
90° elbow (long sweep + long turn ¼ bend) (all pipes)	yes	yes	yes
sanitary tee	yes limits on multiple connection fittings	no	no
wye	yes	yes	yes
tee-wye	yes	yes	yes

Drain + Sewer Pipe Connections + Joints

Changing flow direction from vertical to horizontal using a wye fitting and ⅛ bend.

Changing flow direction from vertical to horizontal using a tee-wye.

Changing flow direction from vertical to horizontal using two ⅛ bends.

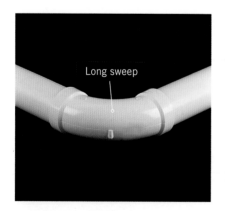

Changing flow direction from horizontal to horizontal using a long sweep fitting.

Changing flow direction from horizontal to horizontal using a wye fitting.

Changing flow direction from horizontal to horizontal using a long-radius tee-wye fitting.

This low-heel inlet bend is improperly installed. Solids from the toilet above may block the inlet.

horizontal (side facing), but not when the inlet is vertical (facing up). The side inlet may accept drainage flow from any fixture except a toilet. Side and heel inlets are usually 1½- or 2-inch openings, and you may not connect a toilet to any opening less than (<) 3 inches.

4. You may connect a dry vent to the quarter bend side or heel inlet only when the inlet is vertical (facing up). You may connect a dry vent to a quarter bend side or heel inlet when the inlet is horizontal (side facing) only when the entire quarter bend fitting is used as part of a dry vent.

Drainage + Sewer Pipe Fittings for Changing Flow Direction

1. Use the fittings in Table 32 to change the direction of flow in drainage and sewer pipes.

Drainage + Sewer Pipe Fittings: Changing from Horizontal to Vertical Using Multiple Fittings

1. You may use multiple fittings and double fittings (such as double sanitary tees) to connect back-to-back fixtures and two or more branch drains on the same level if directly opposite fitting connections are from the same size pipe and if directly opposite fitting connections are from similar fixture types or fixture groups.

2. Do not use a double sanitary tee to receive discharge from back-to-back toilets or from fixtures or appliances with pumping action (such as washing machines and dishwashers). You may use a double sanitary tee if the distance between the center of the closet flange and the inlet of the sanitary tee is at least 18 inches.

Quarter Bends with Heel or Side-Inlet

1. You may not use a heel inlet quarter bend to change flow direction from vertical to horizontal if the fitting serves a toilet. You may use a heel inlet quarter bend to change flow direction from horizontal to vertical without restrictions.

2. You may not connect wet vented fixtures to the low heel inlet of a heel inlet quarter bend.

3. You may use the side inlet of a quarter bend to change the flow direction when the inlet is

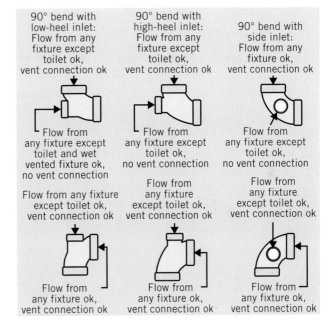

Allowed uses of 90° bends with an inlet

Sanitary tee allowed flow direction change

90° bend allowed direction change

Drain + Sewer Pipe Connections + Joints

ABS Plastic Pipe Joints

1. You may use approved branded couplings to join buried ABS pipes. Do not use branded couplings to join aboveground ABS pipes unless the use is approved by the building official.

2. You may use solvent cement to join ABS pipes above and below ground. Clean and dry pipes and fittings before applying solvent cement to all joint surfaces. Make the joint while the solvent cement is wet. Use solvent cement that complies with ASTM D 2235. Do not use PVC cement with ABS pipe.

3. You may use threaded joints for Schedule 80 and heavier ABS pipe. The threads should be NPT type. Do not place threads on the pipe's interior.

Steel Pipe Joints

1. You may use threaded joints for galvanized steel pipes. The threads should be NPT type.

2. You may use approved branded couplings to join galvanized steel pipes. Install the branded couplings according to manufacturer's instructions.

PVC Plastic Pipe Joints

1. You may use approved branded couplings to join buried PVC pipes. Do not use branded couplings to join aboveground PVC pipes unless the use is approved by the building official.

2. You may use solvent cement to join PVC pipes above and below ground. Clean and dry pipes and fittings before applying primer to all joint surfaces. Apply primer that complies with ASTM F 656 if required by your local jurisdiction. Apply solvent cement that complies with ASTM D 2564. Make the joint while the solvent cement is wet. Do not use ABS cement with PVC pipe.

You may use a product called transition cement to join ABS and PVC pipe if the product is approved by your local jurisdiction. This product is not currently approved by general codes for most applications but is frequently used.

Use the correct solvent cement and primer, if required, for the type of pipe you're using: PVC and CPVC should be connected with PVC solvent cement and primer; ABS requires ABS solvent cement (no primer is required).

3. You may use threaded joints for Schedule 80 and heavier PVC pipe. The threads should be NPT type. Do not place threads on the pipe's interior.

Joints between Different Types of Pipe

1. Use branded couplings approved for joining the different types of pipe. Install all branded couplings according to manufacturer's instructions.

2. Use an approved brass ferrule with a caulked joint or a mechanical compression joint when joining copper tubing to cast-iron pipe.

3. Use a brass converter fitting or a dielectric fitting when joining copper tubing to galvanized steel pipe.

Drain + Sewer Pipe Slope

1. Install horizontal drainage and sewer pipe with a uniform slope and alignment.

2. Install pipe not more than 2½ inches in diameter with at least a ¼ unit in 12 units (2 percent) slope.

3. Install pipe at least 3 inches diameter with at least a ⅛ unit in 12 units (1 percent) slope.

Drain + Sewer Pipe Size Reduction

1. Do not reduce drainage and sewer pipe size in the direction of the waste flow. Example: do not drain a 2-inch trap into a 1½-inch drainpipe.

NOTE: A 4-inch-by-3-inch closet bend fitting is not classified as a reduction in size.

Cast-iron drain pipe joints originally were made with hubbed fittings. Since new cast iron is seldom installed, joinery with cast iron is normally accomplished by connecting the original cast iron to another material, such as PVC, with a branded coupling.

Install and support DWV pipe to maintain the required uniform slope.

Drain + Sewer Cleanout Openings

Cleanout Locations + Spacing

1. Install a cleanout in every horizontal drainpipe so that the distance between cleanouts is not more than 100 feet, measured along the pipe's developed length. Install at least one cleanout for every horizontal drainpipe regardless of drainpipe length. This provision applies to the building drain, building sewer, and horizontal branch drains, not to fixture drains.

2. Install a cleanout within 10 feet of the building drain and building sewer junction. You may install this cleanout inside or outside the building. Make this cleanout accessible. Measure the 10 feet along the developed length of the pipe from the cleanout fitting to the building drain and sewer junction.

3. Install a cleanout at every change of pipe direction more than 45 degrees when the direction change uses one fitting. When multiple direction changes occur in one pipe run, only one cleanout is required, spaced not more than 40 feet apart. This provision applies to the building drain, building sewer, and horizontal branch drains.

Cleanout Size

1. Install cleanouts that are the same size as the largest pipe served by the cleanout. Example: you may not use 1½-inch fixture drain as a cleanout for a 2-inch branch drain.

2. You may install a cleanout in a vertical stack that is one pipe size smaller than the stack pipe size.

Cleanout Accessibility

1. Provide at least 18 inches between the cleanout and any obstruction. Measure the distance perpendicular to the front of the cleanout.

2. Do not conceal cleanouts with permanent finishing materials.

Cleanout required in building sewer ≤ every 100'

One cleanout required in horizontal drainage pipes + building drain ≤ every 100'

Building sewer

Building drain

One cleanout required ≤ 10' from junction of building drain + building sewer, inside or outside foundation

Cleanout required at change in horizontal pipe direction > 45°, not more than one cleanout every 40' if more than one direction change

3. Extend underground cleanouts to or above finished grade. Do not extend cleanouts above surfaces where they may become trip hazards or where they may be damaged by traffic.

Cleanout Plugs

1. Install brass or plastic plugs in cleanout fittings.

2. Make cleanouts gas and liquid tight.

Cleanout Direction

1. Install cleanouts so that they open toward the direction of the waste flow.

Cleanout Fixture Connections

1. Do not connect other pipes or fixtures to an existing cleanout unless you install an alternate cleanout. Example: do not remove a cleanout plug and use the cleanout opening as the drain for a laundry sink.

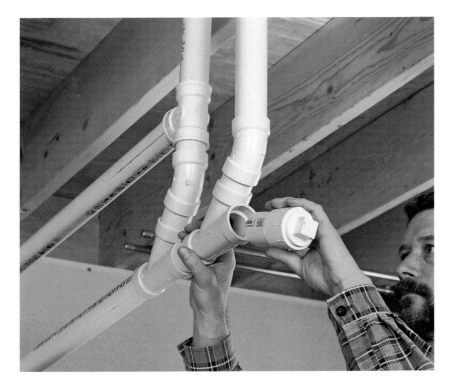

A cleanout is a threaded, removable cap positioned in a drainpipe run to allow access for equipment that clears clogs. Every horizontal line should have a cleanout that is no smaller in diameter than the largest drainpipe in the line.

For your convenience, keep access clear to cleanouts. Position movable objects, such as this washing machine, so they will not interfere with drain cleaning tools. Permanent obstructions must be kept at least 18" away from the cleanout, measured perpendicular to the opening.

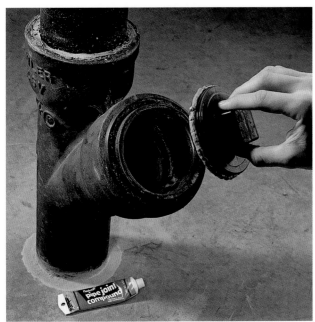

Seal cleanout plugs before capping cleanout fittings.

Plumbing Vents

To understand the purpose of plumbing vents, you must first understand the purpose of plumbing traps. A trap is required for all fixture drains connected to the DWV pipes. A trap can be a separate fitting, such as a P-trap for a sink or a shower, or it can be part of the fixture, such as the trap in a toilet. A trap maintains a water seal that keeps noxious and potentially explosive sewer gas in the DWV pipes and away from the air in the home. Water flows into a fixture and through a trap when you use a fixture. When you stop using the fixture, some of the water remains in the trap and recharges the trap's water seal.

When water flows in a pipe near a trap, the suction caused by the flowing water can create enough negative pressure at the trap to pull the water out of the trap. This is sometimes called siphoning the trap, because it is similar to what happens when you use a hose to siphon fuel out of a fuel tank. If the trap looses its water seal, the home is open to the flow of sewer gas.

A plumbing vent protects the trap's water seal by allowing air into the DWV pipes. The air provided by the vent replaces the air that is drawn along with the flowing water. This replacement air reduces the suction and protects the trap. Without properly sized and installed vents, the DWV system will not function as intended.

Vent pipes should extend in an upward direction from drains. This ensures that wastewater cannot flow into the vent pipe and block it. At the opposite end, a vent pipe should connect to an existing vent stack or stack vent at a point at least 6" above the flood rim of the highest fixture draining into the system.

Vent Slope + Connection to Pipes

Plumbing Vents Required
1. Install an approved vent for every trap and trapped fixture. This means that every plumbing fixture (such as a sink or a shower) and every plumbing fixture with an integrated trap (such as a toilet) must be protected by an individual vent or an approved vent system in which one vent protects multiple fixtures.

2. Terminate at least one vent outdoors. Connect the outdoor vent to the building drain or to a branch or extension of the building drain. The branch or extension cannot be an island fixture vent.

Vent Pipe Slope + Support
1. Install all vent pipes using adequate supports so that the vent pipes slope toward the soil or waste pipe. Moisture in any form should flow toward the soil or waste pipe by gravity. General codes do not specify support intervals for vent pipes. Supporting vent pipes at the same interval required for drain pipes is recommended, but not required.

Vent Pipe Connection to Horizontal Drainage Pipes

1. Connect vent pipes to horizontal drainage pipes above the centerline of the horizontal drainage pipe. This protects the vent pipe from filling with solid material.

Vent Connection Height Minimums

1. Connect dry vent pipes to vent stacks, stack vents, and to stack-type air admittance valves so that the connection point is at least 6 inches above the flood rim level of the highest fixture served by the vent. A common violation of this provision is when a dry vent runs parallel to the drainage pipes under the fixture. This provision helps protect the vent pipe from filling with solid material.

Trap weir

VIOLATION! Do not connect the vent pipe within 2 pipe diameters of the trap weir.

2. Install horizontal branch vent pipes at least 6 inches above the flood rim level of the highest fixture served by the vent.

Vent Rough-in for Future Fixtures

1. Install a vent for roughed-in (future) fixtures that is at least ½ the diameter of the drainpipe rough-in.

2. Connect the roughed-in vent to the vent system or provide another approved means to terminate the roughed-in vent.

3. Label the roughed-in vent pipe to indicate that it is a vent.

Crown Venting

1. Connect the vent fitting at least two pipe diameters from the trap weir.

Connect vent pipes to other vents at least 6" above the highest fixture so that the vent pipe will not become clogged with solid materials.

Vent Termination

Vent Height Above Roof

1. Extend vent pipes above the roof at least 6 inches, or the number of inches required by local snow accumulation and temperature conditions, whichever is higher. Measure vent height from the high side where the vent exits the roof. Obtain the snow accumulation height from the local building official.

Use approved vent flashing boots to seal around the vent projections in a roof. Make sure boot angle is compatible with your roof slope.

2. Extend vent pipes at least 7 feet above any roof used as a balcony, observation deck, or similar accessible walking surface.

Vent Freezing + Frost Closure Protection

1. Protect exterior vent terminals from freezing by using heat, insulation, or both.

2. Increase the diameter of exterior vent terminal pipes to at least 3 inches, beginning at least 1 foot below the roof or inside the wall.

3. These provisions apply only where the 97.5 percent winter design temperature is less than 0 degrees Fahrenheit. Obtain this information from IRC Chapter 3 and from your local building official.

Vent Flashing

1. Use approved flashing to make vent pipes extending through a roof watertight.

2. Use caulk to make vent pipes extending through a wall watertight.

Vent Exterior Termination Locations

1. Locate plumbing vent terminations at least 4 feet below, at least 3 feet above, or at least 10 feet horizontally from any: (a) door or operable window, (b) other air intake opening of the building, and (c) air intake opening of any adjacent building.

2. Locate plumbing vent terminations running through a side wall at least 10 feet from the lot line and at least 10 feet above the highest grade within 10 feet horizontally from the vent termination.

3. Locate plumbing vent terminations at least 7 feet above a roof used for recreational purposes, such as an observation deck or sunbathing.

4. Protect side-wall vent terminations from entry by birds or rodents.

5. Do not locate vent terminations directly under the building's overhang if the overhang contains soffit vents.

Vent Connection Distance from Trap

1. Use Table 33 to determine the maximum length of a fixture drain between a trap weir and a vent fitting. The vent fitting may be at a vent pipe, such as an individual vent, or at a vented pipe, such as a wet vent. Uniform Plumbing Code fixture drain lengths are different.

2. The table does not apply to self-siphoning fixtures, such as toilets. No fixture drain length limitations apply to these fixtures.

Fixture Drain Slope

1. Connect the fixture drain pipe with not more than one pipe diameter of fall between the bottom of the trap outlet and the bottom of the vent fitting inlet. This parallels the distance requirements in Table 33 and reduces the chance that the trap will drain because the fitting is below the trap. Example: 5 feet by ¼ inch per foot equals 1¼ inches. See the first row of Table 33.

2. Connect the top of the fixture drainpipe to the vent fitting above the trap weir. This provision does not apply to toilet fixture drains.

TABLE 33: VENT DISTANCE FROM TRAP

TRAP SIZE	SLOPE	DISTANCE FROM TRAP TO VENT FITTING
1¼	¼" per ft.	5'
1½	¼" per ft.	6'
2	¼" per ft.	8'
3	⅛" per ft.	12'
4	⅛" per ft.	16'

Maximum vent distance from trap

The distance from the trap to the vent fitting is limited. Note that the vent fitting may connect to a vent pipe or to a pipe that is vented, such as a wet vented pipe.

Improper vent connection

Vent connected below flood rim. Waste flow through horizontal vent could occur when drain stack or fixture drain is blocked.

Flood rim

Vent stack

Drain blocked

Proper vent connection

Branch vent

Connect individual and branch vents ≥ 6" above highest fixture flood rim

Flood rim

Flood rim

Vent stack

Individual vents

When a vent is connected to a vent stack, the connection should be at least 6" above the fixture flood rim level. This helps avoid improper waste flow through the trap.

Fall of drain less than 1 pipe diameter

1 pipe diameter

Vent pipe at least 2× pipe diameter from trap weir

2× diameter

Examples of correct individual vent configurations.

Vent Pipe Size

1. Use at least a 1¼-inch-diameter vent pipe or a vent pipe at least ½ the diameter of the drainpipe being vented, whichever is larger, as the dry vent.

2. Increase the vent pipe diameter by at least one pipe size over the entire length of the vent pipe when the vent's developed length is greater than 40 feet.

Vent Pipe Developed Length

1. Measure the developed length of individual, branch, and circuit vents beginning where the vent connects to the drainage system and ending where the vent connects to a vent stack, stack vent, air admittance valve, or the vent's termination point outside the building.

Individual Vents

1. Fixture types: Use an individual vent to protect any fixture.

2. Number of fixtures: Use an individual vent to protect only one fixture.

3. Fixture location: Use an individual vent to protect one fixture located anywhere in the structure.

4. Individual vent connection location: Connect the individual vent on the fixture drain of the fixture being vented or at the fixture drain connection to the drainage system.

Individual vents are the easiest to install. They protect one fixture.

5. Fixture drain length to vent connection: Use Table 33 to determine the maximum distance between the fixture trap weir and the individual vent fitting.

6. Individual vent pipe size: Use at least a 1¼-inch pipe or a pipe at least ½ the size of the drainpipe being vented, whichever is larger.

Common Vents

1. Fixture types: Use a common vent to protect any two fixtures. You may common vent different types of fixtures, such as a sink and a shower or a shower and a toilet.

2. Number of fixtures: Use a common vent to protect only two fixtures.

3. Fixture location: Use a common vent only for fixtures located on the same floor level. You may connect the fixture drains at different vertical levels if the fixtures are on the same floor level.

4. Common vent connection location: You may connect the common vent where the fixture drains intersect. You may connect the common vent downstream from where the fixture drains intersect only when the fixture drains connect to the branch drainpipe at the same horizontal level.

5. Fixture drain length to vent connection: Use Table 33 to determine the maximum distance between each fixture trap weir and the common vent fitting.

6. Common vent pipe size: Use at least 1¼ inches of pipe or a pipe at least ½ the size of the drainpipe being vented, whichever is larger, for the common vent.

Wet Vents

1. Fixture types: Use a wet vent to protect any combination of fixtures from not more than two bathroom groups.

2. Number of fixtures: Use a wet vent to protect not more than two toilets, two bathtubs or showers, two lavatory sinks, or two bidets.

3. Fixture location: Use a wet vent only for approved bathroom fixtures located on the same floor level.

4. Wet vent connection location: (a) Begin the wet vent with an individual or common vent for a lavatory, bidet, shower, or bathtub. This vent does not need to be at the first wet vented fixture in a horizontal wet vent. This vent must be at the first wet vented fixture in a vertical wet vent. End the wet vent at the last wet vented fixture connection to the wet vented pipe. (b) Do not connect more than one fixture upstream from the beginning individual or common vent in a horizontal wet vent. (c) Connect each fixture individually to the wet vented pipe. Do not connect two or more fixtures together and connect that branch drain to the wet vented pipe.

5. Horizontal wet vent fixture drain connection location: (a) Connect each individual fixture drain horizontally to a horizontal wet-vented pipe. Example: you may not install a wye fitting vertically and connect a fixture drain to the vertical opening of the wye in a horizontal wet vent. You may install the wye horizontally and connect the horizontal fixture drain to the horizontal opening of the wye. (b) You may connect a fixture drain vertically to a horizontal wet-vented pipe if you install a dry vent on the vertically connected fixture. Example: you may install a wye fitting vertically if you connect an individual vent to the fixture. (c) Do not connect any fixtures to the horizontal wet-vented pipe other than those fixtures being wet-vented. You may connect other fixtures to the horizontal pipe downstream after the wet vent ends. Example: do not connect a bedroom bar sink to a wet-vented pipe.

Common vent with vent connecting at fixture drain intersection.

6. Vertical wet vent fixture drain connection location: (a) Connect all toilet fixture drains at the same vertical level. (b) Connect fixture drains from bathtubs, showers, lavatory sinks, and bidets at or above where the toilet fixture drains connect to the vertical wet vent.

7. Fixture drain length to wet-vented pipe: Use Table 33 (see page 149) to determine the maximum distance between each fixture trap weir and the fixture drain fitting at the wet-vented drain pipe. You may use individual and common vents to protect any fixture where the fixture drain length limit is a problem.

8. Wet vent pipe size: (a) Use a dry vent that is at least a 1¼-inch pipe or a pipe at least ½ the size of the wet-vented pipe, whichever is larger, for the individual or common vent that begins the wet vent. (b) Use Table 34 to size the horizontal and vertical wet-vented drainage pipe. You may not connect a toilet to a drainage pipe smaller than 3 inches regardless of what is allowed in the table.

Island Fixture Vent

1. Fixture types: Use an island fixture vent to protect only sinks such as those in kitchens and bathrooms. You may connect a dishwasher and disposal to a kitchen sink.

2. Use an island fixture vent to protect any number of approved fixture types.

3. Use an island fixture vent only for fixtures located in the same island and on the same floor level.

4. Pipe configuration: (a) Extend the loop portion of the island fixture vent vertically to above the drain outlet of the fixture being vented before extending the horizontal and/or vertical downward portion. (b) Use drainage fittings and pipe slopes for any portion of the vent below the fixture flood rim level. Do not use vent fittings or slope the vent pipe as a vent below the fixture flood rim level. (c) Connect the downward portion of the vent loop downstream from where the fixture drain connects with the horizontal drainage pipe. Make the connection using a full size fitting. (d) Provide cleanouts at the downward portion of the loop vent and in the vertical portion of the vent pipe before it connects to the exterior vent pipe.

5. Dry vent connection location: (a) Connect the dry vent to the drainage system using a full size fitting. Connect the dry vent to a vertical drain pipe or the top half of a horizontal drain pipe. (b) Extend any dry vent at least 6 inches above the flood rim

TABLE 34: HORIZ. + VERT. WET-VENTED DRAINAGE PIPE SIZE

WET-VENTED PIPE SIZE	MAX. DRAIN FIXTURES LOAD
1½"	1
2"	4
2½"	6
3"	12
4"	32

Horizontal wet vent begins at individual or common vent

Fixtures connecting vertically need separate vent

FDL

Fitting installed horizontally

Wet vented pipe

FDL

All wet vented fixtures connect horizontally to wet vented pipe

Wet vent ends at last wet vented bathroom group fixture

Using a wet vent eliminates the need for an individual vent for each fixture.

level of the highest fixture being vented before any connection to the outside vent.

6. Fixture drain length to vent connection: Use Table 33 to determine the maximum distance between the fixture trap weir and the fixture drain connection to the island vent.

7. Vent pipe size: Use at least a 1¼ inches pipe or a pipe at least ½ the size of the drain pipe size being vented as the dry portion of the vent, whichever is larger.

Air Admittance Valves

1. Install air admittance valves according to manufacturer's installation instructions and general code provisions.

2. You may use air admittance valves to vent individual vents, branch vents, circuit vents, and stack vents. Use individual and branch-type air admittance valves to vent fixtures that are on the same floor level and that are connected to a horizontal branch drain.

3. Use air admittance valves that are rated for the vent size to which the valve is connected.

4. Locate individual and branch-type air admittance valves at least 4 inches above the horizontal branch drain or fixture drain being vented.

5. Locate stack-type air admittance valves at least 6 inches above the flood rim level of the highest fixture being vented.

6. Locate the air admittance valve within the vent's developed length limits.

7. Locate air admittance valves in attics at least 6 inches above insulation.

8. Provide air admittance valves with access and adequate ventilation.

9. Install air admittance valves within 15 degrees of vertical, and do not install air admittance valves outdoors unless allowed by the manufacturer's instructions.

10. Do not use an air admittance valve as the vent for a sewage ejector tank unless the vent system for the tank is designed by a qualified engineer.

11. Look for the UPC symbol on the air admittance valve. Air admittance valves without this symbol are for use only in manufactured homes. They may not be used in homes governed by the IRC.

12. Do not install air admittance valves outside unless allowed by manufacturer's instructions. Do not install them outside to evade vent clearance requirements to air intake openings.

An island fixture vent is a fairly complicated venting configuration used to vent fixtures installed in a kitchen island. To further complicate matters, many codes now require that the vent pipe from the fixture connect to the vent stack at least 6" above the fixture flood rim.

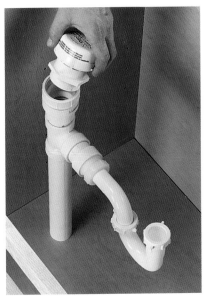

Air admittance valves can be installed in an island cabinet to vent a sink drain line, greatly simplifying the venting process.

Plumbing Traps

Trap Size

1. Use Table 35 to determine the minimum trap size for most plumbing fixtures.

2. Do not install separate traps on toilets, urinals, and other fixtures that have traps in the fixture itself.

3. Do not install a trap that is larger than the drainage pipe into which the trap discharges. Example: do not connect a 2-inch trap to a 1½-inch pipe on the discharge side of the trap.

Trap Seal

1. Install traps with a water seal of at least 2 inches and not more than 4 inches.

2. Install floor drain traps that have a deep seal (near 4 inches) design or a trap primer. Connect trap primer valves above the trap seal level.

TABLE 35: MINIMUM TRAP SIZE FOR PLUMBING FIXTURES

PLUMBING FIXTURE	MINIMUM TRAP SIZE
Bathtub (equipped or not equipped with shower head or whirlpool)	1½"
Bidet	1¼"
Clothes washing machine standpipe	2"
Dishwasher (separately trapped)	1½"
Floor drain	2"
Kitchen sink (equipped or not equipped with dishwasher or disposal + trapped using one or two traps)	1½"
Laundry tubs (≥ 1 compartments)	1½"
Lavatory	1¼"
Shower (total flow rate of all showerheads + body sprays) ≤ 5.7 gallons per minute (gpm) > 5.7 gpm + ≤ 12.3 gpm > 12.3 gpm + ≤ 25.8 gpm > 25.8 gpm + ≤ 55.6 gpm	1½" 2" 3" 4"

Measure the water seal from the trap dip to the crown weir.

Trap dip

VIOLATION! Install traps so that the water seal is level. Traps set out of level may lose their water seal and will not drain properly.

Trap Installation

1. Set traps level with respect to their water seal.

2. Protect traps from freezing.

3. Provide access to traps with slip joints at the trap inlet or outlet.

4. Do not install more than one trap per fixture.

5. Limit the vertical distance between the fixture drain outlet and the trap weir to not more than 24 inches.

6. Limit the horizontal distance between the fixture drain outlet and the center of the trap inlet to not more than 30 inches. Note that this 30-inch horizontal distance may be eliminated or not enforced in some jurisdictions. Verify if this provision applies in your jurisdiction.

Prohibited Traps

1. Do not install the following types of traps: bell traps, drum traps, S-traps, traps with moving parts, and building traps.

Plumbing Appliances + Fixtures

The installation and hookup of appliances that are part of your home plumbing system is the part of the plumbing process that DIYers are most likely to attempt. The information in this section provides a good general backdrop for making plumbing hookups, but be sure to read the manufacturer's installation recommendations carefully. As always, manufacturer instructions take precedence over codes.

2. Do not install fuel-fired water heaters in bedrooms or bathrooms unless the water heater is installed in a sealed enclosure where combustion air does not come from the living space. This restriction does not apply to direct vent water heaters.

3. You may provide access to water heaters located in attics or crawl spaces through bedrooms, bathrooms, or their closets if ventilation of the bedroom, bathroom, or closet complies with codes.

Water Heaters

Replacing a water heater is a relatively easy DIY plumbing task as long as it is a like-for-like replacement. In an ideal situation, you'd replace the old unit with one of the exact same size and make, and thereby avoid having to move any gas, water, or electrical lines. But if you choose to upgrade or downgrade in size, or perhaps replace an old electric water heater with a gas water heater that costs less to run, you'll find that relocating the necessary lines isn't that difficult. Be sure to check with your local building department to determine if a permit is required to replace a water heater. A permit probably is required.

Water heaters for primary duty in residences range in size from 30 gallons to 65 gallons. For a family of four, a 40- or 50-gallon model should be adequate. While you don't want to run out of hot water every morning, you also don't want to pay to heat more water than you use. Base your choice on how well your current water heater is meeting your demand.

Prohibited Locations for Water Heaters

1. Do not install fuel-fired water heaters in rooms used as storage closets. You may install water heaters in closets used solely to store the water heater if you provide adequate combustion air in the closet. You may install electric water heaters in any closet when allowed by the manufacturer.

Water heaters typically last for at least 10 years, but once they start to show signs of aging, it's a good idea to replace them with a new, more efficient appliance. A new water heater may be larger than the existing appliance even if it holds the same amount of water. Measure the space to confirm that the new water heater will fit.

Water Heater Relief Valves

1. Install either a separate temperature relief valve and a separate pressure relief valve or a combination temperature and pressure relief valve on all appliances used to heat or store hot water. Combination temperature and pressure relief valves (T+P valves) are used almost exclusively in modern water heaters. This provision applies to tank-type, tankless, and swimming pool water heaters.

2. Install the temperature relief or T+P valve on the top of the water heater or on the side of the water heater within 6 inches of the top. Do not install an extension pipe between the water heater and the T+P valve.

3. Do not install a check valve or shutoff valve anywhere that might interfere with the operation of the relief valve or the flow of water or steam from the discharge pipe.

The T+P valve is a critical safety device that is required on all water heaters.

T+P valves should be installed on your water heater prior to placing the appliance in position. Many water heaters today come with the T+P valve preinstalled.

Water Heater Relief Valve Discharge Pipe

1. Use water distribution pipe listed in Table 28 (see page 131) as the relief valve discharge pipe. Copper and CPVC are the most commonly used discharge pipes. It is difficult to maintain uniform slope and fall on flexible pipes, such as PEX.

2. Install the discharge pipe so hot water and steam will not cause personal injury or property damage if the relief valve discharges.

3. Install the discharge pipe so that any leaking from the pipe outlet is readily observable by the building occupants.

4. Use a discharge pipe that is at least as large as the relief valve opening. The size is usually ¾ inch in diameter. Use 1-inch-diameter pipe or tubing if insert fittings are installed in the discharge pipe. PEX tubing is the most common example of this situation.

5. Run the discharge pipe full size to the floor, to an indirect waste receptor (such as a floor drain) inside the building, to the water heater drip pan, or outside the building. If the area is subject to freezing, terminate the discharge pipe through an air gap into an indirect waste receptor located inside the building. You may use other discharge points in areas subject to freezing, if approved by the local building official.

6. Slope the discharge pipe so that it drains by gravity from the relief valve to the discharge point.

7. Do not connect the discharge pipe directly to the building's drain, waste, and vent system. Leave an air gap between the discharge pipe and the floor, ground, or other termination point.

8. Do not install a trap or a valve or a threaded outlet in the discharge pipe.

9. Terminate the discharge pipe through an air gap not more than 6 inches and not less than 1½ inches above the floor.

10. Do not connect more than one appliance to a discharge pipe.

> ### ⚠ SAFETY TIP
>
> T+P valve manufacturers recommend testing the valve at least once per year. They also recommend having a licensed plumber inspect the valve at least every 3 years. Minerals in the water can collect on the sensor and render the valve inoperable. Check and follow the safety instructions for your T+P valve.

The vent for a gas water heater should be connected securely to the draft hood at the top of the appliance.

Install a drip pan under a water heater when water leaks might damage surrounding areas. Use at least a ¾"-diameter discharge pipe to drain the drip pan. Use a larger discharge pipe if the connection to the drip pan is more than ¾" diameter.

Water Heater Drip Pans

1. Install a drip pan under storage tank water heaters located where leakage could cause damage. These locations often include attics and all areas within the conditioned area of the home, including finished basements. Drip pans are not required under tankless water heaters, unless required by local codes.

2. Use a drip pan at least 1½ inches deep and made with at least 24-gauge galvanized steel or other approved materials. Use a pan with a size and shape to catch all leaks and condensation from the water heater. Do not install a plastic pan under a gas-fired water heater unless the pan is listed for installation under a gas-fired water heater.

3. Run the discharge pipe to an indirect waste receptor (such as a floor drain) or to the outside of the building. Terminate the pipe not more than 24 inches or not less than 6 inches above the ground or a waste receptor, such as a floor drain.

4. You are not required to install a pan under a replacement water heater if no pan is currently installed.

Do not connect PEX supply tubing directly to a gas water heater. Install metal connector tubes to the inlet ports first, and then attach the PEX to the tubes.

Toilets

You can replace a poorly functioning or inefficient toilet with a high-efficiency, high-quality new toilet in just a single afternoon. All toilets made since 1994 have been required to use 1.6 gallons or less per flush, which has been a huge challenge for the industry. Today, the most evolved 1.6-gallon toilets have wide passages behind the bowl and wide (3-inch) flush valve openings—features that facilitate short, powerful flushes. This means fewer second flushes and fewer clogged toilets. These problems were common complaints of the first generation of 1.6-gallon toilets and continue to beleaguer inferior models today. See what toilets are available at your local home center in your price range, then go online and see what other consumers' experiences with those models have been. New toilets often go through a "debugging" stage when problems with leaks and malfunctioning parts are more common.

Most toilet tanks today are equipped with a float cup style fill valve rather than the float ball types that were common previously. Some have power-assisted flush mechanisms to boost today's low-flow toilets.

Your criteria should include ease of installation, good flush performance, and reliability. With a little research, you should be able to purchase and install a high-functioning, economical gravity-flush toilet that will serve you well for years to come.

General Requirements

1. Install toilets with an approved flushing mechanism that provides enough water to clear and refill the toilet bowl and refill the toilet's internal trap. Approved flushing mechanisms are the common gravity feed flush tanks (one- and two-piece tanks) and power-assisted tanks or valves.

2. Install toilets that use an average of not more than 1.6 gallons per flush.

3. Provide the toilet with an adequate supply of water. Control the water supply with an automatic device (such as a float valve) that will refill the toilet tank after each flush and completely stop the flow of water to the tank when the tank is full. The device should also supply enough water to refill the toilet.

4. Install toilets with a flush valve seat in the toilet tank that is at least 1 inch above the flood level of the toilet bowl. An alternate design (used by low-profile one-piece toilets) is acceptable. This design closes the flush valve when the toilet is clogged and prevents water from flowing back into the tank.

5. Provide toilet tanks with an overflow pipe or mechanism that is sufficient to prevent the tank from flooding if the fill valve malfunctions.

6. Provide access to all parts in the toilet tank for repair and replacement. Do not install permanent counter tops or similar obstructions that restrict access to the tank.

7. Use toilet seats made of smooth, non-absorbent material properly sized for the toilet bowl.

8. Use corrosion-resistant screws, nuts, bolts, and washers to secure toilets to the closet flange.

Backflow Protection of Toilet Fill Valves

1. Protect toilets with an approved antisiphon fill valve.

2. Locate the backflow preventer at least 1 inch above the opening of the overflow pipe. Fill valves with all parts below the tank water line usually violate this provision.

Toilet (Closet) Flange

1. Install a closet flange that is firmly attached to a structural support (floor) to connect a toilet to drainage piping. Use a closet flange that is compatible with the connected drainage pipe. Example: do not use a PVC closet flange with ABS pipe. Do not use the closet flange to provide structural support to the toilet.

2. Use non-corrosive bolts and an approved gasket (O-ring) or other approved setting compound to secure the toilet and closet flange and to make the seal watertight.

An overflow tube must be provided inside the toilet tank to keep water from rising out of the tank if the fill valve is malfunctioning.

The water inlet of a fill valve should usually be above the tank's water line to reduce backflow of wastewater into the drinking water system.

The closet flange and O-ring seal the plumbing connection. The closet flange does not support the toilet.

Dishwashing Machines

General Requirements

1. You may discharge a dishwashing machine, a disposal, and a kitchen sink into one 1½-inch-diameter drain (trap). Use a ¾-inch-diameter dishwashing machine drain tube when discharging the dishwashing machine into either a sink drain (trap) or a disposal. Connect the dishwashing machine drain tube to a wye fitting in the sink tailpiece when connecting the drain line directly to the sink tailpiece. Loop the dishwashing machine drain line as high as possible in the sink cabinet and securely fasten or install an air gap device. An air gap device is not necessary in the dishwashing machine drain tube unless required by local codes.

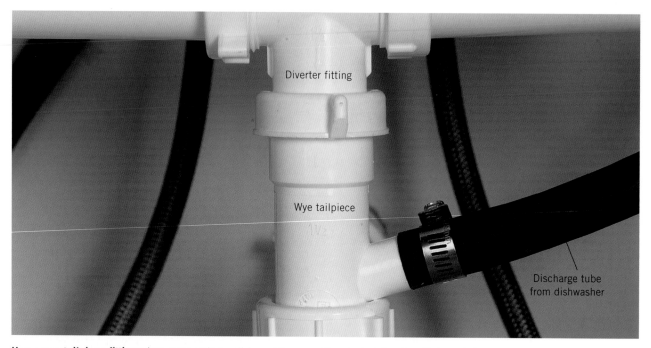

Diverter fitting

Wye tailpiece

Discharge tube from dishwasher

Use a wye tailpiece fitting when connecting a dishwashing machine drain tube directly to a sink.

A dishwashing machine drain tube high loop is one method of backflow prevention. Secure the tube as high as possible in the sink base cabinet.

A dishwashing machine drain air gap device is one method of backflow prevention. Install the device according to manufacturer's instructions. These are required in some jurisdictions instead of a high loop.

Food Disposers

Fittings

1. Use an approved directional fitting on the tailpiece when connecting a disposal or dishwashing machine. This helps direct the waste down into the plumbing drain system and avoids blockage and blow back up the tailpiece when these appliances discharge under pressure. Examples of directional fittings include the waste tee with a baffle and a sanitary tee.

A sanitary tee fitting is one possible directional fitting when draining a dishwashing machine or food disposer into a kitchen sink.

A waste tee with a baffle is one possible directional fitting when draining a dishwashing machine or food disposer into a kitchen sink.

Clothes Washing Machines

Fittings

1. Discharge the wastewater from a clothes washing machine through an air gap. Do not connect the clothes washing machine drain line directly to the plumbing waste pipes. Inserting the clothes washing machine drain hose into the standpipe is the most common acceptable method of providing the required air gap.

2. Install a water-hammer arrestor where required to control water flow and reduce the possibility of water hammer. A water-hammer arrestor may be used near a quick-closing valve, such as in a clothes washing machine.

Water-hammer arrestors may be required in some jurisdictions at clothes washing machine hose connections.

Whirlpool Bathtubs (Jetted Baths)

General Requirements

1. Install whirlpool tubs according to manufacturer's instructions. This includes testing the tub for leaks and pump operation, usually prior to installation, and providing adequate support for the tub, water, and occupants. Some whirlpool tub manufacturers allow plaster as a tub support method. Plaster is not the same as drywall joint compound. Do not use drywall joint compound to support bathtubs unless it is specifically approved by the tub manufacturer.

2. Provide a door or access panel large enough to allow service personnel to repair and replace the pump. The door size will depend on where the pump is located relative to the door. The door may have to be larger than the specified minimum size if the pump is located far away from the door.

3. Make the access opening at least 12 inches by 12 inches if the manufacturer does not specify an opening size. Make the access opening at least 18 inches by 18 inches if the pump is located more than 2 feet away from the opening. Do not place obstructions, such as tub support framing and pipes, between the access opening and the pump.

4. Locate the circulation pump above the crown weir of the trap.

5. Install circulation pipes and pump drain line so that they are self-draining and retain minimum possible water after using the tub.

6. Install whirlpool bathtub motors on a GFCI protected circuit. Do not use the bathroom receptacle circuit for this purpose.

7. Install a copper bonding wire at least #8 AWG connecting all metal pipes, pump motors, and other electrical equipment associated with the whirlpool bathtub. Do not bond grounded double insulated whirlpool bathtub pump motors.

Whirlpool tub motors need access for maintenance and replacement. The access opening must be large enough to allow effective access to the motor. Connect a bonding wire between the tub motor and metal water pipes for electrical safety.

A bathtub can crack and drain connections can loosen and leak unless it is properly supported. Here, the tub is installed on a bed of hardened mortar.

Showers

Shower Size

1. Provide showers with a finished area of at least 900 square inches and a finished minimum dimension of at least 30 inches. Maintain the minimum dimensions from the top of the threshold to at least 70 inches above the shower drain outlet. Measure the shower from the centerline of the threshold (curb). You may install valves, showerheads, soap dishes, and grab bars that encroach into the minimum dimensions. You may install a fold-down seat in the shower if the minimum dimensions are maintained when the seat is up.

2. You may provide a shower with a finished minimum dimension of at least 25 inches if the finished area is at least 1,300 square inches.

3. Provide shower compartment access of at least 22-inch finished width.

4. Swing hinged shower doors out from the shower stall. Hinged doors may swing into the shower stall if they also swing out. Sliding shower doors are also allowed.

Water Supply Riser

1. Secure the pipe between the shower valve and the showerhead to the permanent structure. This provision applies whether the riser is visible or concealed. Securing the riser helps avoid leaks if the riser twists and becomes loose at joints.

Shower Receptor Construction

1. You are not required to install a raised curb or threshold at the entrance to a shower. Showers designed for wheelchair access will not have a curb or threshold.

2. Install a shower curb or threshold (when used): (a) at least 1 inch below the sides and back of the receptor; and (b) at least 2 inches and not more than 9 inches above the top of the drain.

3. Slope the shower floor at least ¼ unit in 12 units (2-percent slope) and not more than ½ unit in 12 units.

4. Use a flanged shower floor drain that provides a watertight seal at the floor.

A sufficiently large shower stall is more than a convenience—it is a safety issue.

Attaching the shower riser pipe to framing helps avoid water leaks caused when adjusting the showerhead loosens the pipe fittings.

Proper installation of a site-built shower receptor is critical to avoiding costly water leaks.

5. Use hot-mopped felt, sheet lead, sheet copper, approved plastic liner material, or approved trowel-applied liquid material when installing a site-built shower receptor. Plastic liners (such as chlorinated polyethylene and plasticized polyvinyl chloride) are the most common modern site-built liner materials.

6. Extend the lining material at least 2 inches beyond or around the rough jambs of the shower receptor. Extend the lining material at least 2 inches above the finished threshold or curb.

7. Attach the lining material to an approved backing. Nail or perforate the lining at least 1 inch above the finished threshold. Seal joints in plastic lining material according to manufacturer's instructions.

8. Install an approved flanged shower drain that is equipped with weep holes into the drain and is equipped with a flange that makes a watertight seal between the lining material and the drain.

WATER SUPPLY BACKFLOW PREVENTION

An important part of the design and use of the drinking (potable) water supply system is preventing contamination of potable water. Contamination can occur when the potable water supply is intentionally or unintentionally connected to a contaminant source. A cross-connection is a connection between the potable water supply and a potential contaminant source. Backflow is when material (usually liquid) travels in the reverse of the intended direction within a cross-connection. Contamination occurs when contaminated material backflows into the potable water system through a cross-connection.

Some cross-connections are intended. Examples of intended cross-connections include toilet tank fill valves, automatic fill systems for swimming pools, and lawn irrigation systems. Some cross-connections are unintended. Examples of unintended cross-connections include spray hoses connected to a laundry tub faucet and garden hoses attached to chemical sprayers. In these examples, a sudden loss of water pressure in the potable water supply system or an increase in pressure at the contaminant source could allow a contaminant to be drawn back into the potable water system. If the liquid were weed killer in a spray bottle at the end of a garden hose, the weed killer could be drawn into the potable water system.

Backflow into the potable water system can occur by backpressure or by backsiphonage. Backpressure occurs when the pressure in the cross-connection source exceeds the pressure in the potable water supply system. Contaminated material is forced under pressure into the potable water system. Sources of backpressure include pumps, liquid storage tanks at a higher elevation than the cross-connection point, and thermal expansion from a heat source, such as a water heater. Backsiphonage occurs when the pressure in the potable water supply system falls below atmospheric pressure. Air pressure can force contaminated material into the potable water supply system or negative pressure in the potable water supply system can draw contaminated material into the potable water supply system.

The IRC requires protections of all potable water supply outlets and all intentional cross-connections by an air gap or by an approved backflow prevention device.

AIR GAP TERMS

Air gap: An air gap is the unobstructed distance between a water supply fixture outlet opening and the flood rim level of a receptor. Example: the vertical distance between a sink spout and the highest level that the water in the sink could reach without overflowing is the air gap.

Air gap distance measurement: Measure the air gap distance between the plumbing fixture outlet opening and the flood rim of the fixture or receptor. Measure the fixture outlet opening diameter without the aerator attached. Measure the vertical air gap distance with the aerator attached.

Air gap minimum distances: Provide an air gap distance based on the effective size of the fixture outlet opening. In most cases this distance is twice the fixture outlet opening diameter. Example: if a bathroom sink faucet outlet opening is ½", then the minimum vertical air gap between the faucet outlet opening and the flood rim of the sink is 1".

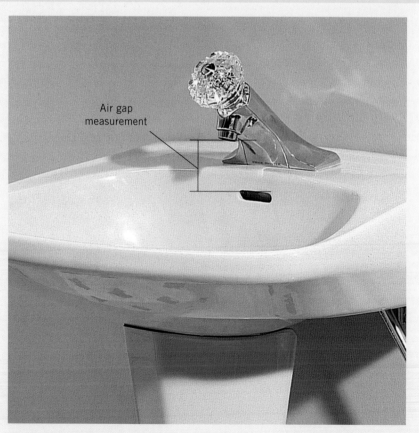

Air gap measurement

Most commercially available faucets are designed to provide the required minimum air gap distance.

Irrigation Systems

1. Protect lawn irrigation system water connections by installing an atmospheric vacuum breaker, a pressure vacuum breaker, or a reduced pressure backflow preventer.

2. Do not install a valve downstream from an atmospheric vacuum breaker.

3. Install a reduced pressure backflow preventer if chemicals are introduced into the irrigation system.

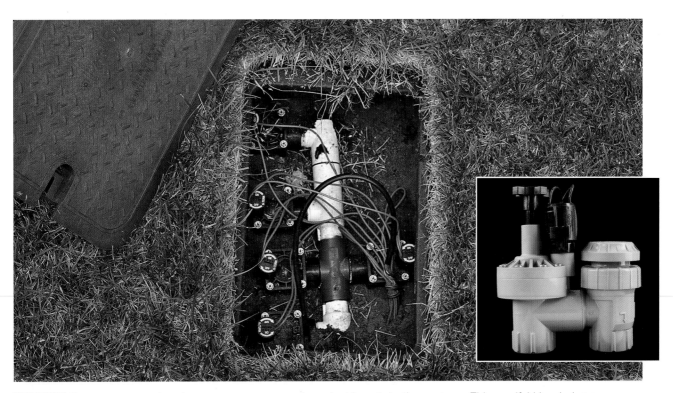

VIOLATION! Pressure vacuum breakers are a common way to protect lawn irrigation systems. This manifold is missing a backflow preventer (inset photo) and is a code violation.

PVC supply tubing is a good choice for bringing water to a home irrigation system: ¾" inside diameter schedule 40 is shown here.

Sprinkler heads in many irrigation systems are tied into the water supply with thin riser flex pipes. The union is typically made with a barbed fitting.

Electrical System

Home wiring is a very popular do-it-yourself subject that is fundamentally hazardous. When it comes to electricity, mistakes and accidents do pose threats, including fire, injury, and death. Therefore, safety is the primary focus of the electrical code provisions.

In this chapter you will find many of the rules governing safe installation of electrical wires, electrical equipment—including conduit, electrical receptacles, switches, lights, and other fixtures. Use this information to inspect your wiring and make sure it all conforms to code. If it does not, or if you are unsure about it, have a professional electrician upgrade your electrical system.

In this chapter:
- Understanding Electrical Circuits
- Electrical Grounding + Bonding
- Electrical Branch Circuit Requirements
- Electrical Receptacle Installation
- Ground-Fault (GFCI)
  + Arc-Fault (AFCI) Protection
- Junction Boxes, Device Boxes + Enclosures
- Switch Installation
- Light Fixture Installation
- Satellite Dishes, Television + Radio Antennas
- Broadband Cable Wiring

Accessible (readily): Electrical components are readily accessible if they can be reached quickly without moving or climbing over obstructions (such as pictures and work benches) and without using a portable ladder. Locks may be used to secure readily accessible components; however, the key or combination should be readily accessible to all occupants at all times. Panelboards and service disconnect equipment must be readily accessible in case circuits need to be shut off during an emergency.

Accessible (wires): Wires are accessible if they can be exposed without removing or damaging permanent parts of the building and if a person can reach them for inspection, repair, or maintenance. Examples: wires are accessible if they are behind suspended ceiling panels or if access requires opening a door, removing an access panel, or climbing a ladder. Wires are not accessible if you must cut drywall to expose the wires or if they are located in an area that cannot be reached for repair, inspection, or maintenance.

Bonding: Metallic components are bonded if they are physically and electrically connected together. Example: a bonding wire should connect a swimming pool motor and nearby metal parts of the electrical supply system. Example: metal conduit should be electrically and mechanically connected where it enters a panelboard cabinet.

Bonded metallic components are part of an electrically conductive path that will safely conduct current imposed by a ground fault. Example: when metal conduit containing a damaged wire becomes energized, this is a ground fault. A proper bonding connection will conduct the fault current on the conduit safely to the electrical panel and allow proper operation of the circuit breaker or fuse. Otherwise, a person touching the energized conduit could become the electrical circuit, and that person could receive a dangerous shock or the current flow could generate enough heat to start a fire.

Branch circuit: A branch circuit begins at a circuit breaker or fuse in a panelboard and conducts electricity to where it is used. A branch circuit can serve one device, such as an oven, or it can serve multiple devices, such as receptacles and light fixtures.

Cable: Any two or more wires contained in an insulating sheath or jacket. Most wire used in residential construction is actually a cable called nonmetallic cable and abbreviated NM. "Romex" is a common brand name belonging to one manufacturer of NM cable.

Grounded: The ground in an electrical system is the return path through which alternating current electricity flows to return to its source (the utility's transformer and ultimately to the power generating station). A grounded conductor is

connected to the earth or to some body that serves as the earth. A grounded connection may be intentional (as in a circuit's grounded conductor) or it may be unintentional (as in a ground fault).

Grounding electrode: A component in contact with the earth that provides the grounding connection for the electrical system. Common residential grounding electrodes include a copper rod driven at least 8' into the ground, a metal water service pipe, or a piece of reinforcing steel embedded in the footing.

Grounding wire: A grounding conductor, also called an equipment grounding conductor, connects electrical equipment to the grounding electrode system. This connection usually occurs at a grounding bus or terminal bar at the service equipment that is in turn connected to a grounding electrode. Grounding conductors are bare wires or may be covered with green insulation.

Grounded wire: A grounded conductor, broadly defined, is any conductor that is intentionally grounded. The common term for the grounded conductor in residential electrical systems is the "neutral" wire. The grounded conductor is a current-carrying conductor. You should treat it as such when working with electrical circuits. Grounded conductors are usually insulated with white or light gray insulation.

Grounding electrode wire: The grounding electrode conductor is a wire that connects the grounding electrode to the grounded conductors. In most residential electrical systems, the only connection between the grounding electrode conductor and the grounded conductors should occur at the service equipment.

Ground fault: A ground fault occurs when metal that is not normally energized becomes energized. Examples of a ground fault: (a) the hot (ungrounded) wire in a motor is damaged or disconnected and touches the motor's case, energizing the case; (b) a screw penetrates the insulation of a hot (ungrounded) wire in an electrical panelboard and energizes the cabinet; (c) damaged insulation on a hot (ungrounded) wire allows the conductor to touch copper water pipe, energizing the pipe.

Location (damp): Damp locations are subject to moderate levels of moisture but are not subject to direct saturation by liquids. Examples of damp locations include covered porches and some basements. Many inspectors consider ceilings over showers and bathtubs as damp locations, but general codes do not specifically cite these as damp locations.

Location (wet): Wet locations are subject to direct contact with liquids or the elements. Examples of wet locations include exterior house walls not protected by a roof, concrete and masonry in contact with the earth, and any components buried or in contact with the earth.

Multiwire branch circuit: A multiwire branch circuit is a three-wire branch circuit with two hot (ungrounded) wires and one neutral (grounded) wire. In residential electrical systems, the voltage between the two hot wires is 240 volts, and the voltage between the hot wires and the neutral wire is 120 volts. When a multiwire branch circuit is operating as intended, the current on the shared neutral wire is balanced. An indication that a multiwire branch circuit is not operating as intended is when some lights are dim and some are much brighter than normal. Split-wired receptacles that provide the required two 20-amp kitchen countertop receptacle circuits are one example of a multiwire branch circuit. Clothes dryer and range circuits are another example. Water heater and air conditioning condenser circuits are usually not multiwire branch circuits, because there is no neutral wire in the circuit.

Outlet: An outlet is a connection point where electricity is taken for use. An outlet could be a receptacle, a light fixture box, a junction box connected to an oven, or an air conditioning condenser disconnect box. Switch boxes, junction boxes, and panelboards are not outlets.

Overcurrent protection device: An overcurrent protection device automatically interrupts the flow of electricity if the current flowing through the device exceeds a design maximum amount. Common examples in residential electrical systems are fuses and circuit breakers.

Receptacle: A device into which a plug is inserted and through which electricity flows to equipment that uses electricity. Receptacles include the familiar single (one plug) and duplex (two plug) 120-volt devices and the 240-volt devices most often seen in laundry rooms to serve electric clothes dryers.

Service drop: The service drop describes overhead electrical wires beginning at the power pole and ending where the service drop wires connect to the service entrance wires. This is usually at the service point near the mast on the roof.

Service entrance wires: Service entrance wires run from the service point to the service equipment. Typically, the service entrance wires mark the point in your home wiring system where the equipment is the responsibility of the homeowner and not the utility company.

Ungrounded conductor: An ungrounded conductor is one that intentionally carries electricity. The common term for an ungrounded conductor in residential electrical systems is the "hot" or "live" wire or conductor. Ungrounded conductors are usually covered with red or black insulation.

Multiwire branch circuits.

Split-wired receptacle

240V receptacle

Shared-neutral receptacles

Typical Home Wiring System

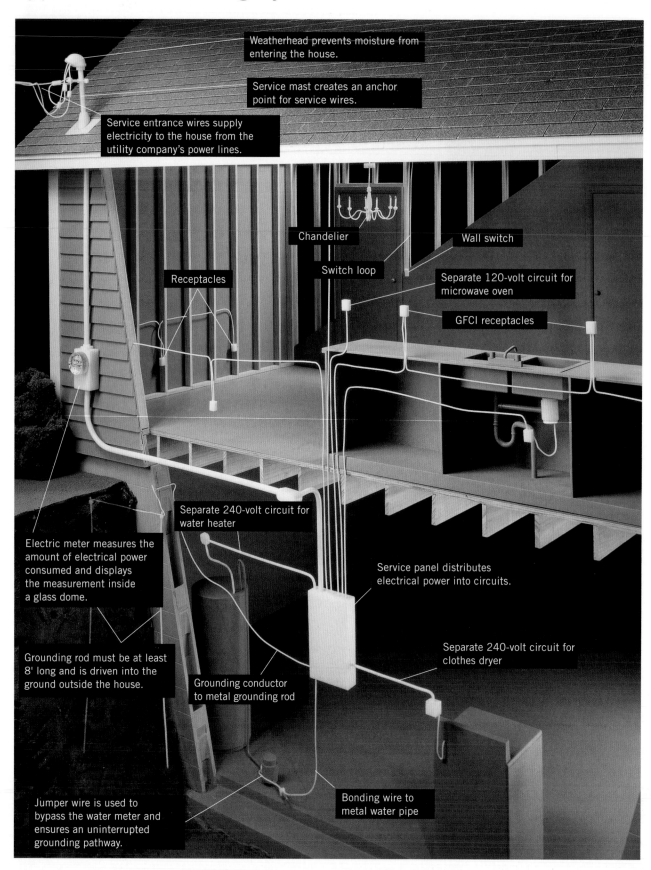

Weatherhead prevents moisture from entering the house.

Service mast creates an anchor point for service wires.

Service entrance wires supply electricity to the house from the utility company's power lines.

Chandelier

Wall switch

Switch loop

Separate 120-volt circuit for microwave oven

Receptacles

GFCI receptacles

Separate 240-volt circuit for water heater

Service panel distributes electrical power into circuits.

Electric meter measures the amount of electrical power consumed and displays the measurement inside a glass dome.

Separate 240-volt circuit for clothes dryer

Grounding rod must be at least 8' long and is driven into the ground outside the house.

Grounding conductor to metal grounding rod

Jumper wire is used to bypass the water meter and ensures an uninterrupted grounding pathway.

Bonding wire to metal water pipe

Understanding Electrical Circuits

An electrical circuit is a continuous loop. Household circuits carry current from the main service panel, throughout the house, and back to the main service panel. Several switches, receptacles, light fixtures, or appliances may be connected to a single circuit.

Current enters a circuit loop on hot wires and returns along neutral wires. These wires are color coded for easy identification. Hot wires are black or red, and neutral wires are white or light gray. For safety, most circuits include a bare copper or green insulated grounding wire. The grounding wire conducts current when wires or equipment are malfunctioning and helps reduce the chance of severe electrical shock. The service panel also has a bonding wire connected to any metal water pipes.

If a circuit carries too much current, it can overload. A fuse or a circuit breaker protects each circuit in case of overloads.

Current returns to the service panel along a neutral circuit wire. Current then leaves the house on a large neutral service wire that returns it to the utility pole transformer.

WIRING SAFETY

Safety should be the primary concern of anyone working with electricity. Although most household electrical repairs are simple and straightforward, always use caution and good judgment when working with electrical wiring or devices. Common sense can prevent accidents.

The basic rule of electrical safety is: Always turn off power to the area or device you are working on. At the main service panel or subpanel, remove the fuse or shut off the circuit breaker that controls the circuit you are servicing. Then check to make sure the power is off by testing for power with a voltage tester. Restore power only when the repair or replacement project is complete.

Follow the safety tips shown on these pages. Never attempt an electrical project beyond your skill or confidence level. Never attempt to repair or replace your main service panel or service entrance head. These are jobs for a qualified electrician and require that the power company shuts off power to your house.

General Requirements

Minimum Service Current Capacity Requirements

1. Provide at least 100-amp service to a single family home.

2. Provide at least 60-amp service to an accessory structure. Exceptions to the 60-amp minimum service exist for one- and two-circuit 120-volt service to accessory structures.

3. You may use the following wire sizes as a feeder when the load at the accessory structure is limited to one or two 15- or 20-amp, 120-volt branch circuits: (a) use at least #10 AWG copper or #8 AWG aluminum wire if the accessory structure has not more than two 15 or 20 amp, 120 volt branch circuits; (b) use at least #14 AWG copper or #12 AWG aluminum if the accessory structure has only one 15 amp, 120 volt branch circuit and use at least the same size feeder wire as used for the branch circuit.

4. Provide an equipment grounding wire with the feeder wires, and refer to the grounding requirements section if there are more than two branch circuits in the accessory structure.

Closure of Unused Openings

1. Close all openings in boxes, conduit bodies, and cabinets with material that provides protection equal to the original opening cover. This means using plastic or metal knockout covers. Tape and cardboard do not provide equal protection.

2. Recess metal knockout covers in non-metallic boxes and conduit bodies at least ¼ inch from the surface of the box or conduit body.

3. Cover open outlet boxes with a blank cover, a blank plate, or fixture canopy. Switch plates and receptacle plates do not provide complete closure for electrical boxes.

4. Ground metal covers and plates.

Identification of Circuits in Electrical Panels

1. Provide a legible and permanent marking or label that identifies the purpose of circuit breakers, fuses, and other equipment used to disconnect power from a circuit. Identify the circuit in enough detail that it can be distinguished from all other circuits. Example: do not identify a circuit as general lighting. Identify the specific rooms or outlets served by the circuit. A marking or label is not required if the purpose of the disconnecting equipment is self-evident. Use marking or labeling materials that will withstand the environment where the disconnecting equipment is located.

2. Locate the circuit identification on the face of the panelboard enclosure on the inside panelboard door or at an approved location adjacent to the panelboard.

Prohibited Locations for Electrical Panels

1. Do not locate electrical panels and circuit breakers and fuses in clothes closets, bathrooms, over stairway steps, or in spaces designated for storage.

Cover open conduit knockouts in electrical boxes with an approved plastic or metal cap (inset).

Label each circuit in all electrical panels so that the purpose of each circuit is clear.

Working Clearances around Electrical Panels

1. Inspect your electrical enclosures (cabinets) to make sure they conform to code. If not, hire a professional electrician to relocate them. The following rules apply to electrical enclosures (cabinets) that require access while interior parts are energized. Examples of these enclosures include electrical panels and subpanels, and air conditioner and furnace service-disconnect boxes.

2. Provide a clear working space around electrical enclosures that is at least 36 inches deep, at least 30 inches wide (or as wide as the enclosure if it is wider than 30 inches), and at least 78 inches high (or as high as the enclosure if it is higher than 78 inches). Measure the clear working space from any exposed energized parts or from the cover in front of covered energized parts.

3. The enclosure should have enough clearance that the enclosure door can be opened at least 90 degrees.

4. Provide a light near electrical enclosures. A light includes a switched receptacle. The light should be switch-controlled when located in an attic or a crawl space; otherwise, it may be a pull-chain or a similar fixture.

5. Do not locate equipment, pipes, and ducts that are not associated with the electrical system directly above or below an indoor enclosure from the floor to the ceiling or 6 feet above the enclosure, whichever is less.

6. Do not locate anything not associated with the electrical system directly above or below an outdoor enclosure from grade to 6 feet above the enclosure. Examples include hose bibbs, exhaust duct terminations, and appliance vents.

7. Provide access to the clear working space around the enclosure (cabinet). Do not block access with shelves, workbenches, or other difficult to move objects.

8. Install electrical panels and circuit breakers and fuses so that the circuit breaker handle or fuse is not more than 79 inches above the floor or ground when the center of the handle is in its highest position.

9. You may install electrical panels rated not more than 200 amps in existing buildings where the working space height is less than 78 inches. This does not apply to new construction.

Ideal height 60" (eye level)

Minimum 78" high unobstructed access

Minimum 36" deep unobstructed access in front

Minimum 30" wide unobstructed access

Your equpment should include a safe space above, in front of, and below all electrical panels and similar electrical equipment. If your panel does not meet these standards, have it relocated by a professional.

Minimum: two 14-gauge wires

Maximum: four 12-gauge (or three 10-gauge) wires

Minimum: two 16-gauge wires

Maximum: four 14-gauge wires

Maximum: two 14-gauge wires

Minimum: two 18-gauge wires

Use wire connectors rated for the wires you are connecting. Wire connectors are color-coded by size, but the coding scheme varies by manufacturer. The wire connectors shown above come from one major manufacturer. To ensure safe connections, each connector is rated for both minimum and maximum wire capacity. These connectors can be used to connect both conducting wires and grounding wires. Green wire connectors are used only for grounding wires.

Splicing Wires

1. Splice (join) wires using only listed devices, such as appropriate-sized wire connectors. Use the wire connector according to manufacturer's recommendations regarding the minimum and maximum number and size of wires that the connector can accommodate.

2. Cover spliced wires with material equal to the original insulation. This does not include electrical tape or similar materials.

3. For splice wires that will be buried in the ground, use only devices listed for direct burial and install them according to manufacturer's instructions.

4. Provide access to spliced wires unless the splice and splicing device are specifically allowed to be concealed. Access is usually provided by an accessible, covered junction box.

5. Do not place wire splices in a raceway, such as conduit or tubing, unless the raceway has a removable cover.

Twist wire connectors over the ends of individual conductors that have been stripped of insulation. Pre-twist wires together with pliers or linesmans' pliers (optional). Do not leave bare wire exposed beneath the bottom of the connector.

Push-in connectors are a relatively new product for joining wires. Instead of twisting the bare wire ends together, you strip off about ¾" of insulation and insert them into a hole in the connector. The connectors come with two to four holes sized for various gauge wires. These connectors are perfect for inexperienced DIYers, because they do not pull apart like a sloppy twisted connection can.

Splicing Aluminum + Copper Wires

1. Splice (join) aluminum and copper wires together using devices listed for splicing aluminum and copper wires. Look for a mark or label, such as AL/CU, on the device or on the package for assurance that the device is listed for splicing aluminum and copper wires. Some wire nuts sold for residential use are not listed for splicing aluminum and copper wires.

2. Use only inhibitors and antioxidant compounds that are approved for splicing aluminum and copper wires. These materials should not degrade or damage the wires, wire insulation, or equipment. Read and follow manufacturer's instructions.

Length of Wires Extending from Boxes

1. Extend wires at least 3 inches beyond the opening of any electrical box, junction, or switch point if the opening is less than 8 inches in any direction. This applies to most switch, receptacle, and light fixture mounting boxes used in residential electrical systems.

2. Extend wires at least 6 inches beyond where the wires emerge from the raceway or cable sheathing. Example: NM cable enters a single residential switch box with 1 inch of intact sheathing (outer cover). Begin the 6 inches measurement where the sheathing ends. The cable should extend at least 7 inches from the rear of the box. The NM cable should also extend at least 3 inches beyond the outside edge of the box.

Extend wires past the box opening at least 3".

Connecting Wires to Terminals

1. Remove insulation from wires and connect wires to terminals without damaging the wire. Do not connect damaged wires to terminals. Example: if you nick, damage, or cut strands from a stranded wire, cut the wire back to where it is full size and use the full, undamaged wire.

2. Connect more than one wire to a terminal only if the terminal is identified to accept multiple wires. Example: general codes require one wire per terminal for the grounded (neutral) wires and allow two or more same-gauge wires per terminal for the equipment grounding wires. Example: many circuit breakers allow only one hot (ungrounded) wire per circuit breaker terminal.

3. Connect aluminum wires to terminals only if the terminal is identified to accept aluminum wires.

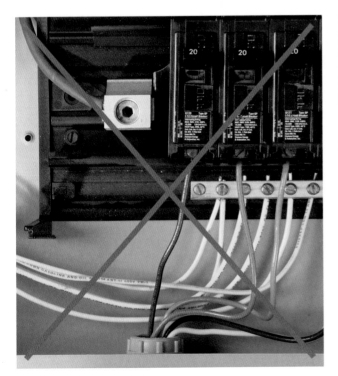

VIOLATION! Do not connect multiple neutral or hot wires to a terminal (the neutral bus bar seen here has two neutral conductors connected to single terminal).

VIOLATION! Never connect multiple hot wires to the same terminal on circuit breakers or other electrical devices unless specifically allowed by the manufacturer.

Wire Color Codes

1. Use wires with white or gray insulation or wires with three white stripes on other than green insulation as neutral (grounded) wires.

2. Use wires with green insulation, or wires with green insulation and at least one yellow stripe as equipment grounding wires. You may use uninsulated (bare) wires as equipment grounding wires in most circuits.

3. You may use any color other than white, gray, or green as hot (ungrounded) wires. The common colors are red and black.

4. You may use a wire with white or gray insulation as a hot (ungrounded) wire if the wire is part of a cable (such as NM) and if you permanently mark it as a hot (ungrounded) conductor at all places where the wire is visible and accessible. This marking is usually done by wrapping the end of the wire with black or red electrical tape. The marking must encircle the insulation.

Neutral + Equipment Grounding Wire Continuity

1. Connect neutral (grounded) wires together in device boxes if the neutral wire is part of a multiwire branch circuit. Do not rely on any device, such as a receptacle or light fixture, to provide the connection for the neutral wire in a multiwire branch circuit.

2. Connect equipment grounding wires together in all device boxes. Do not rely on any device, such as a receptacle or light fixture, to provide the connection for the equipment grounding wire in any circuit.

3. Install a wire (called a pigtail) between the connected wires and any device in the box.

Pigtail

Use a pigtail when you need to connect multiple wires together and use one wire to connect to a terminal.

WIRE COLOR CHART

WIRE COLOR		FUNCTION
	White	neutral wire: at zero voltage in many, but not all, circuits
	Black	hot wire carrying current at full current + voltage
	Red	hot wire carrying current at full current + voltage
	White, Black markings	hot wire carrying current at full current + voltage
	Green	serves as a grounding pathway
	Bare copper	serves as a grounding pathway

Individual wires are color-coded to identify their function. In some circuit installations, the white wire serves as a hot wire that carries voltage. If so, this white wire may be labeled with black tape or paint to identify it as a hot wire.

WIRE SIZE CHART

WIRE GAUGE		WIRE CAPACITY + USE
	#6	55 amps; central air conditioner, electric furnace
	#8	40 amps; electric range, central air conditioner
	#10	30 amps; window air conditioner, clothes dryer
	#12	20 amps; light fixtures, receptacles, microwave oven
	#14	15 amps; light fixtures, receptacles
	#16	light-duty extension cords
	#18 to 22	thermostats, doorbells, security systems

Wire sizes (shown actual size) are categorized by the American Wire Gauge system. The larger the wire size, the smaller the AWG number. Amp ratings in this chart assume that the wires are contained in NM cable.

Shut off power at the main electrical service panel before beginning any work. In some cases you may shut off individual circuits, but the safer precaution is always to throw the main breaker.

Service + Main Service Panel

Disconnecting Electrical Service

1. Provide equipment to disconnect all electrical service to a building using not more than six sets of switches or six sets of circuit breakers. The disconnecting equipment may be in one cabinet or in a group of cabinets in the same location.

2. Label the service disconnecting equipment as such. The label must be permanent and clearly marked.

3. Use only service disconnecting equipment listed and labeled for that purpose. The electric meter and meter enclosure are not service equipment. Do not rely on removing the electric meter to disconnect electrical service.

4. The service disconnecting equipment should be installed in a readily accessible place where every building occupant has access.

5. The service disconnecting equipment may be located outside the building or inside the building as close as possible to where the service entrance conductors enter the building. Check with the local building official for information concerning your area. Fifteen feet is one typical maximum, but the distance may be less in some jurisdictions.

6. Service disconnecting equipment should not be located in bathrooms.

7. Service disconnecting switches or circuit breakers should not be installed more than 79 inches above the floor or ground.

8. Install emergency disconnecting equipment in a readily accessible location outside of the building. This equipment may be the service disconnecting equipment, or it may be up to six additional emergency disconnecting switches or circuit breakers. Label this emergency disconnecting equipment as required by code.

9. Install a permanently installed Type I or Type II surge protection device (SPD) at the service disconnecting equipment or at another location allowed by code. This requirement applies to new construction and when the service disconnecting equipment is replaced.

Aboveground service. In this common configuration, the service wires from the closest transformer (called the service drop) are connected to the power distribution system in your house through a protective hood called a weatherhead. The service entrance wires are routed to a power meter that's owned by your utility company but housed in a base that may be your property. From the meter the entrance wires enter your house through the wall and are routed to the main service panel, where they are connected to the service equipment. Other aboveground configurations are allowed.

Weatherhead

Service wires

Service entrance wires

Conduit

Emergency disconnecting equipment

Power meter

Service entrance wires

Meter base

Underground service lateral.
Increasingly, homebuilders are choosing to have power supplied to their new homes through underground service wires instead of an overhead service drop. Running the wires in the ground eliminates problems with power outages caused by ice accumulation or fallen trees, but it entails a completely different set of wire and conduit requirements. For the homeowner, however, the differences are minimal because the hookups are identical once the power service reaches the meter.

Power meter

Meter base

Emergency disconnecting equipment

Strap

Conduit

Underground service wires

Service entrance wires

SERVICE DROP CLEARANCES TO OPENINGS

(1) 3' CLEARANCE REQUIRED   (2) CLEARANCE NOT REQUIRED

Overhead Service Drop Wire Clearances

1. Provide at least 3 feet of clearance between service drop and service entrance wires and porches, decks, stairs, ladders, fire escapes, balconies, sides of doors, and sides and bottoms of operable windows (not the tops of operable windows even if the top sash is operable). Clearance is required only to service drops and service entrance wires that consist of individual wires that are not protected by a raceway or outer jacket. This means that clearances are usually required for utility service drop wires and are not required for SE type service entrance cable and for wires or cables installed in conduit or tubing.

2. Provide at least 8 feet of vertical clearance between service drop wires and a roof not designed for regular pedestrian traffic, with a slope less than 4 inches in 12 inches. Access to such a roof would usually be by a ladder, through a window, or through a maintenance hatch.

3. You may reduce the 8-foot vertical clearance to at least 3 feet of vertical clearance if: (a) the voltage between wires is not more than (≤) 300 volts and (b) the roof is guarded or isolated; or if (c) the roof slope is at least 4 inches in 12 inches. Many residential service drops comply with this exception.

4. Provide at least 10 feet of vertical clearance between service drop wires and a roof designed for regular pedestrian traffic. Access to such a roof would usually be by stairs or by a door, and the roof edges would be protected by a guard.

5. Provide at least 18 inches of vertical clearance between service drop wires and a roof if: (a) the wires pass only over the overhang portion of the roof, and (b) not more than 6 feet of wire pass over not more than 4 lineal feet of roof surface measured horizontally, and (c) the wires enter a through-the-roof mast or terminate at an approved support.

6. Maintain all required clearances above the roof for at least 3 feet in all directions from the roof's edge.

Service Drop Clearance Aboveground

1. Measure the vertical clearance between service drop wires and the ground, walkway, driveway, or street beginning at the lowest point of the service drop wires and ending at the surface under the wire's lowest point. The lowest point of the service drop wires is often at the drip loop, but it could be at the point of attachment to the house or it could be where the wires enter the house.

2. Provide at least 10 feet of vertical clearance between service drop wires and areas or sidewalks accessed by pedestrians only.

3. Provide at least 12 feet of vertical clearance between service drop wires and residential property and driveways.

4. Provide at least 18 feet of vertical clearance between service drop wires and public streets, alleys, roads, or parking areas subject to truck traffic.

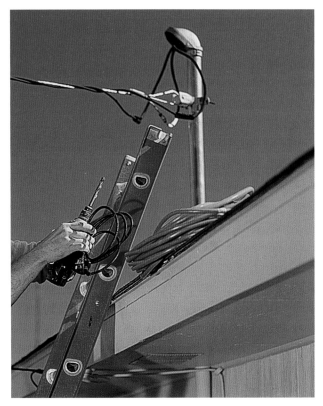

The service drop must occur at least 10' above ground level, and as much as 18' in some cases. Occasionally, this means that you must run the conduit for the service mast up through the eave of your roof and seal the roof penetration with a boot.

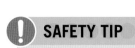

SAFETY TIP ●●●●●●●●●●●●●

If your electrical service entry does not conform to the codes, hire a professional to update it.

SERVICE DROP CLEARANCES ABOVE GROUND

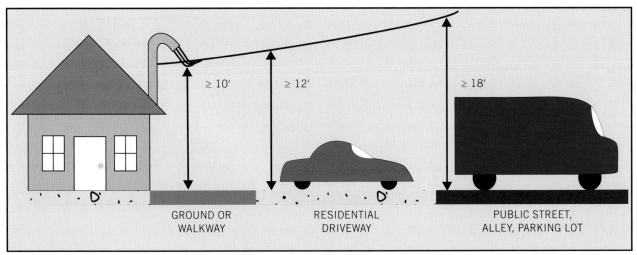

≥ 10'   ≥ 12'   ≥ 18'

GROUND OR WALKWAY   RESIDENTIAL DRIVEWAY   PUBLIC STREET, ALLEY, PARKING LOT

Safe clearance between service drop wires and the ground.

Electrical Grounding + Bonding

One of the important purposes of grounding and bonding can be summarized in this simple rule: Electricity wants to return to its source and will take all available paths to get there. When the electrical system is working as intended, electricity enters through the hot (ungrounded) wire, does its work, and returns to its source (usually the utility's transformer) through the neutral (grounded) wire.

When electricity finds its way out of the intended path, things get dangerous. Example: a rat sits on copper water pipe and chews through the insulation on electrical cable exposing the hot (ungrounded) wire. After electrocuting the unfortunate rat, the exposed wire lands on the water pipe. If the water pipe is connected without electrical interruption to the electricity's source (through bonding), the electricity thinks that the water pipe is the neutral (grounded) wire and happily starts flowing through the water pipe. This is a ground fault. The electric current should quickly rise to the point where it trips a circuit breaker or blows a fuse, clearing the fault.

But what if the water pipe is not bonded? Perhaps a water softener has been added to the system, interrupting the electrical continuity of some or all of the water pipe. In our example, the water pipe is still energized, but there is no way for the electricity to return to its source; that is, until someone grabs a metal water faucet handle and is standing on the ground or on some conducting surface. At that time, the electricity finds its path to its source through the person. The person is injured or killed.

When trying to understand grounding and bonding, think like electricity. If metal can become energized, however unlikely that is, you must assume that it will become energized. Bonding metal together and connecting the metal to ground in an approved manner lets you, not the electricity, decide how electricity will flow in a fault condition.

Normal current flow: Current enters the electrical box along a black hot wire, then returns to the service panel along a white neutral wire.

Ground fault: Current is detoured by a loose wire in contact with the metal box. The grounding wire picks it up and channels it safely back to the main service panel where the circuit breaker trips or the fuse blows.

Inspect Electrical Panels for Proper Grounding

Grounding + Bonding at Service Panels + Subpanels

1. The neutral (grounded) wire should be connected to the grounding electrode wire at the nearest accessible point at or before the service equipment (main disconnect). The service equipment is usually the most convenient accessible grounding point, because the meter enclosure and points before it are usually locked or secured and not accessible. The grounding electrode wire connects the neutral (grounded) wire to a grounding electrode.

2. The neutral (grounded) wire should not be connected to ground at any other place downstream from the service equipment grounding point. An exception to this rule exists when two buildings are supplied by one electric service.

3. All metal parts of the electrical system should be connected to the neutral (grounded) wire. This includes service equipment and panelboard cases, any metal electrical conduit or tubing, and all metal pipes in the building (such as metal water and gas pipe).

Metallic conduit must be physically and electrically connected to panel cabinets. A bonding bushing may be required, in some cases, where all of a knockout is not removed.

Neutral bus

Grounding bus

The neutral and grounding wires should not be connected to the same bus in most subpanels. The grounding bus should be bonded to the subpanel cabinet. The neutral bus should not be bonded to the subpanel cabinet.

Parts of a common electrical service configuration.

Installing Electricity to a Detached Building

Running electricity to a detached building, such as a storage shed or a workshop, is a popular DIY project. Details about how to do this are covered in other books in the Black + Decker series. This discussion provides the basic general code requirements.

Detached Building with One or Two Branch Circuits

1. Install at least #15 AWG copper cable to the detached building if there is only one 15 amp branch circuit in the building.

2. Install at least #10 AWG copper cable to the detached building if there are only one or two 15 or 20 amp branch circuits in the building.

3. Use cables with an equipment grounding conductor.

4. Note that long cable runs (about 75 feet or more) may require increasing the cable size to avoid voltage drop that can cause wire overheating and equipment damage.

Detached Building with a Subpanel

1. Install a feeder cable with an equipment grounding conductor (four-wire feeder) between the main building and the detached building. The feeder cable size depends on the subpanel load and on the length of the feeder cable.

2. Install a grounding electrode at the detached building and connect it to the subpanel grounding bus.

3. Connect the feeder cable equipment grounding wire to the subpanel grounding bus, and bond the grounding bus to the subpanel enclosure.

4. Connect the feeder cable neutral neutral wire to the subpanel neutral bus. Do not bond the neutral bus to the subpanel enclosure.

5. Connect the branch circuit equipment grounding wires to the grounding bus, and connect the branch circuit neutral wires to the neutral bus. Do not connect the grounding wires to the neutral bus, and do not connect the neutral wires to the grounding bus.

Grounding Electrodes + Electrode Wires

General Requirements

1. Every electrical service should be provided at least one approved type of grounding electrode. The most common grounding electrodes are underground metal water pipe, driven rod and pipe, and concrete encased.

2. All grounding electrodes that may be available at a building should be bonded together. General codes do not require that all possible types of grounding electrodes be installed. They require that if a grounding electrode is installed, it must be connected (bonded) to all other grounding electrodes and to the neutral (grounded) wire.

3. A bonding jumper at least as large as the grounding electrode wire should be used to connect (bond) the grounding electrodes. Bonding jumpers may be connected between grounding electrodes at any convenient point.

4. The grounding electrode wire may be connected at any convenient grounding electrode. Protect grounding electrode wires that are subject to physical damage with approved conduit or tubing, such as intermediate metallic conduit or PVC conduit.

5. Protect grounding electrode wires that are smaller than #6 AWG with approved conduit regardless of whether the wire is subject to physical damage.

6. Install a grounding electrode wire based on the size of the service entrance conductors. Most grounding electrode wires should be #6 or #8 copper.

7. Metal gas pipe should never be used as a grounding electrode.

Wiring diagram for wiring a feeder from the main service panel to a subpanel in a separate building.

Underground Water Pipe Electrodes

1. Use metal underground water pipe that is in contact with the ground for at least 10 feet as a grounding electrode. This includes all metal water pipe materials, such as copper and steel, and all metal water pipes, such as water service pipes, metal well casing pipe, and metal irrigation system pipes.

2. You must consider all underground water pipe that satisfies the previous conditions as a grounding electrode and connect (bond) underground water pipe to all other grounding electrodes.

3. Do not connect a grounding electrode wire to any interior metal water pipe at a point that is more than 5 feet from where the underground water pipe enters the building. Do not use any interior metal water pipe that is more than 5 feet from where the water pipe enters the building as a conductor for a grounding electrode. Example: do not connect the grounding electrode wire at a water heater cold water pipe if the pipe is more than 5 feet from where the water pipe enters the building.

4. Do not use underground metal water pipe as the only grounding electrode. Install at least one other type of grounding electrode and connect (bond) it to the underground metal water pipe.

5. Install bonding jumper wires around devices that might interrupt electrical continuity. Such devices include water meters, water pressure reducers, water softeners, and water filtration systems.

Rod + Pipe Electrodes

1. You may use metal pipe or conduit that is at least ¾ inch in diameter and at least 8 feet long as a grounding electrode. Use galvanized materials or other corrosion-resistant coating on iron and steel pipes.

2. You may use a stainless steel, zinc-coated or copper-coated steel, or copper rod that is at least ⅝-inch diameter and at least 8 feet long as a grounding electrode.

3. Do not use aluminum as rod and pipe electrodes.

4. Do not use one rod or pipe electrode as the only grounding electrode. Install at least one other grounding electrode of any approved type. Bond all grounding electrodes together. This provision does not apply if the rod or pipe electrode has a resistance to earth of not more than 25 ohms.

Concrete Encased Electrodes

1. You may use at least ½-inch-diameter reinforcing bar or at least #4 AWG bare copper wire as a concrete encased grounding electrode. The electrode material must be at least 20 feet long. Do not use reinforcing bar that is not electrically conductive or that is coated in non-conductive material.

2. Encase the reinforcing bar or wire in at least 2 inches of concrete. Place the bar or wire in either the horizontal or vertical part of the concrete that is in direct contact with the ground. Do not place a moisture barrier between the concrete and the ground.

3. Do not expose the reinforcing bar to contact with the earth without protecting the reinforcing bar from corrosion. Corrosion protection includes the part of the reinforcing bar that extends above the foundation where it is connected to the grounding electrode wire.

4. You may use wire ties or similar means to connect (bond) reinforcing bars together to achieve the 20-foot minimum length.

5. Concrete encased electrodes are also called ufer grounding electrodes after the man who designed this grounding electrode system.

Grounding Electrode Wire Installation

Aluminum Grounding Electrode Wires

1. Do not use aluminum or copper-clad aluminum grounding electrode wires if the wire is in direct contact with masonry or the ground or if the wire is in a corrosive environment.

2. Do not install aluminum or copper-clad aluminum grounding electrode wires within 18 inches of the ground when the wire is installed outside.

Connecting Grounding Electrode Wires to the Electrode

1. Use one of the following methods to connect grounding electrode wires to grounding electrodes: (a) a pipe fitting, pipe plug, or other approved device screwed into a pipe or pipe fitting or (b) a listed bolted clamp made of cast bronze or brass or of plain or malleable iron.

2. You may use a listed metal strap ground clamp to connect indoor communications equipment grounding electrode wires to a grounding electrode.

3. Make accessible the connection point of grounding electrode wires and bonding jumpers to grounding electrodes. The connection point need not be accessible for buried or concrete encased grounding electrodes.

4. Clean grounding electrode wire connection points and all clamps and fittings of non-conductive materials, such as paint.

Connections around Equipment + Insulated Fittings

1. Install bonding jumpers around equipment such as water meters, pressure reducing valves, water softeners, water filtration equipment, dielectric fittings, and other equipment and fittings that interrupt the electrical continuity of metal piping.

2. Make bonding jumpers long enough to permit removal of the equipment and maintain electrical continuity.

3. Use bonding jumpers that are at least the same wire size as the grounding electrode wire.

Proper CSST bonding is very tricky to determine and has very high danger potential if incorrect. Have a qualified electrician determine if CSST in your house is properly bonded.

Metal Water Pipe Bonding

1. Connect (bond) interior metal water pipes to the service equipment enclosure, the neutral (grounded) wire at the service equipment, the grounding electrode conductor, or to any grounding electrode.

2. Use a bonding jumper or wire that is at least the same wire size as the grounding electrode wire.

3. Make the bonding connection point accessible.

Metal Gas Pipe Bonding

1. Connect (bond) interior metal gas pipes and other metal pipes to the service equipment enclosure, the neutral (grounded) wire at the service equipment, the grounding electrode conductor, or to any grounding electrode.

2. You may use the equipment grounding wire that serves the gas appliance as the bonding wire. Number 10 AWG copper wire is the largest equipment grounding wire for almost all residential branch circuits. This means that: (a) a separate bonding wire between the gas pipe and the service equipment is usually not necessary (although some jurisdictions require one anyway), and (b) #10 AWG copper wire is usually the largest required gas pipe bonding wire.

3. Make the bonding connection point accessible.

Bonding Corrugated Stainless Steel Gas Tubing

1. Install a #6 AWG copper bonding wire that is connected to a listed clamp on gas supply systems using corrugated stainless steel gas tubing (CSST). Limit the length of the wire to not more than 75 feet. This bonding connection is for lightning protection.

2. Install the bonding connection at the first length of steel or copper pipe before the CSST. This is usually at the gas meter or where the propane pipe enters the home.

3. Some CSST is arc-resistant and does not need a separate bonding connection. This CSST usually has a black jacket. Verify CSST bonding requirements using manufacturer's instructions and by contacting your building inspector.

Electrical Branch Circuit Requirements

Every electrical circuit has its limits. Among the more basic tasks in evaluating your existing wiring system or planning a system expansion is to identify which loads will be drawing from which circuits so you can establish what each circuit capacity will need to be. In addition to letting you plan the circuits wisely, specific load knowledge lets you create a more balanced service panel, lessening the chances that you'll trip breakers.

A duplex receptacle (A) contains two outlets. A single receptacle (B) contains one outlet.

Branch Circuit Load Limits

15-amp + 20-amp Circuits

1. Use only 15-amp and 20-amp, 120-volt circuits for multiple outlet branch circuits. A multiple outlet branch circuit has more than one light fixture and/or receptacle on the same circuit. One duplex receptacle counts as two receptacles. A circuit that serves one duplex receptacle is a multiple outlet branch circuit. This provision does not apply to a circuit that serves one single receptacle or one single light fixture.

2. Use only 120-volt branch circuits to supply residential light fixtures, receptacles for plug-and-cord connected loads not more than 1,440 watts, and motor loads less than .25 horsepower.

3. You may use either 120- or 240-volt branch circuits to supply one plug-and-cord connected or one permanently wired appliance rated more than 1,440 watts. This means that branch circuits rated more than 120 volts are effectively limited to serving a single receptacle or permanently wired fixed equipment.

4. Do not connect one or more fixed devices that in total exceed 50 percent of a multiple outlet branch circuit's amperage rating. Fixed devices do not include light fixtures. This means that all fixed devices (such as a permanently wired disposal or hot water circulating pump) on a multiple outlet branch circuit may not exceed 7.5 amps (about 900 watts) on a 15-amp multiple outlet branch circuit and may not exceed 10 amps (about 1,200 watts) on a 20-amp multiple outlet branch circuit.

30-amp Circuits

1. Do not connect one plug-and-cord device that exceeds 80 percent of a 30-amp branch circuit's amperage rating. This means that one device (such as a clothes dryer) may not exceed 24 amps (about 5,760 watts) on a 30-amp, 240-volt branch circuit.

2. Do not use a 30-amp branch circuit to serve loads other than a fixed device, such as a water heater, or a single plug-and-cord connected device, such as a welder.

Water Heater Circuits

1. Use wires and circuit breakers that are rated at least 125 percent of a storage tank–type water heater's total rated current load if the water heater capacity is 120 gallons or less. This applies to almost all residential water heaters.

Space Heating Equipment Circuits

1. Use wires and circuit breakers that are rated at least 125 percent of an electric space heater's total rated current load, including any motors such as the circulation fan.

2. Use wires and circuit breakers that are rated not more than 30 amps for branch circuits that serve two or more electric space heaters, such as baseboard heaters.

Continuous Loads

1. Use wires and circuit breakers that are rated at least 125 percent of a branch circuit's total rated current load if the branch circuit serves any combination of continuous and noncontinuous loads. Receptacles for charging electric vehicles, electric water heaters, and electric heaters and furnaces are examples of a continuous load.

SAFETY TIP

Always work with your local electrical inspector and an experienced wiring installer when adding electrical circuits.

Room Air Conditioner Circuits

1. Use wires that are rated at least 125 percent of a window or through-wall air conditioner's total rated current load if: (a) the air conditioner is connected to a receptacle by a plug-and-cord, (b) the air conditioner's total rated current load is shown on its nameplate (not just the individual motor load), (c) the air conditioner's total rated current load on the nameplate is not more than 40 amps and 250 volts, and (d) the branch circuit overcurrent protection device does not exceed the branch circuit wire ampacity rating and the ampacity rating of the receptacle. Example: a plug-and-cord connected room air conditioner's total rated current load is 17 amps. Use wires rated for 1.25 times 17 amps, which equals 21.25 amps (#10 copper wire).

2. Do not install a window or through-wall air conditioner on a 15- or a 20-amp multiple outlet branch circuit if the air conditioner's total rated current load is more than 50 percent of the branch circuit's rating (80 percent for dedicated circuits).

Kitchen Small Appliance Circuits

1. Provide at least two 20-amp, 120-volt branch circuits to serve only receptacles in the kitchen, pantry, breakfast and dining areas, and similar rooms. You may use the kitchen receptacle circuits to power a refrigerator, a wall clock, and the electrical requirements for gas cooking equipment. You may not use the kitchen branch circuits to supply light fixtures or other outlets in these rooms, and you may not use the kitchen branch circuits to supply outlets in other rooms or outside the house.

Air-conditioner load ratings can be found on the nameplate.

2. Provide a separate dedicated branch circuit for the kitchen range hood receptacle, if a range hood receptacle is installed. It is recommended, but not required, that this be a 20-amp, 120-volt branch circuit.

Bathroom Receptacle Circuit

1. Provide at least one 20-amp, 120-volt branch circuit to serve only receptacles located in the bathroom(s). You may not use the bathroom branch circuit to supply light fixtures or other outlets in the bathroom, and you may not use the bathroom branch circuit to supply outlets in other rooms.

2. You may provide each bathroom with its own dedicated 20-amp, 120-volt branch circuit. In this case, you may use the branch circuit to supply other bathroom outlets, such as light fixtures and exhaust fans.

Laundry Receptacle Circuit

1. Provide at least one 20-amp, 120-volt branch circuit to serve only receptacles located in the laundry area. You may not use the laundry branch circuit to supply light fixtures or other outlets in the laundry, and you may not use the laundry branch circuit to supply outlets in other rooms. Electric clothes dryers require a dedicated 240-volt, 30-amp circuit.

Garage Receptacle Circuit

1. Provide at least one 20-amp, 120-volt branch circuit to serve only receptacles located in the garage and readily accessible receptacles located outside the house. You may not use the garage receptacle branch circuit to supply light fixtures or other outlets in the garage.

2. Provide at least one receptacle outlet for each vehicle storage bay in attached garages and in detached garages that are provided with power. Locate these receptacles not more than 66 inches above the floor.

Multiwire Branch Circuits

1. Run multiwire branch circuit wires from adjacent slots on the same panelboard. It is safer to originate a multiwire branch circuit from adjacent slots on the same side of the panelboard. This helps avoid overloading the shared neutral (grounded) wire.

2. Use a two-pole overcurrent device or two single pole devices that are connected by an approved handle tie to protect most multiwire branch circuits. Do not connect circuit breaker handles with nails, wires, or other unapproved handle tie substitutes.

3. Use wire ties or similar devices to group all ungrounded (hot) and grounded (neutral) wires of each multiwire branch circuit in the cabinet where the circuit originates.

The receptacle yoke is removed (A) when it is split-wired using a multiwire branch circuit.

Connect both handles of circuit breakers protecting a multiwire branch circuit with an approved handle tie.

 QUANTITY OF RECEPTACLES ON A BRANCH CIRCUIT

A widely held belief exists that the IRC limits the number of receptacles on a residential branch circuit. This belief is incorrect. The IRC only requires that the number of branch circuits is sufficient to supply the connected load and that the load on any branch circuit does not exceed the IRC limits. This belief may come from restrictions on the number of outlets (both lights and receptacles) allowed for commercial electrical circuits. Commercial applications allow about 13 outlets on a 20-amp circuit and about 10 outlets on a 15-amp circuit. Wiring residential general lighting branch circuits based on these commercial outlet limits is often a good idea but is not required by the IRC.

Current Wiring Methods

Table 36 lists the wiring methods currently allowed in residential construction. **Note that certain wiring methods may not be used in certain applications.**

Approved Uses for Wiring Methods

1. Table 37 lists when a wiring method may be used in a specific application. Note that some wiring methods have restrictions or limitations shown by the following superscripts: (1) use less than 6 feet of LFC if the conduit walls are not reinforced, (2) insulate the neutral (grounded) wire unless the cable is used to supply other buildings on the same property, (3) insulate the neutral (grounded) wire, (4) use wires approved for wet locations and seal raceways to prevent water entry, (5) use materials listed as sunlight resistant, (6) protect metal raceways from corrosion, (7) use Schedule 80 RNC, (8) use materials listed as sunlight resistant if exposed to direct sunlight, (9) use less than 6 feet of conduit.

TABLE 36: CURRENT WIRING METHODS

WIRING METHOD	ABBREVIATION
Armored cable	AC
Electrical metallic tubing	EMT
Electrical nonmetallic tubing	ENT
Flexible metal conduit	FMC
Intermediate metal conduit	IMC
Liquidtight flexible conduit	LFC
Metal-clad cable	MC
Nonmetallic sheathed cable	NM
Rigid PVC conduit	RNC
Rigid metallic conduit	RMC
Service entrance cable	SE
Surface raceways	SR
Underground feeder cable	UF
Underground service cable	USE

TABLE 37: CURRENT WIRING METHODS ALLOWED USES

ALLOWED APPLICATION	AC	EMT	ENT	FMC	IMC RMC RNC	LFC[1]	MC	NM	SR	SE	UF	USE
Branch circuits	OK	OK	OK	OK	OK	OK	OK	OK	OK	OK[3]	OK	NO
Damp locations	NO	OK	OK	OK[4]	OK	OK	OK	NO	NO	OK	OK	OK
Direct burial	NO	OK[6]	NO	NO	OK[6]	OK	OK[6]	NO	NO	NO	OK	NO
Embedded in concrete below grade	NO	OK[6]	OK	NO	OK[6]	NO	NO	NO	NO	NO	NO	NO
Embedded in concrete in dry location	NO	OK	OK	NO	OK	NO	NO	NO	NO	NO	NO	NO
Embedded in masonry	NO	OK	OK	NO	OK[6]	OK	OK	NO	NO	NO	NO	NO
Embedded in plaster in dry location	OK	OK	OK	OK	OK	OK	OK	NO	NO	OK	OK	NO
Exposed not subject to damage	OK	OK	OK	OK	OK	OK	OK	OK	OK	OK	OK	OK
Exposed subject to damage	NO	NO	NO	NO	OK[7]	NO	NO	NO	NO	NO	NO	NO
Feeder	OK	OK	OK	OK	OK	OK	OK	NO	OK[2]	OK	OK	OK[2]
Fished in masonry voids	OK	NO	NO	OK	NO	OK	OK	NO	OK	OK	OK	NO
In masonry voids + cells in damp location or below grade	NO	OK[6]	OK	OK[4]	OK[6]	OK	OK	NO	NO	OK	OK	NO
In masonry voids + cells in dry location	OK	OK	OK	OK	OK	OK	OK	OK	NO	OK	OK	NO
Indoors (e.g., in stud walls)	OK	OK	OK	OK	OK	OK	OK	OK	OK	OK	OK	NO
Service entrance	NO	OK	OK[8]	OK[9]	OK	OK[9]	OK	NO	NO	OK	NO	OK
Wet locations + exposed to sunlight	NO	OK	OK[8]	OK[4]	OK	OK	OK	NO	NO	OK	OK[5]	OK[5]

Rules for NM + UF Cable

1. Use Table 38 to determine the maximum ampacity and overcurrent protection of NM and UF cable. NM and UF cable is often referred to by the trade name *Romex*. This table applies to almost all branch circuit and feeder wiring in modern residential electrical systems. Example: the maximum rating for a circuit breaker protecting Number 12 copper wire is 20 amps.

Rigid metal conduit has threaded ends for making watertight connections with female-threaded fittings and couplings.

Electrical nonmetallic tubing (A) may be used inside, and outside if it is rated as sunlight resistant. Liquid-tight flexible conduit can be non-metallic (B) or it can be metallic conduit with a non-metallic sheath (C).

TABLE 38: NM + UF CABLE MAXIMUM AMPACITY

WIRE SIZE (AWG)	COPPER WIRE (AMPS)	ALUMINUM WIRE (AMPS)
14	15	--
12	20	15
10	30	25
8	40	30
6	55	40
4	70	55
3	85	65
2	95	75
1	110	85

Non-metallic sheathed cable (right three cables) and underground feeder cable (left two cables) are available in the most common gauges used in residential construction.

TABLE 39: MAXIMUM HOLE OR NOTCH SIZE IN STUDS + JOISTS

FRAMING MEMBER	MAXIMUM HOLE SIZE	MAXIMUM NOTCH SIZE
2 × 4 load-bearing stud	1⁷/₁₆" diameter	⅞" deep
2 × 4 nonload-bearing stud	2⅛" diameter	1⁷/₁₆" deep
2 × 6 load-bearing stud	2¼" diameter	1⅜" deep
2 × 6 nonload-bearing stud	3⁵/₁₆" diameter	2³/₁₆" deep
2 × 6 joists	1⅞" diameter	⅞" deep
2 × 8 joists	2⅜" diameter	1¼" deep
2 × 10 joists	3¹/₁₆" diameter	1½" deep
2 × 12 joists	3¾" diameter	1⅞" deep

This framing member chart shows the maximum sizes for holes and notches that can be cut into studs and joists when running cables. When boring holes, there must be at least ⅝" of wood between the edge of a stud and the hole and at least 2" between the edge of a joist and the hole. Joists can be notched only in the end ⅓ of the overall span, never in the middle ⅓ of the joist.

NM + UF Cable Installation

1. Use NM and UF cable where the cable is not subject to physical damage. The term "subject to physical damage" is undefined and subject to interpretation. Your local building inspector will define what this means in your area. Locations that may be considered subject to physical damage include those within easy reach. Examples may include inside cabinets, in unfinished walls, and attached to finished walls below about 7 feet above the floor. Cable run in attics and crawl spaces is not usually considered subject to physical damage.

2. Protect NM and UF cable using RMC, IMC, EMT, or Schedule 80 RNC when the cable is subject to physical damage. Extend the protection at least 6 inches above the floor when the cable runs through the floor.

3. Protect NM and UF cable using nail guards or other approved physical protection when the cable is installed: (a) through holes, notches, or grooves that are closer than 1¼ inches to the edge of a stud or joist; (b) in notches and grooves in places such as drywall, plaster, and under carpet, unless the groove or notch is deeper than 1¼ inches; (c) through holes in metal framing (use grommets or bushings); and (d) parallel to the edge of a stud, joist, or furring strip when the cable is closer than 1¼ inches to the edge of the framing member.

4. Support NM, UF, AC, and MC cable every 4½ feet. Use wire staples or other approved fasteners to support vertical runs of NM, UF, AC, and MC cable. Staple the cable only on the flat edge. Note that wiring methods need not always be secured to be considered supported. Cable run across the tops of joists and truss chords is usually considered supported without being secured to the joists. Cable must be secured to be considered supported when it is run vertically and when it is run on the sides and bottoms of framing members.

VIOLATION! Do not install NM and UF cable inside cabinets.

5. Secure NM and UF cable not more than 8 inches from boxes and terminations that do not have cable clamps. This includes most plastic boxes. Secure NM and UF cable not more than 12 inches from boxes and terminations that have cable clamps. This includes most metal boxes. Measure the support distance from where the cable sheathing ends in the box, not from the box itself.

6. Use NM cable only in dry locations that are indoors and not within concrete or masonry that is exposed to the ground. Do not use NM cable in conduit that is buried in the ground. Buried conduit is considered a wet location. You may use UF cable in wet locations, including outdoors and underground if it is not subject to damage.

7. Do not bend NM, UF, and SE cable so that the bend radius measured at the inside edge of the bend is less than five times the diameter of the cable.

VIOLATION! Do not install NM and UF cable in exposed walls and ceilings. You may install NM and UF cable in exposed basement ceilings and attics under certain conditions.

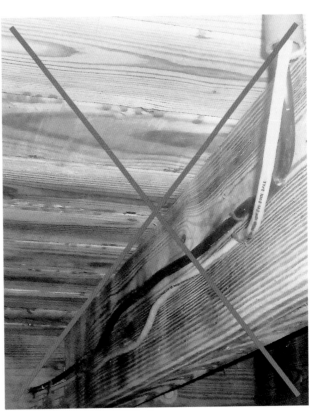

VIOLATION! Do not install NM cable outdoors. Outdoors includes buried conduit. You may install UF cable outdoors if it is protected from physical damage.

Support NM and UF cable at least every 4½'. Cable on top of ceiling joists is considered supported.

Secure NM and UF cable within 8" from where the cable enters or leaves a plastic box. Measure from where the cable sheathing ends in the box, not from the edge of the box.

Conduit + Tubing Installation

1. Apply the following installation requirements to EMT, IMC, RMC, ENT, FMC, LFC, and RNC: (a) limit the number of 90-degree bends between junction boxes to not more than four; (b) install bushings where conduit or tubing enters a box, fitting, or enclosure, unless the device provides equivalent protection against damage to any wires that may be pulled into the device; (c) remove rough edges from the ends of all conduit and tubing that may damage wires; (d) support EMT, IMC, and RMC not more than every 10 feet and within 3 feet of junction boxes or terminations; (e) support ENT not more than every 3 feet, unless the ENT is in an accessible ceiling, such as a drop ceiling, and if the distance between light fixtures is not more than 6 feet; and (f) support FMC and LFC not more than every 4½ feet and within 12 inches of junction boxes and terminations, unless the FMC and LFC is in an accessible ceiling, such as a drop ceiling, and if the distance between light fixtures is not more than 6 feet.

2. You may allow not more than 36 inches between the last support and a light fixture or other equipment that may need to be moved for service or replacement.

3. Seal the ends of conduit and tubing where the conduit or tubing may be subjected to different temperatures such that condensation could occur. Example: where conduit or tubing runs through a wall between conditioned space and unconditioned space. Use sealants that are listed as compatible with the conduit, tubing, and cables or wires inside.

Wiring Support Requirements

1. Table 40 lists the on center support requirements for wiring methods. Note that some wiring methods have special requirements shown by the following superscripts: (1) support is not required in accessible ceilings, such as drop ceilings, if the distance between light fixtures is not more than 6 feet; (2) you may allow not more than 24 inches between the last support and a light fixture or other equipment that may need to be moved for service or replacement; (3) you may allow not more than 36 inches between the last support and a light fixture or other equipment that may need to be moved for service or replacement; (4) support NM and UF cable not more than 8 inches from boxes and terminations that do not have cable clamps.

TABLE 40: WIRING METHODS SUPPORT

	AC	MC	EMT IMC RMC	ENT	FMC LFC	NM UF	RNC	SE USE (SERVICE)	SE (BRANCH CIRCUIT OR INDOOR FEEDER)
MAXIMUM SUPPORT SPACING	4.5[1]	6[1]	10'	3[1]	4.5[1]	4.5'	3[6]	2.5'	4.5'
MAXIMUM SUPPORT DISTANCE TO BOX OR TERMINATION (INCHES)	12[1,2]	12[1,2]	36"	36"	12[1,3]"	8[4]-12[5]"	36"	12"	12"

Use wood or other substantial guards to protect NM and UF cable installed perpendicular to rafters within the protection area.

Use wood or other substantial guards to protect NM and UF cable installed on top of ceiling joists within the protection area.

This includes most plastic boxes. Measure the support distance from where the cable sheathing ends in the box, not from the box itself; (5) support NM and UF cable not more than 12 inches from boxes and terminations that have cable clamps. This includes most metal boxes. (6) support RNC not more than 5 feet for conduit sizes between 1¼ and 2 inches.

Wiring Protection in Attics

1. Protect electrical cables in accessible attics by using substantial guard strips that are at least as tall as the electrical cables when: (a) access to the attic is by permanent stairs or ladders (such as a pull-down attic ladder), and the cables are within 7 feet vertically from the top of attic floor joists or truss bottom chords, or the cables run across the face (shortest dimension) of rafters, studs, or truss webs or chords, or (b) access to the attic is by scuttle hole or similar opening and the cables described in (a) are within 6 feet horizontally from the nearest point of the attic access opening.

2. You need not protect electrical cables in accessible attics when the cables are installed: (a) running parallel to the edge of the framing and at least 1¼ inches from the edge of the framing or (b) in holes that are at least 1¼ inches from the edge of the framing.

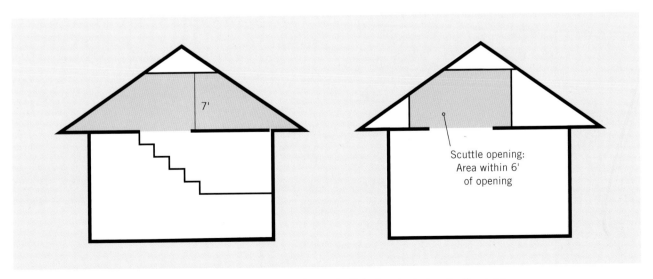

Protect exposed NM and UF cable installed in accessible attics and within the shaded protection area.

Electrical Receptacle Installation

Whether you call them outlets, plug-ins, or receptacles, these important devices represent the point where the rubber meets the road in your home wiring system. From the basic 15-amp, 120-volt duplex receptacle to the burly 50-amp, 240-volt appliance receptacle, the many outlets in your home do pretty much the same thing: connect power to a load.

Learning the essential differences between receptacles does not take long. Amperage is the main variable, as each receptacle must match the amperage and voltage of the circuit in which it is installed. A 15-amp circuit should be wired with 15-amp receptacles; a 20-amp circuit needs 20-amp receptacles (identified by the horizontal slot that Ts into each tall polarized slot). A 20-amp multi-receptacle circuit may use either 15- or 20-amp receptacles. Receptacles for 240-volt service have unique slot configurations so you can't accidentally plug in an appliance that's not rated for the amperage in the circuit. Some receptacles can be wired using the push-in wire holes, but this is not recommended. Some receptacles provide built-in, ground-fault circuit protection. These are easy to identify by reset and test buttons.

General Receptacle Installation Requirements

1. Use only grounding type (3-slot) when installing new receptacles in 15-amp and 20-amp branch circuits. You may replace existing 2-slot receptacles with a new 2-slot receptacle.

2. Mount receptacles in boxes that are recessed from the wall by seating the receptacle's extension ears at the top and bottom of the receptacle against the wall surface.

3. Mount receptacles in boxes that are flush with the wall by seating the receptacle's mounting yoke or strap against the box.

4. Do not allow the receptacle to move when a plug is inserted. This can, over time, cause wires to loosen, allow arcing, and cause a fire.

5. Install receptacle faceplates so that the plate completely covers the receptacle and so that the faceplate is flush against the wall. No gaps should exist between the receptacle and the faceplate or between the faceplate and the wall.

6. Install receptacles so that the face of the receptacle is either flush with or projects out from a nonmetallic faceplate.

7. Install receptacles so that the face of the receptacle projects out from a metallic faceplate at least (≥) $\frac{1}{64}$ inch.

8. Install receptacles so that the wiring terminals are not exposed to physical contact.

Receptacles Near Bathtubs and Showers

1. Do not install receptacles that are located in an exclusion zone measuring 3 feet horizontally from the base of a tub or shower stall threshold and 8 feet vertically from the top of the tub rim or shower stall threshold. This exclusion zone includes the area above the bathtub or shower.

2. You may install a receptacle on the wall farthest from the bathtub or shower in a small bathroom where there is no other place to install a receptacle.

3. Check with your local building official if this rule conflicts with other receptacle rules, such as the rule requiring a receptacle within 3 feet from each sink in a bathroom.

Long (neutral) slot • Stamp of approval • Mounting strap • Push-in fitting • Wire ratings • Silver (neutral) screw terminals • Short (hot) slot • Grounding hole • Connecting tab • Wire type • Brass (hot) screw terminals • Voltage rating • Amperage rating • Green (grounding) screw terminal

FRONT   BACK

Tamper-Resistant Receptacles

1. Install tamper-resistant receptacles in 120-volt, 15- and 20-amp general purpose branch circuits. These receptacles usually have an opening that moves to allow access to the receptacle. This requirement includes interior and exterior receptacles unless an exception applies. This requirement includes replacement of existing three-slot receptacles.

2. You do not need to install tamper-resistant receptacles if the receptacle: (a) is located more than 66 inches above the floor, (b) is part of a light fixture or appliance, or (c) is a single or duplex dedicated appliance receptacle into which one or two not easily movable appliances will be plugged.

Non-Grounding Type Receptacles

1. You may replace a non-grounding type receptacle (2-slot) with another non-grounding type receptacle.

2. You may replace a non-grounding type receptacle (2-slot) with a grounding type receptacle (3-slot) if: (a) the replacement receptacle is a GFCI receptacle and (b) the cover plate is labeled "No Equipment Ground."

3. You may replace a non-grounding type receptacle (2-slot) with a grounding type receptacle (3-slot) if: (a) the replacement receptacle is supplied by a GFCI protected circuit and (b) the cover plate is labeled "GFCI Protected and No Equipment Ground."

4. Use 1, 2, and 3 above only if no equipment grounding wire is available in the receptacle box. You must use a grounding type receptacle, and you must use the equipment grounding wire if it is available.

Example of countertop receptacle spacing in a typical kitchen.

5. You may run an equipment grounding wire to the nearest box containing an equipment grounding wire if all hot, neutral, and grounding wires originate at the same panelboard.

6. Do not connect the neutral wire to the receptacle grounding lug. These "bootleg grounds" are a dangerous code violation.

Receptacle Installation in Rooms

1. Apply the following provisions to receptacles in living rooms, family rooms, bedrooms, dens, sunrooms, recreation rooms, dining rooms, breakfast rooms, libraries, and similar living areas. Kitchens, bathrooms, hallways, garages, laundry rooms, and exterior receptacles have their own installation requirements.

2. Install the required interior receptacles so that any point along a wall is not more than 6 feet from a receptacle. When measuring a wall, do not include operable doors, fireplaces, closet interiors, or similar openings, or fixed cabinets that do not have countertops or similar work surfaces. A wall begins at the edge of an opening and continues around any corners to the next opening. Walls include fixed (not sliding) panels in doors that are at least 2 feet wide. Walls include partial height walls that serve functions, such as room dividers, and walls that form breakfast bars and similar bar-type counters. Walls include guards and railings at balconies, raised floors, and other areas where furniture could be placed.

Example of receptacle spacing requirements in a typical room. Measure receptacle spacing distance along the wall line. Install receptacles along partial height walls and along balcony guards in lofts and similar areas.

VIOLATION! Running a pigtail from the neutral terminal to the grounding screw on a receptacle is called a bootleg ground. It is usually done to make an ungrounded circuit appear to be grounded. It is very dangerous.

You must install receptacles behind a sink or cooking appliance if the countertop behind the sink or cooking appliance is at least 18" deep in a corner cabinet.

A GFCI protected receptacle must be installed within 36" of each bathroom sink basin.

3. Locate floor receptacles intended to serve as required interior receptacles not more than 18 inches from the wall. You may install interior floor receptacles at any safe place, but you may count only receptacles not more than 18 inches from the wall among the required receptacles.

4. Install receptacles not more than 66 inches above the finished floor. You may install receptacles at any height, but you may count only receptacles not more than 66 inches above the finished floor among the required receptacles.

Kitchen Countertop Receptacle Installation

1. Install a GFCI protected receptacle at every kitchen countertop that is at least 12 inches wide.

2. Kitchen countertops include similar horizontal work surfaces, such as desks, that are located in the kitchen area. Receptacles include multiple outlet assemblies that are sometimes installed in place of or in addition to receptacles that are installed in the backsplash above the countertop.

3. Install kitchen countertop receptacles so that all points along the countertop wall are not more than 2 feet from a receptacle. A wall begins at the edge of an opening or appliance, and continues around any corners, and ends at the next opening or appliance. Include windows when measuring the wall unless the window is above a sink or cooking appliance.

4. Count every 12 inches of a multiple outlet assembly as one receptacle. Multiple outlet assemblies contain two or more outlets in one horizontal strip.

5. Install receptacles behind a sink or cooking appliance located along a straight wall if the countertop behind the sink or cooking appliance is at least 12 inches deep. Install receptacles behind a sink or cooking appliance located along a wall corner if the countertop behind the sink or cooking appliance is at least 18 inches deep.

6. Install receptacles not more than 20 inches above the countertop. You may install receptacles at any height, but you may include only receptacles not more than 20 inches above the countertop among the required kitchen countertop receptacles.

7. Do not include among the required kitchen countertop receptacles: (a) receptacles located in appliance garages, (b) receptacles dedicated for a fixed-in-place appliance, or (c) receptacles not readily accessible for use by small appliances.

8. Do not install receptacles face up on work surfaces unless the receptacle is listed for this type of installation.

9. Locate the receptacle for the dishwasher in a space adjacent to the dishwasher, if installing a dishwasher receptacle. This does not apply to a hard-wired dishwasher outlet. Protect the dishwasher power cord with a grommet, bushing, or another approved method where the cord runs through a partition, such as a cabinet wall.

Kitchen Island + Peninsula Receptacles

1. Install at least one GFCI protected receptacle to serve the first 9 square feet of an island or a peninsula countertop. At least one receptacle is required if the island or peninsula countertop is less than 9 square feet.

An exterior-rated receptacle should be installed on both the front and back exterior walls of your house.

2. Install at least one GFCI protected receptacle to serve every 18 additional square feet of an island or a peninsula countertop. At least one receptacle is required if the additional island or peninsula countertop area is less than 18 square feet.

3. Install the peninsula receptacle within 2 feet from the outer end of a peninsula countertop. Measure a peninsula countertop from where the peninsula countertop intersects with the wall, or where the peninsula countertop connects with another countertop.

4. You may install receptacles not more than 12 inches below an island or a peninsula countertop. You may not install this receptacle below a breakfast bar or other countertop that extends more than 6 inches beyond the supporting base.

Bathroom Sink Receptacles

1. Install at least one GFCI protected receptacle not more than 36 inches from the outside edge of each sink basin in a bathroom. You may install the receptacle along a wall adjacent to the sink.

2. Do not install receptacles faceup on work surfaces unless the receptacle is listed for this type of installation.

Laundry Receptacles

1. Install at least one 20-amp, 120-volt receptacle in the laundry area. This required receptacle usually serves the clothes washing machine. The required laundry receptacle is in addition to any required garage or basement receptacle if the laundry is in the garage or basement.

2. Provide GFCI protection for all 15- and 20-amp, 120-volt receptacles in the laundry area. This includes any dedicated receptacle for the clothes washing machine and for the clothes dryer.

Exterior Receptacles

1. Install at least one GFCI protected, 15- or 20-amp, 120-volt receptacle on the front and back exterior wall of every home. Locate the receptacle so that it is accessible from grade level and is not more than 78 inches above finished grade level.

2. Install at least one GFCI protected, 15- or 20-amp, 120-volt receptacle within the perimeter of any balcony, deck, or porch that: (a) is accessible from inside the home and (b) has a usable area of at least 20 square feet. Locate the receptacle not more than 78 inches above the balcony, deck, or porch.

Basement Receptacles

1. Install at least one GFCI protected, 15- or 20-amp, 120-volt receptacle in an unfinished basement. This receptacle is in addition to any receptacles that are dedicated to other appliances or equipment. Install at least one GFCI protected receptacle in the unfinished part of a basement that is partially finished.

2. You are not required to provide GFCI protection to a receptacle that is dedicated to serving a fire or security alarm system.

Garage + Accessory Building Receptacles

1. Install one GFCI protected, 15- or 20-amp receptacle for each motor vehicle parking space in an attached garage and in a detached garage that is supplied with electricity. Locate the receptacle not more than 66 inches above the floor. You are not required to supply electricity to detached garages and accessory buildings, but if you do you must install a receptacle. Accessory buildings include work sheds, storage sheds, tack sheds, barns, and similar buildings.

2. You may not serve any other outlets from the circuit serving garage receptacles except for readily accessible receptacles located outside the house. This means that garage lights and exterior lights and receptacles must be served by one or more separate circuits.

Ground-Fault (GFCI) + Arc-Fault (AFCI) Protection

Ground-Fault Location Requirements

1. Kitchen receptacles. Install ground-fault circuit-interrupter (GFCI) protection on all 120-volt through 250-volt receptacles that serve kitchen countertops. This does not include receptacles under the kitchen sink and receptacles located on kitchen walls that do not serve the countertop.

2. Kitchen. Install GFCI protection on the outlets that supply dishwashing machines. This includes receptacles and hard-wired connections.

3. Bathroom receptacles. Install GFCI protection on all 120-volt through 250-volt receptacles located in bathrooms. This applies to all receptacles regardless of where they are located in the bathroom and includes receptacles located at countertops, inside cabinets, and along bathroom walls. This also applies to bathtubs and shower stalls that are not located in a bathroom. Install GFCI protection on all circuits serving electrically heated floors in bathrooms, kitchens, and around whirlpool tubs, spas, and hot tubs.

4. Garage and accessory building receptacles. Install GFCI protection on all 120-volt through 250-volt receptacles located in garages and grade-level areas of unfinished accessory buildings.

5. Exterior receptacles. Install GFCI protection on all 120-volt through 250-volt receptacles located outdoors. This does not apply to receptacles that are dedicated for deicing equipment and are located under the eaves. This does apply to holiday lighting receptacles located under the eaves.

6. Basement receptacles. Install GFCI protection on all 120-volt through 250-volt receptacles located in unfinished basements. An unfinished basement is not intended as habitable space and is limited to storage and work space. A receptacle dedicated for a permanently installed fire or security alarm is exempt from this requirement.

7. Crawl space outlets. Install GFCI protection on all 120-volt through 250-volt outlets and lights located in crawl spaces. Receptacles in crawl spaces are

Ground-fault receptacles and circuit breakers detect unwanted current running between an energized wire and a grounded neutral wire.

A combination ARC-fault circuit breaker detects sparking (arcing) faults along damaged energized wires and detects these faults between wires. A branch ARC-fault circuit breaker only detects arcing faults between wires.

not required unless equipment requiring service is located there.

8. Sink receptacles. Install GFCI protection on all 120-volt through 250-volt receptacles that are located within 6 feet of the top inside edge of a sink. This includes wall, floor, and countertop receptacles.

9. Boathouse receptacles. Install GFCI protection on all 120-volt receptacles located in boathouses. Install GFCI protection on all 120-volt through 250-volt and 240-volt receptacles that serve boat hoists.

10. Laundry area receptacles. Install GFCI protection on all 120-volt through 250-volt receptacles located in the laundry area. This includes the receptacle for an electric clothes dryer, if installed.

11. Indoor damp and wet area receptacles. Install GFCI protection on all 120-volt through 250-volt receptacles located in indoor damp and wet areas. This is intended to extend GFCI protection to any indoor damp and wet areas that are not specifically covered by other provisions.

12. Spas, tubs, and other circuits requiring ground-fault protection. Install GFCI protection on all circuits serving spa tubs, whirlpool tubs, hot tubs, and similar equipment. Refer to the general codes for more information about receptacles serving these components.

13. Install GFCI circuit breakers and receptacles so that they are readily accessible.

Arc-Fault Location Requirements

1. Install a combination type or an outlet (receptacle) type arc-fault circuit-interrupter (AFCI) on all 15- and 20-amp, 120-volt branch circuits serving sleeping, family, dining, living, sun, and recreation rooms, kitchens, laundry areas, and parlors, libraries, dens, hallways, closets, and similar rooms and areas. This means that 15- and 20-amp, 120-volt branch circuits serving most interior spaces in a home are required to have AFCI protection. Note that garages, basements, utility and mechanical rooms, and exterior branch circuits are not included in this list, although local building officials may include these areas by interpretation.

2. You may provide AFCI protection for the entire branch circuit by installing a combination-type AFCI circuit breaker in the electrical panel where the branch circuit originates.

3. You may provide AFCI protection to a branch circuit using several different combinations of branch-circuit type AFCI circuit breakers and branch-circuit type AFCI receptacles. Refer to general codes or your local building inspector for details about these alternate methods.

4. Provide AFCI for branch circuits that are modified, replaced, or extended. You may use either of the following methods: (a) install a combination-type AFCI circuit breaker in the electrical panel where the branch circuit originates or (b) install a branch-circuit type AFCI receptacle at the first receptacle in the existing branch circuit. Refer to your local building inspector for details about requirements in your situation.

5. Install AFCI circuit breakers and receptacles so that they are readily accessible.

Receptacles for whirlpool tubs must be GFCI protected and readily accessible

Junction Boxes, Device Boxes + Enclosures

All electrical boxes are available in different depths. A box must be deep enough so a switch or receptacle can be removed or installed easily without crimping and damaging the circuit wires. Replace an undersized box with a larger box using Table 42 the Electrical Box Fill Chart (see page 206) as a guide. **The NEC also says that all electrical boxes must remain accessible. Never cover an electrical box with drywall, paneling, or wall coverings.**

Box Installation

1. Use non-metallic boxes with NM cable or with non-metallic cable, conduit or tubing. You may use non-metallic boxes with metallic conduit or tubing if you maintain the electrical continuity of the metallic cable, conduit or tubing by installing a bonding jumper through the box. In many situations it is easier to use a metallic box with metallic conduit or tubing.

2. Extend the sheathing of NM cable, and other cables with non-metallic sheaths, at least ¼ inch into a box knockout opening and at least ¼ inch past any cable clamp inside the box.

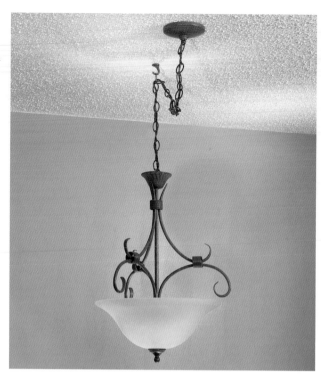

Do not support heavy light fixtures using only the light fixture electrical box. The eye hook supporting this chandelier is driven into the same ceiling joist to which the electrical box is mounted.

3. Secure NM cable, and other non-metallic cable, conduit, and tubing to each box. You may secure cable with cable clamps inside the box or with compression tabs provided where the cable enters the box. You do not need to secure NM cable to a standard single-gang box (2¼ by 4 inches) mounted in a wall or ceiling if you fasten the cable not more than 8 inches from the box and if the sheathing enters the box at least ¼ inch. Measure the 8 inches along the length of the sheathing, not from the outside of the box.

Light Fixture Box Installation

1. Use boxes designed for mounting light fixtures if a light fixture is to be mounted to the box. These boxes are usually 4-inch round or octagonal.

2. You may use other boxes to mount light fixtures on walls if the fixture weighs less than 6 pounds and is secured to the box using at least #6 screws.

3. Support light fixtures weighing at least 50 pounds independently from the light fixture box unless the box is labeled as being designed to support a heavier light fixture. You may use the light fixture box to support light fixtures weighing less than 50 pounds. Note that ceiling fans are not light fixtures.

Box shape is related to function, as electrical fixtures are created to fit on boxes of a particular shape. Octagonal and round boxes generally are designed for ceiling mounting, while square and rectangular boxes are sized for single-pole, duplex, and other standard switch and receptacle sizes.

Box Contents Limitations

1. Limit the number of wires, devices (such as switches and receptacles), and fittings in a box. This limitation is primarily based on the heat generated by the wires and devices in the box. The actual size of the box relative to its contents is a secondary consideration.

2. Use the cubic inch volume printed on the box or provided in the box manufacturer's instructions to determine box volume. Do not attempt to measure the box volume. Do not estimate box volume from the volume of similar size boxes. You will probably not get the same volume as provided by the manufacturer.

3. Use Table 41 to determine the volume units required by wires, devices, and fittings in a box.

Box Installation Tolerances

1. Install boxes in non-combustible material, such as masonry, drywall, plaster, or tile, so that the front edge is set back not more than ¼ inch from the finished surface.

2. Install boxes in walls and ceilings made of wood or other combustible material so that the box's front edge is flush with the finished surface or projects from the finished surface. You may use an extension ring, plaster ring, or similar device to extend the box to the finished wall surface.

Boxes must be installed so the front edges are flush with the finished wall surface and the gap between the box and the wall covering is not more than ⅛".

TABLE 41: WIRE VOLUME UNIT

WIRE SIZE (AWG)	WIRE VOLUME
14	2.00 in.³
12	2.25 in.³
10	2.50 in.³
8	3.00 in.³
6	5.00 in.³

Mechanically secure the extension device to the box.

3. Cut openings for boxes in drywall and plaster so that the opening is not more than ⅛ inch from the perimeter of the box.

VOLUME UNITS

Calculate the volume units required by wires, devices, and fittings based on the following definitions:

Volume units for current-carrying wires. Allow one volume unit for each individual hot (ungrounded) and neutral (grounded) wire in the box. Use Table 41 to determine the volume units of common wire sizes. Example: two pieces of #14/2 NM are in a box. Each piece of this cable contains one hot (ungrounded) and one neutral (grounded) wire and one grounding wire. From Table 41, each #14 wire uses 2.00 cu. in. in the box. The total volume units required by the hot (ungrounded) and neutral (grounded) wires is 8 cu. in.

Volume units for devices. Allow two volume units for each device (switch or receptacle) in the box. Base the volume units on the largest hot (ungrounded) or neutral (grounded) wire in the box. Example: NM cable size #14 and #12 are in a box. From Table 41, #14 wire uses 2.00 cu. in. and #12 wire uses 2.25 cu. in. Allow 4.5 cu. in. volume units (2 × 2.25 cu. in.) for each switch or receptacle in the box based on the volume of the larger #12 NM cable.

Volume units for grounding wires. Allow one volume unit for all grounding wires in the box. Base the volume unit on the largest hot (ungrounded) or neutral (grounded) wire in the box.

Volume units for clamps. Allow one volume unit for all internal cable clamps in the box, if any. Base the volume unit on the largest hot (ungrounded) or neutral (grounded) wire in the box.

Volume units for fittings. Allow one volume unit for all fittings in the box, if any. Base the volume unit on the largest hot (ungrounded) or neutral (grounded) wire in the box.

TABLE 42: ELECTRICAL BOX FILL CHART

BOX SIZE + SHAPE (If volume not labeled by manufacturer)	MAXIMUM NUMBER OF VOLUME UNITS PERMITTED (SEE NOTES BELOW)			
	14 AWG	12 AWG	10 AWG	8 AWG
JUNCTION BOXES				
4 × 1¼" R or O	6	5	5	4
4 × 1½" R or O	7	6	6	5
4 × 2⅛" R or O	10	9	8	7
4 × 1¼" S	9	8	7	6
4 × 1½" S	10	9	8	7
4 × 2⅛" S	15	13	12	10
4¹¹⁄₁₆ × 1¼" S	12	11	10	8
4¹¹⁄₁₆ × 1½" S	14	13	11	9
4¹¹⁄₁₆ × 2⅛" S	21	18	16	14
DEVICE BOXES				
3 × 2 × 1½"	3	3	3	2
3 × 2 × 2"	5	4	4	3
3 × 2 × 2¼"	5	4	4	3
3 × 2 × 2½"	6	5	5	4
3 × 2 × 2¾"	7	6	6	4
3 × 2 × 3½"	9	8	7	6
4 × 2⅛ × 1½"	5	4	4	3
4 × 2⅛ × 1⅞"	6	5	5	4
4 × 2⅛ × 2⅛"	7	6	5	4

Notes:
- R = Round; O = Octagonal; S = Square or rectangular
- Each hot or neutral wire entering the box is counted as one volume unit.
- Grounding wires are counted as one volume unit in total—do not count each one individually.
- Raceway fittings and external cable clamps do not count. Internal cable connectors and straps count as one volume unit.
- Devices (switches and receptacles mainly) each count as two volume units.
- When calculating total volume units, any non-wire components should be assigned the gauge of the largest wire in the box.
- For wire gauges not shown here, contact your local electrical inspections office.

Box Support in Walls, Ceilings + Floors

1. Provide support for boxes that rigidly and securely fasten them in place. You may use nails or screws to support these boxes.

2. Protect screws inside boxes so that the threads will not damage the wires.

3. Wood braces used to support boxes must be at least 1 × 2 inches.

4. Use "cut-in" or "old work" retrofit boxes only if they have approved clamps or anchors that are identified for the location where they are installed.

Damp Locations

1. Install a receptacle box cover that is weatherproof when the cover is closed and a plug is not inserted into a receptacle located in a damp location. This applies to 15-amp and 20-amp receptacles. A damp area is protected from direct contact with water. Refer to the definition of damp location. You may use a receptacle cover suitable for wet locations in a damp location (see page 168).

2. Install a watertight seal between a flush-mounted receptacle and its faceplate. This will require a gasket or sealant between the finished surface (such as stucco, brick, or siding) and the faceplate.

Wet Locations

1. Install a receptacle box cover that is weatherproof when the cover is closed on any receptacle located in a wet location. This applies to 15-amp and 20-amp receptacles in any indoor or outdoor wet location. This applies regardless of whether or not a plug is inserted into the receptacle. Refer to the definition of wet location (see page 168).

2. Install a watertight seal between a flush-mounted receptacle and its faceplate. This will require a gasket or sealant between the finished surface (such as stucco, brick, or siding) and the faceplate.

Box Support by Raceways

1. Do not support any junction or device boxes using only conduit or tubing if the box volume is larger than 100 cubic inches.

2. Support boxes that do not contain switches, receptacles, or light fixtures by using at least two

lengths of conduit threaded wrench-tight into the box. Secure the conduit not more than 3 feet from the box if the conduit enters from different sides of the box. Secure the conduit not more than 18 inches from the box if the conduit enters from the same side of the box. Example: if the conduit enters the box from the top and bottom of the box, then secure the conduit not more than 3 feet from the box. Example: if the conduit enters the box from only the top or only from the bottom, then secure the conduit not more than 18 inches from the box.

3. Support boxes that contain switches or receptacles or light fixtures by using at least two lengths of conduit threaded wrench-tight into the box. Secure the conduit not more than 18 inches from the box.

4. You may use RMC or IMC metal conduit to support light fixtures under certain conditions. Refer to the IRC for the exceptions.

Secure each cable to a cabinet using an approved cable clamp.

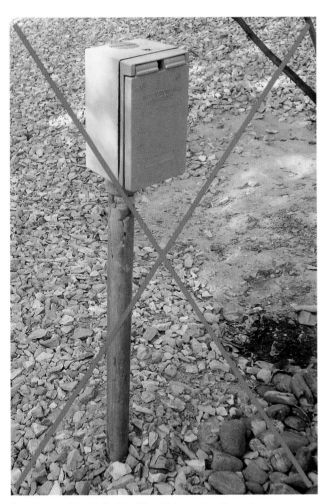

One piece of conduit should not be used as the sole means to support a box.

Panel boxes, including the main service panel and subpanel boxes, also require the use of properly sized cable clamps wherever cables enter or exit the box.

Cables Secured to a Cabinet

1. Secure each individual cable to panelboard cabinets and to similar enclosures, unless the exception applies.

2. You may run NM cable into the top of a surface-mounted cabinet through an accessible rigid raceway under certain conditions. Refer to IRC Chapter 39 for the conditions.

Electrical Box Types

3½"-deep plastic boxes with preattached mounting nails are used for any wiring project protected by finished walls. Common styles include single-gang (A), double-gang (B), and triple-gang (C). Double-gang and triple-gang boxes require internal cable clamps.

Metal boxes should be used for exposed installations in an unfinished basement. Metal boxes also may be used for wiring that will be covered by finished walls.

Plastic retrofit light fixture boxes let you install a new fixture in an existing wall or ceiling.

Plastic light fixture boxes with brace bars let you position a fixture between framing members.

Metal light fixture boxes with heavy-duty brace bars are recommended when installing heavy light fixtures or hanging a ceiling fan.

GFCI damp area plates

Duplex damp area plates

Cast aluminum boxes are required for outdoor electrical fixtures connected with metal conduit. Sealed seams and threaded openings keep moisture out. A variety of cover plates are available.

PVC plastic boxes are used with PVC conduit in outdoor wiring and exposed indoor wiring. PVC cover plates are available to fit switches, standard duplex receptacles, and GFCI receptacles.

Box Installation Specifications

High-quality non-metallic boxes are rigid and don't contort easily. A variety of adapter plates are available, including single-gang (A), double-gang (B), light fixture (C), and junction box cover plate (D). Adapter plates come in several thicknesses to match different wall constructions.

Boxes larger than 2 × 4" and all retrofit boxes must have either compression tabs or internal cable clamps. After installing cables in the box, tighten cable clamps over the cables so they are gripped firmly, but not so tightly that the cable sheathing is crushed.

Bonding screw

Pigtail

Metal boxes must be bonded to the circuit grounding system. Connect the circuit grounding wires to the box with a pigtail wire and wire connector (as shown) or with a grounding clip.

Cables entering a metal box must be clamped. A variety of clamps are available, including plastic clamps (A, C) and threaded metal clamps (B).

Circuit Breaker Panels

The circuit breaker panel is the electrical distribution center for your home. It divides the current into branch circuits that run throughout the house. Each branch circuit is protected by a circuit breaker or fuse that protects the wires from dangerous current overloads. When installing new circuits, the last step is to connect the wires to new circuit breakers at the panel. Follow basic safety procedures and always shut off the main circuit breaker and test for power before touching any parts inside the panel. Never touch the service wire lugs. If unsure of your own skills, hire an electrician to make the final circuit connections. (If you have an older electrical service with fuses instead of circuit breakers, always have an electrician make these final hookups.)

If a circuit breaker panel does not have enough open slots for new full-size circuit breakers,

120-volt branch circuits

Main circuit breaker panel distributes the current entering the home into branch circuits.

Neutral service wire carries current back to the source after it has passed through the home.

Main circuit breaker protects the panelboard from overloads and disconnects current to all circuits in the panel.

Neutral bus bar has setscrew terminals for linking all neutral circuit wires to the neutral service wire.

Double-pole breaker wired for a 120/240 circuit transfers current from the two hot bus bars to red and black hot wires in a three-wire cable.

Grounding conductor leads to metal grounding rods driven into the earth or to other grounding electrodes.

Two hot service wires provide 120/240 volts to the main circuit breaker. These wires are always HOT.

The green screw is the bonding connection to the cabinet. It should be removed in a subpanel.

Grounding bus bar has terminals for linking grounding wires to the main grounding conductor. It is bonded to the neutral bus bar.

Two hot bus bars run through the center of the panel, supplying current to the circuit breakers. Each carries 120 volts.

Subpanel feeder breaker is a double-pole breaker. It is wired in the same way as a 120/240-volt circuit.

you may be able to install ½-height (slimline) circuit breakers. Otherwise, you will need to install a subpanel.

Before installing any new wiring, evaluate your electrical service to make sure it provides enough current to support both the existing wiring and any new circuits. If your service does not provide enough current, you will need to upgrade to a higher amp rating panel with enough extra breaker slots for the new circuits you want to install.

SAFETY WARNING

Never touch any parts inside a circuit breaker panel until you have checked for power. Circuit breaker panels differ in appearance, depending on the manufacturer. Never begin work in a circuit breaker panel until you understand its layout and can identify the parts.

Circuit breaker subpanel can be installed when the main circuit breaker panel does not have enough space to hold circuit breakers for new circuits you want to install.

Two hot feeder wires supply 120 volts each to the two hot bus bars.

Neutral feeder wire connects the neutral bus bar in the subpanel to the neutral bus bar in the main service panel.

Feeder cable brings current from the main circuit breaker panel. A 30-amp, 240-volt subpanel requires a 10/3 feeder cable controlled by a 30-amp double-pole circuit breaker.

Neutral bus bar has setscrew terminals for linking neutral circuit wires to the neutral feed wire.

Single-pole circuit breaker transfers 120 volts from one hot bus bar to the black hot wire in a two-wire cable.

Grounding bus bar has setscrew terminals for connecting circuit grounding wires. In a circuit breaker subpanel, the grounding bus bar is not bonded to the neutral bus bar.

120-volt branch circuit

120-volt isolated ground circuit

240-volt branch circuit

Two hot bus bars pass through the center of the service panel, supplying power to the individual circuit breakers. Each carries 120 volts.

Double-pole breaker wired for 240 volts transfers current from both hot bus bars to white and black hot wires in a two-wire cable. This 240-volt circuit has no neutral wire connection; the white wire is tagged with black tape to identify it as a hot wire.

Switch Installation

Switch Current Load Limitations

1. Switches that control light fixtures and switched receptacles may include devices, such as dimmers, that activate lights when someone enters the room (occupancy sensors), and computer-controlled (smart) devices.

2. Do not use a switch in a circuit if the current load on the circuit exceeds the current rating of the switch. Example: a 15-amp snap switch may be overloaded if it switches ten 200-watt, 120-volt flood lights. Beware of overloads if the switch controls multiple high wattage flood lights or other high current draw equipment.

3. Use switches that are rated at least 80 percent of a motor's full load current rating.

4. Install switches that have at least the same current rating as the circuit breaker or fuse protecting the branch circuit when the switch controls plug-and-cord connected equipment either by switching the receptacle or by switching a permanently

Cover exposed electrical connections in timer boxes using the manufacturer-supplied cover.

connected cord. Example: a switch controls half of a receptacle in a bedroom. If the branch circuit is 20 amps, the switch should be rated at 20 amps or more.

5. Run the grounded (neutral) wire of a general purpose branch circuit to the switch box when the switch controls lighting loads. Refer to the IRC for exceptions that may occur in some unusual conditions.

Three-way switches and four-way switches are required for circuits with fixtures controlled by multiple switches. A four-way switch is seen here. Note that ON and OFF are not indicated on the toggle because these settings can change based on which switch was used last.

Push-in fittings

Grounding screw

Wire compatibilty ratings

Screw terminals

Amperage + voltage ratings

Underwriters Laboratories (UL) approved

Mounting screw

Mounting strap

Grounding lug screw

Wire strip gauge

Wire release opening for push-in fittings

FRONT

BACK

A typical 15-amp single pole switch seen front and back.

Connect the grounding wire to the switch grounding terminal when mounting the switch in a plastic box.

Switch Orientation

1. Install single-throw switches so that ON is in the up position when the device is installed vertically. You may install single-throw switches horizontally.

2. Use switches that clearly indicate whether the switch is in the ON or OFF position. This does not apply to three-way and four-way switches. This requirement is frequently waived when rocker type switches are used.

Timer Switches

1. Use timer switches with energized parts that are enclosed in the switch's case or enclose the timer switch in a cabinet or box.

2. Install a barrier to guard against contact with energized parts.

Switch Height

1. Locate switches not more than 79 inches above the finished floor or finished grade. Measure to the center of the handle when in the up position.

2. Locate switches in readily accessible places.

Grounding of Switches, Boxes + Faceplates

1. Ground metal boxes containing switches, the switches themselves (including dimmers and similar devices), and metal faceplates covering switches. Ground the switch by mounting the switch to a grounded metal box using metal screws or by connecting an equipment grounding wire to the switch. Connect switches to the equipment grounding wire when using non-metallic boxes.

2. You may replace an existing ungrounded switch with another ungrounded switch if the wiring method has no equipment grounding wire. Protect these ungrounded switches that are located not more than 8 feet vertically or 5 feet horizontally from the ground or from grounded metal objects by: (a) installing a non-combustible and non-conductive faceplate using nonmetallic screws or (b) using a switch with a non-metallic strap or yoke or (c) installing GFCI protection on the circuit.

Switches in Wet Locations

1. Enclose switches and circuit breakers installed in wet locations in a weatherproof cabinet or enclosure.

2. Do not locate switches in shower or tub spaces unless the switch is part of a listed tub or shower assembly.

Switch Mounting in Boxes

1. Mount switches in boxes that are recessed from the wall by seating the switch's extension ears at the top and bottom of the switch against the wall surface.

2. Mount switches in boxes that are flush with the wall by seating the switch's mounting yoke or strap against the box.

3. Do not allow the switch body to move when the switch is operated. This can, over time, cause wires to loosen, potentially causing arcing and a fire.

Switch Faceplate Installation

1. Install switch faceplates so that the plate completely covers the switch and so that the faceplate is flush against the wall. No gaps should exist between the switch handle and the faceplate or between the faceplate and the wall.

Computer-Controlled Devices

1. Install computer-controlled (smart) devices according to manufacturer's instructions.

 SWITCH ONLY HOT WIRES

Switch only the hot (ungrounded) wire unless the switch simultaneously disconnects all wires in the circuit. Maintain required wire color-coding throughout three-way and four-way circuits.

Light Fixture Installation

Energy Efficiency

1. Install high-efficacy light fixtures and lamps. High-efficacy usually means LED or fluorescent lamps (bulbs). This does not apply to lamps in appliances such as range hoods.

2. Control light fixtures using a dimmer, occupancy sensor, or by a similar method. This does not apply to bathrooms, hallways, exterior lights, and security lights.

3. Use exterior lights that automatically shut off during the day if the light consumes more than 30 watts.

4. Do not install gas lights that have a continuously running pilot light.

5. Confirm interpretation and enforcement of these provisions with your local building official.

Lights Required in Habitable Rooms

1. Switches that control light fixtures and switched receptacles may include devices, such as dimmers, that activate lights when someone enters the room (occupancy sensors), and computer-controlled (smart) devices.

2. Install at least one switch-controlled light in every habitable room, kitchen, and bathroom. This light may be a switched (half-hot) receptacle in habitable rooms other than kitchens and bathrooms. In kitchens and bathrooms, the outlet must be a switched wall or ceiling lighting outlet.

Lights Required in Other Interior Spaces

1. Install at least one wall switch–controlled wall or ceiling light in every hallway, stairway, attached garage, and detached garage if the detached garage is provided with electricity.

2. Install at least one wall switch to control stairway lights if the stairs have at least (≥) 6 risers. Install a switch at: (a) each floor and (b) each landing that provides access to an interior or exterior entry opening.

3. Do not install two or more dimmers to control stairway lights unless all dimmers allow the lights to be turned all the way on and off.

Lights Required at Exterior Doors

1. Install at least one switch-controlled wall or ceiling light on the exterior side of every exterior door with grade level access. Exterior lights are not required at garage vehicle doors.

Lights Required in Attics, Crawl Spaces + Basements

1. Install at least one light outlet in attics, crawl spaces, utility rooms, and basements if the area is used for storage or if it contains equipment that requires service. Locate the light outlet near any equipment that requires service.

2. Locate a switch for the light at all points of entry into the area.

Light Fixture Support

1. You may use a securely attached box to support light fixtures weighing less than 50 pounds. Note that ceiling fans are not considered light fixtures.

2. Do not use the screw shell of a light fixture to support anything that weighs more than 6 pounds or is more than 16 inches in any dimension.

Recessed Lights

1. Use recessed lights that are labeled as being thermally protected. Thermal protection shuts off power to the light at high temperatures. Thermal protection is not required if the recessed light is made, labeled, and installed so that it functions as if it were thermally protected.

2. Use insulation contact (IC) rated recessed lights when the recessed parts are installed in an insulated attic. IC rated recessed lights may not require clearance to insulation or to combustible materials.

3. Provide at least 3 inches of clearance between insulation and recessed lights that are not labeled as being insulation contact (IC) rated. Do not install insulation above non-IC rated recessed lights.

Keep all parts of ceiling fans, hanging lights, and track lights at least 3' horizontally and 8' vertically from bathtubs and showers.

Look for heavy-duty ceiling boxes that are specifically rated for ceiling fans and heavy light fixtures.

A sturdy metal brace with an integral box that is installed between ceiling joists can be used to support ceiling fans and heavy light fixtures.

Lights in Wet + Damp Locations

1. Install lights in wet and damp locations so that water cannot enter or accumulate in the wiring or energized parts.

2. Use only lights labeled SUITABLE FOR WET LOCATIONS when installing lights that may be subject to direct contact with water. Refer to the definition of wet location (see page 168).

3. Use lights labeled either SUITABLE FOR WET LOCATIONS or SUITABLE FOR DAMP LOCATIONS when installing lights in damp locations. Refer to the definition of damp location (see page 168). Light fixtures, including ceiling fans, intended for indoors may not be installed in either wet or damp locations.

Ceiling Fans

1. Support ceiling fans weighing not more than 70 pounds using boxes listed and labeled to support the fan.

2. Support ceiling fans weighing more than 70 pounds independently from the box.

3. Install boxes that are either listed and labeled to support a ceiling fan, or that are attached to framing in a manner that allows the box to support a ceiling fan, when installing boxes where a ceiling fan may be installed. This is required regardless of whether a ceiling fan currently is installed or whether a ceiling fan is specified to be installed. For example, ceiling boxes in bedrooms and family rooms usually should be capable of supporting a ceiling fan.

Ceiling Fans + Lights Near Tubs + Showers

1. Install ceiling fans, cord-connected lights, lights suspended by cords, chains, or cables, and track lights so that no part of the light or fan falls within an exclusion zone measuring 3 feet horizontally from the base of the tub or shower stall threshold and 8 feet vertically from the top of the tub rim or shower stall threshold. Parts include fan blades, bulb enclosures, hanging chains, and other parts connected to or hanging from the light or fan.

2. Use light fixtures that are listed for damp locations if the fixture is: (a) located within the tub or shower area and (b) within 8 feet from the top of the tub rim or shower threshold.

3. Use light fixtures that are listed for wet locations if the fixture is: (a) located within the tub or shower area, (b) within 8 feet from the top of the tub rim or shower threshold, (c) subject to shower spray.

Closet Lights

Applicable Code Definitions for Closets:

Clothes closet: A space intended for storage of clothing, a clothes closet usually contains a horizontal rod for hanging clothing. This definition implies that this section does not apply to storage areas such as linen closets and pantries. As with all codes, application of this section depends on interpretation by the local building official.

Closet storage area: Clearances to light fixtures required by this IRC Section are between light fixtures and the closet storage area. The closet storage area is a space consisting of a hanging rod storage area and a shelf storage area. The required clearance applies to both areas. The clearances to light fixtures apply whether or not shelves or hanging rods are currently installed in the closet. This means that if a shelf or rod could be installed on a clothes closet wall, you must assume that one will be installed and that the clearances to light fixtures apply.

Hanging rod storage area: This area begins at the closet floor and ends 6 feet above the closet floor or at the highest hanging rod, whichever is higher. The hanging rod storage area includes all of the space within 24 inches horizontally from the back and sides of the closet walls.

Shelf storage area: This begins 6 feet above the closet floor or at the highest hanging rod, whichever is higher, and ends at the closet ceiling. The shelf storage area includes all of the space within 12 inches horizontally from the back and sides of the closet walls or within the width of the shelf, whichever is wider.

Light Fixture Clearances in Clothing Closets

1. Do not install any incandescent or LED light fixture in a clothes closet if any part of the lamp is exposed. This includes both surface mounted and recessed light fixtures. This includes incandescent light fixtures that have lamps such as compact fluorescent installed because the fluorescent lamp could be replaced with an incandescent lamp. This includes hanging light fixtures.

2. Provide at least 12 inches between surface mounted incandescent or LED light fixtures and the closest point of the closet storage area.

3. Provide at least 6 inches between recessed incandescent and LED light fixtures and the closest point of the closet storage area.

4. Provide at least 6 inches between fluorescent light fixtures and the closest point of the closet storage area.

5. You may install surface-mounted fluorescent and LED light fixtures within the closet storage area if the fixture is identified for use within the area.

Using Flexible Cords with Equipment

1. Use flexible cords only to connect an appliance to a receptacle and only if the appliance manufacturer's instructions allow connection by a flexible cord.

2. Do not run or conceal flexible cords in walls, ceilings, floors, or raceways.

3. Do not splice or tap flexible cords.

4. Provide power to flexible cords through an attachment plug. Do not hard-wire flexible cords directly to a power source.

5. Do not use flexible cords as a substitute for permanent wiring.

Closet hanging rod and shelf storage areas.

ELECTRIC EQUIPMENT GROUNDING

1. Ground metal parts in an electrical system including equipment cases, cabinets, boxes, conduit, tubing, light fixtures, and water pumps. Equipment cases include furnaces, air conditioning condensers, water heaters, dishwashers, and similar equipment.

2. You may ground metal parts in an electrical system by using any currently accepted wiring method that provides a mechanically and electrically continuous path to the service grounding connection. These methods include: (a) grounding wires contained in NM cable, (b) separate equipment grounding wires, and (c) metal conduit and tubing when the fittings at terminations are listed for grounding.

3. Do not use a separate earth ground as the only means of grounding equipment. Example: do not install a separate driven ground rod to ground an air conditioning condenser.

4. In older homes, the electrical wires do not have a separate grounding wire. Some people install a wire between the grounding screw of a grounded receptacle and the neutral terminal. This is not safe.

Modern NM (nonmetallic) cable, found in most wiring systems installed after 1965, contains a bare wire that provides grounding for receptacle and switch boxes.

Armored cable has a metal sheath that can serve as the grounding pathway.

Polarized receptacles have a long slot and a short slot. Used with a polarized plug, the polarized receptacle keeps electrical current directed for safety.

Three-slot receptacles are required by code for all new installations. They are usually connected to a standard two-wire cable with ground.

Satellite Dishes, Television + Radio Antennas

This material applies to receiving antennas, such as satellite dishes, and traditional radio and television antennas. It does not apply to cable TV system wiring, and it does not apply to network-powered broadband communication system wiring. This material also applies to radio transmission antennas and towers, such as those used by amateur radio operators.

Antenna Prohibited Installation Locations

1. Do not attach or secure (guy) antennas to electric service entrance masts, poles that support electric power wires, plumbing vent pipes, or furnace vent pipes.

2. Do not attach or secure (guy) large antennas to chimneys, including framed and brick veneer chimneys. These chimneys are not designed to bear the loads imposed by large antennas. Consult a qualified contractor or chimney sweep before attaching or securing large antennas to chimneys.

3. Provide clearance between antennas and masts and electric power wires so that if the antenna falls, it is unlikely to fall on the electric power wires.

Antenna Wire + Cable Clearance to Electric Power Lines

1. Do not install outdoor, aboveground antenna wires and cables so that they cross over electric power wires. Avoid, if possible, installing outdoor, aboveground antenna wires that cross under electric power wires. Electric power wires include wires on overhead power poles, overhead service drop wires, and any electric power wires running between buildings.

2. Provide at least 2 feet of clearance between outdoor, aboveground antenna wires and cables and electric power lines that can swing freely.

3. Provide at least 4 inches between outdoor antenna wires and cables and most residential electric power wires when both are secured so that they cannot move.

4. Provide at least 12 inches of clearance between underground antenna wires and underground cables and electric power wires.

5. Provide at least a 2-inch clearance between indoor antenna wires and cables and indoor electric power wires.

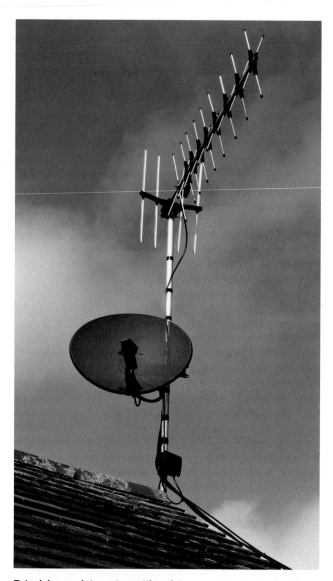

Television aerials and satellite dishes must be located well away from power lines. They should be properly grounded and protected against lightning strikes.

Grounding Antennas, Masts, Wires + Cables

1. Install a ground/bonding wire between metal antenna masts, towers, and support poles and an approved grounding point. Metal antenna masts include the short metal mast commonly found on satellite dishes.

2. Install a grounding/bonding wire between the coaxial cable shield and an approved grounding/bonding point. You must ground/bond both the coaxial cable shield and any metal antenna mast.

3. Use at least #10 AWG copper wire or #17 copper clad steel wire as the grounding/bonding wire for receiving equipment only. You may use a #8 AWG aluminum or copper-clad aluminum grounding/bonding wire for receiving equipment only if it is not in contact with masonry, and is not installed in a corrosive environment, and is installed at least 18 inches above the ground at all points, including at the connection to the grounding/bonding point.

4. Use at least #10 AWG copper, bronze, or copper-clad steel as the grounding/bonding wires for transmitting/receiving stations. Use a larger wire if the lead-in wires are larger than #10 AWG. Insulation is not required on any grounding/bonding wire. You may use solid or stranded grounding/bonding wires for transmitting or receiving stations.

5. Run the grounding/bonding wire in as straight a line as possible to an approved grounding point.

6. Connect the grounding/bonding wire(s) to one of the following approved grounding/bonding points: (a) the intersystem bonding connection terminal; (b) the building's grounding electrode, grounding electrode wire, or other metal part of the building grounding electrode system; (c) a metal water service pipe not more than 5 feet from where the water service pipe enters the building; (d) the service equipment cabinet or non-flexible metal service equipment raceway; or (e) the other system grounding/bonding connection described in the IRC.

7. Do not connect the antenna mast or coaxial cable to its own ground rod unless the ground rod is bonded to the building grounding electrode system using at least #6 AWG copper wire.

8. Secure and support the grounding/bonding wire by fastening it to the building or other substantial structure. Insulating supports are not required.

9. Protect the grounding/bonding wire if it is exposed to physical damage. Use a wiring method, such as metallic conduit, that is approved for use in physical damage environments.

10. Bond (connect) both ends of any metallic conduit and tubing used to protect the grounding/bonding wire to the bonding/grounding wire.

Grounding Wire Connection to the Grounding Point

1. Use a listed clamp, listed pressure connector, or other listed means to connect the grounding wire to the grounding point.

2. Install the listed connector so that it is both physically and electrically connected to the grounding point. This means removing paint, lacquer, rust, and other non-conductive material before attaching the listed connector to the grounding point.

3. Connect not more than one grounding wire to a listed connector unless the connector is listed to accept more than one wire.

4. Use a listed connector that is compatible with both the grounding point and the grounding wire material. Example: an iron or steel clamp is not compatible with a copper water pipe. Both materials will corrode over time.

SOURCE FOR THIS MATERIAL

The material in this section is based on the National Electrical Code (NEC)®, 2020 Edition. Most local building officials use the NEC as a supplement to or in place of the IRC when dealing with residential electrical issues. The IRC does not address antennas, so the NEC is usually the appropriate source for rules regarding installation of antennas and the wires that connect them to the receiving equipment. Verify with the local building official which version, if any, of the NEC is adopted in your area.

Broadband Cable Wiring

This material applies to network-powered broadband communication system wiring. These systems usually deliver television, telephone, Internet, and similar services. They operate at up to 150 volts and 100 watts. This material does not apply to standard cable TV system wiring, and it does not apply to satellite TV antenna wiring. Some new communication systems use fiber-optic cables. This article does not apply to fiber-optic cables.

Overhead Broadband Cable Clearance

1. Install outdoor, aboveground broadband communication cables above electric power wires whenever possible.

2. Avoid installing outdoor, aboveground broadband communication cables near electric power wires that can swing freely. Electric power wires include wires on overhead power poles, overhead service drop wires, and any electric power wires running between buildings. Provide at least 12 inches of clearance between outdoor, aboveground broadband communication cables and electric power lines that can swing freely. Increase clearance to at least 40 inches at the power pole.

3. Provide at least 4 inches between outdoor broadband communication cables and most residential electric power wires when both are secured so that they cannot move.

4. Measure the vertical clearance between overhead broadband cables and the ground, walkway, driveway, or street beginning at the lowest hanging point of the cables and ending at the surface under the lowest point.

5. Provide at least 9½ feet vertical clearance between broadband cables and finished grade, sidewalks, or platforms accessed by pedestrians only.

6. Provide at least 11½ feet vertical clearance between overhead broadband cables and residential property and driveways.

7. Provide at least 15½ feet vertical clearance between overhead broadband cables and public streets, alleys, roads, or parking areas subject to truck traffic.

8. Provide the same clearance between overhead broadband cables and swimming pools, spas, and hot tubs as for electrical wires.

9. Provide at least 8 feet vertical clearance between broadband cables and most low-slope roofs.

10. Provide at least 18 inches of vertical clearance between broadband cables and roof overhangs if not more than 4 feet of cable passes over the roof and if the cable terminates at a through-the-roof raceway or support. This is similar to clearances allowed for service drop wires.

11. Provide at least 3 feet vertical clearance between broadband cables and roofs with a slope of at least 4 inches in 12 inches.

Broadband Cable Burial Depth

1. Bury broadband cables at least 18 inches deep when the cables are not covered by concrete or enclosed in conduit or other raceways. You may reduce the depth to at least 12 inches when the cables are under concrete residential driveways, patios, and similar concrete slabs. Refer to the NEC for burial depths when the cables are enclosed in conduit or raceways.

Grounding Broadband Cables

1. Install a copper (or other corrosion-resistant material) grounding/bonding wire at least #14 AWG between the broadband cable shield and an approved grounding/bonding point.

2. Connect the grounding/bonding wire to the broadband cable shield at a point as close as possible to where the outside cable terminates

---

⊘ LOW + MEDIUM POWER BROADBAND SYSTEM DEFINITION

Low power broadband systems operate at not more than 100 volts, and medium power systems operate at not more than 150 volts. Verify voltage rating and system classification with the broadband service provider. The operating voltage of the system affects how the cables are installed.

outside the building. If the outside cable enters the building, make this connection at a point as close as possible to where the outside cable enters the building.

3. Run the grounding/bonding wire in as straight a line and as short a distance as possible from the broadband cable shield grounding/bonding connection point to an approved grounding/bonding point.

4. Limit the length of the grounding/bonding wire to not more than 20 feet. If the broadband cable shield ground/bonding point is more than 20 feet from an approved grounding point, you may install at least an 8-foot-long ground rod near where the cable enters the building and bond the ground rod to the electrical service grounding system using at least #6 AWG copper wire.

5. Connect the grounding/bonding wire(s) to one of the following approved grounding/bonding points in other than manufactured homes: (a) the intersystem bonding connection terminal; (b) the building's grounding electrode, grounding electrode wire, or other metal part of the building grounding electrode system; (c) a metal water service pipe not more than 5 feet from where the water service pipe enters the building; (d) the service equipment cabinet or non-flexible metal service equipment raceway; or (e) the other system grounding/bonding connection described in the IRC.

6. Connect the grounding/bonding wire(s) to one of the approved grounding/bonding points described above at manufactured homes if the home has service equipment or a grounded power disconnecting means located not more than 9 feet from the nearest wall of the home.

7. Connect the grounding/bonding wire(s) to the manufactured home's grounding electrode if the home does not have service equipment or a grounded power disconnecting means located not more than 9 feet from the nearest wall of the home. Use at least #6 AWG copper wire to make this connection.

8. Connect the broadband cable shield to the metal frame of the manufactured home if the grounding/bonding connection is made as described in #7 above. Use at least #12 AWG copper wire to make this connection.

9. Protect the grounding/bonding wire if it is exposed to physical damage. Use a wiring method, such as metallic conduit, that is approved for use in physical damage environments.

Broadband Cable + Electric Power Wire Separation

1. Do not run low-power or medium-power broadband cables in the same conduit, tubing, raceway, junction and device box, or enclosure with electric power wires unless an exception applies.

2. You may install low-power and medium-power broadband cables and electric power wires in the same cabinet or box when the electric power wires are intended to supply power to the broadband cable system, such as for an amplifier.

3. Separate indoor broadband cables and electric power wires by at least 2 inches.

4. Separation described in number 3 is not required if the electric power wires or broadband cables are enclosed in conduit, tubing, metal cable armor or if the electric power wires and cables are permanently separated from each other by a continuous non-conductive material.

5. Separation described in number 3 is not required if the electric power wires are contained in a jacket, such as with types NM, UF, and AC cable. This means that, in most cases, separation between broadband cables and electric power wires is required only when individual electric wires are installed in conduit or tubing.

6. Provide, if possible, at least 6 feet of separation between coaxial cables and any part of a lightning protection system.

APPENDIX

Common Mistakes

An electrical inspector visiting your home might identify a number of situations that are not up to code. These situations may not be immediate problems. In fact, it is possible that the wiring in your home has remained trouble free for many years.

Nevertheless, any wiring or device that is not up to code carries the potential for problems, often at risk to your home and your family. In addition, you may have trouble selling your home if it is not wired according to accepted methods.

Most local electrical codes are based on the National Electrical Code (NEC), a book updated and published every three years by the National Fire Protection Agency. This code book contains rules and regulations for the proper installation of electrical wiring and devices. Most public libraries carry reference copies of the NEC.

All electrical inspectors are required to be well versed in the NEC. Their job is to know the NEC regulations and to make sure these rules are followed in order to prevent fires and ensure safety. If you have questions regarding your home wiring system, your local inspector will be happy to answer them.

While a book cannot possibly identify all potential wiring problems in your house, we have identified some of the most common wiring defects here and will show you how to correct them. When working on home wiring repair or replacement projects, refer to this section to help identify any conditions that may be hazardous.

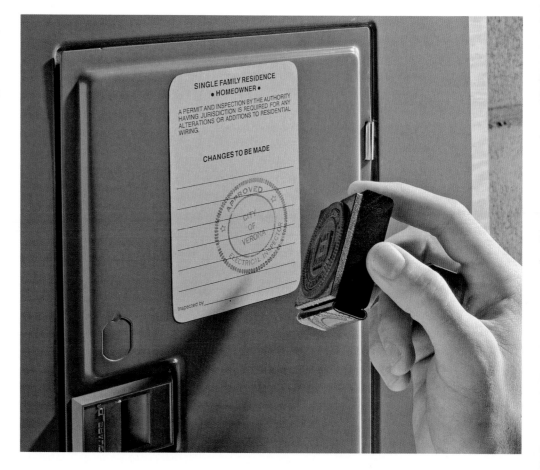

Electrical inspectors are on the lookout for common mistakes. The following pages detail problems to avoid so you will pass inspection on the first try.

Service Panel Inspection

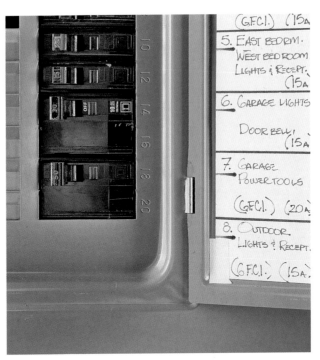

Problem: Rust stains are found inside the main service panel. This problem occurs because water seeps into the service head outside the house and drips down into the service panel.

Solution: Have an electrician examine the service head and the main service panel. If the panel or service wires have been damaged, new components must be installed.

Problem: This problem is actually a very old and very dangerous one. A penny or a knockout behind a fuse effectively bypasses the fuse, preventing an overloaded circuit from blowing the fuse. This is very dangerous and can lead to overheated wiring.

Solution: Remove the penny and replace the fuse. Have a licensed electrician examine the panel and circuit wiring. If the fuse has been bypassed for years, wiring may be dangerously compromised, and the circuit may need to be replaced.

Problem: Two wires connected to one single-pole breaker is a sign of an overcrowded panel and also a dangerous code violation unless the breaker is approved for such a connection.

Solution: If there is room in the panel, install a separate breaker for the extra wire. If the panel is overcrowded, have an electrician upgrade the panel or install a subpanel.

 ## RECOGNIZING ALUMINUM WIRE

Solid-conductor aluminum wire was used in place of copper in many wiring systems installed beginning around 1964 and continuing until the late 1970s. Aluminum wire is identified by its silver color and by the AL stamp on the cable sheathing.

By the late 1960s, reports of house fires were traced to solid-conductor aluminum wire. Investigators discovered a couple of causes. One cause was aluminum's tendency to oxidize (rust), especially when connected to copper at switches, receptacles, and other wires. The other cause was that the aluminum wire being used until about 1972 tended to shrink and swell at a different rate than other materials. These problems increased heat at the connections and caused the fires.

By about 1974, the problems had been corrected and inventories of existing wire and devices had been depleted. The aluminum wire alloy was changed to reduce the shrink and swell problem. Switches and receptacles were changed to the CO/ALR type, which reduced the oxidation problem. By about 1980, though, solid-conductor aluminum wire had such a bad reputation that its use in the United States was minimal. It's unusual to find solid-conductor aluminum wire in houses built after about 1980, although some #8 AWG is being installed even today.

Here is some general advice about dealing with solid-conductor aluminum wiring. A qualified electrician who is familiar with the issues should work on wiring installed between 1964 and about 1974. The aluminum wire produced during this period may not be entirely safe even when connected to CO/ALR devices. Aluminum wire installed after 1974 should be safe when connected to CO/ALR devices; however, connecting aluminum wire to copper wire should only be done using connectors designed for this purpose.

You should not confuse solid-conductor aluminum wire with similar wire and with wire that looks similar but is not aluminum. Stranded aluminum wire continues to be used for large appliance circuits, feeders, and service entrance wires. It is safe when properly installed with anti-oxidant paste at terminals.

Copper-coated aluminum wire was produced in the 1970s. It is treated like aluminum wire but does not share the same problems. Copper-coated aluminum wire is uncommon. "Tin-coated" copper wire was installed mainly during the

1940s and 1950s. This wire looks like aluminum wire but is copper. This wire's safety may be questionable because of deterioration of its insulation, not because of the wire itself.

Inspecting the Bonding Jumper Wire

Problem: Grounding system jumper wire is missing or is disconnected. In most homes the grounding jumper wire attaches to water pipes on either side of the water meter.

Solution: Attach a jumper wire to the water pipes on either side of the water meter using pipe clamps. Use wire that is the same size and type as the grounding electrode wire.

Common Cable Problems

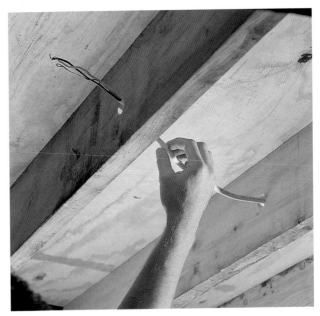

Problem: Cable running across joists or studs is attached to the edge of framing members. Electrical codes forbid this type of installation in exposed areas, such as unfinished basements or walk-up attics.

Solution: Protect cable by drilling holes in framing members at least 2" from exposed edges and threading the cable through the holes.

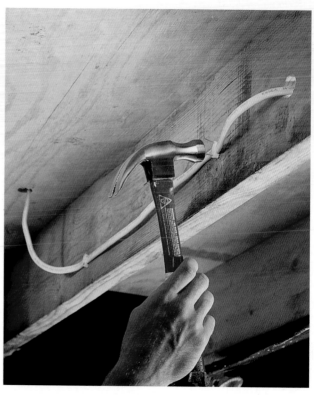

Problem: Cable running along joists or studs hangs loosely. Loose cables can be pulled accidentally, causing damage to wires.

Solution: Anchor the cable to the side of the framing members at least 1¼" from the edge using plastic staples. NM (non-metallic) cable should be stapled every 4½' and within 8" of each electrical box.

Cable shown cutaway

Problem: Cable threaded through studs or joists lies close to the edge of the framing members. NM (non-metallic) cable (shown cutaway) can be damaged easily if nails or screws are driven into the framing members during remodeling projects.

Solution: Install metal nail guards to protect cable from damage. Nail guards are available at hardware stores and home centers.

Problem: Unclamped cable enters a metal electrical box. Edges of the knockout can rub against the cable sheathing and damage the wires.

NOTE: With plastic boxes, clamps are not required if cables are anchored to framing members within 8" of the box.

Solution: Anchor the cable to the electrical box with a cable clamp. Several types of cable clamps are available at hardware stores and home centers.

Problem: Cables are spliced outside an electrical box. Exposed splices can spark and create a risk of shock or fire.

Solution: Bring installation up to code by enclosing the splice inside a metal or plastic electrical box. Make sure the box is large enough to accommodate the number of wires it contains.

Checking Wire Connections

Problem: Two or more wires are attached to a single-screw terminal. This type of connection is seen in older wiring but is now prohibited by the NEC.

Pigtail

Solution: Disconnect the wires from the screw terminal, then join them to a short length of wire (called a pigtail) using a wire connector. Connect the other end of the pigtail to the screw terminal.

Exposed wire

Problem: Bare wire extends past a screw terminal. Exposed wire can cause a short circuit if it touches the metal box or another circuit wire.

Solution: Clip the wire and reconnect it to the screw terminal. In a proper connection, the bare wire wraps completely around the screw terminal, and the plastic insulation just touches the screw head.

Problem: Wires are connected with electrical tape. Electrical tape was used frequently in older installations, but it can deteriorate over time, leaving bare wires exposed inside the electrical box.

Solution: Replace electrical tape with wire connectors. You may need to clip away a small portion of the wire so the bare end will be covered completely by the connector.

Problem: Nicks and scratches in bare wires interfere with the flow of current. This can cause the wires to overheat.

Solution: Clip away the damaged portion of the wire, then restrip about ¾" of insulation and reconnect the wire to the screw terminal.

Electrical Box Inspection

Armored cable

Sharp edges

Protective sleeve

Problem: No protective sleeve on armored cable. Sharp edges of the cable can damage the wire insulation, creating a shock hazard and fire risk.

Solution: Protect the wire insulation by installing a plastic sleeve around the wires. Sleeves are available at hardware stores. Wires that are damaged must be replaced.

Problem: Insulation on wires is cracked or damaged. If damaged insulation exposes bare wire, a short circuit can occur, posing a shock hazard and fire risk.

Solution: Wrap damaged insulation temporarily with plastic electrical tape. Damaged circuit wires should be replaced by an electrician.

Problem: Open electrical boxes create a fire hazard if a short circuit causes sparks (arcing) inside the box.

Solution: Cover the open box with a solid metal cover plate, available at any hardware store. Electrical boxes must remain accessible and cannot be sealed inside ceilings or walls.

Problem: Short wires are difficult to handle. The NEC requires that each wire in an electrical box have at least 6" of workable length.

Solution: Lengthen circuit wires by connecting them to short pigtail wires using wire connectors. Pigtails can be cut from scrap wire but should be the same gauge and color as the circuit wires and at least 6" long.

Problem: A recessed electrical box is hazardous, especially if the wall or ceiling surface is made from a flammable material, such as wood paneling. The NEC prohibits this type of installation.

Solution: Add an extension ring to bring the face of the electrical box flush with the surface. Extension rings come in several sizes and are available at hardware stores.

Problem: Open electrical boxes create a fire hazard if a short circuit causes sparks (dust and dirt in an electrical box can cause hazardous, high-resistance short circuits). When making routine electrical repairs, always check the electrical boxes for dust and dirt buildup.

Solution: Vacuum the electrical box clean using a narrow nozzle attachment. Make sure power to the box is turned off at the main service panel before vacuuming.

Problem: Crowded electrical box (shown cutaway) makes electrical repairs difficult. This type of installation is prohibited because heat in the box may cause a fire.

Solution: Replace the electrical box with a deeper electrical box.

Problem: Light fixture is installed without an electrical box. This installation exposes the wiring connections and provides no support for the light fixture.

Solution: Install an approved electrical box to enclose the wire connections and support the light fixture.

Inspecting Receptacles + Switches

Problem: Octopus receptacle attachments used permanently can overload a circuit and cause overheating of the receptacle.

Solution: Use a multi-receptacle power strip with built-in overload protection. This is for temporary use only. If the need for extra receptacles is frequent, upgrade the wiring system.

Problem: Scorch marks near screw terminals indicate that electrical arcing has occurred. Arcing usually is caused by loose wire connections.

Solution: Replace the receptacle. Make sure wires are connected securely to screw terminals.

Problem: Exterior receptacle box allows water to enter the box when receptacle slots are in use.

Solution: Replace the old receptacle box with an in-use box that has a bubble cover to protect plugs from water while they are in the slots.

Problem: White neutral wires are connected to a switch. Although the switch appears to work correctly in this installation, it is dangerous because the light fixture carries voltage when the switch is off.

Solution: Connect the black hot wires to the switch, and join the grounded white wires together with a wire connector.

Problem: White neutral wires are connected to the brass screw terminals on the receptacle, and black hot wires are attached to silver screw terminals. This installation is hazardous because live voltage flows into the long neutral slot on the receptacle.

Solution: Reverse the wire connections so that the black hot wires are attached to brass screw terminals and white neutral wires are attached to silver screw terminals. Live voltage now flows into the short slot on the receptacle.

Measurement Conversions

ENGLISH TO METRIC

TO CONVERT:	TO:	MULTIPLY BY:
Inches	Millimeters	25.4
Inches	Centimeters	2.54
Feet	Meters	0.305
Yards	Meters	0.914
Square inches	Square centimeters	6.45
Square feet	Square meters	0.093
Square yards	Square meters	0.836
Ounces	Milliliters	30.0
Pints (US)	Liters	0.473 (Imp. 0.568)
Quarts (US)	Liters	0.946 (Imp. 1.136)
Gallons (US)	Liters	3.785 (Imp. 4.546)
Ounces	Grams	28.4
Pounds	Kilograms	0.454

TO CONVERT:	TO:	MULTIPLY BY:
Millimeters	Inches	0.039
Centimeters	Inches	0.394
Meters	Feet	3.28
Meters	Yards	1.09
Square centimeters	Square inches	0.155
Square meters	Square feet	10.8
Square meters	Square yards	1.2
Milliliters	Ounces	.033
Liters	Pints (US)	2.114 (Imp. 1.76)
Liters	Quarts (US)	1.057 (Imp. 0.88)
Liters	Gallons (US)	0.264 (Imp. 0.22)
Grams	Ounces	0.035
Kilograms	Pounds	2.2

Resources

Air Diffusion Council (ADC)
Flexible air ducts
847-706-6750
www.flexibleduct.org

American Concrete Institute
Document ACI 332
248-848-3800
www.concrete.org

American Society of Home Inspectors (ASHI)
Information and references
847-759-2820
www.ashi.org

American Wood Council
"Prescriptive Residential Deck
   Construction Guide"
202-463-2766
www.awc.org

Black + Decker Corporation
Power tools + accessories
800-544-6986
www.blackanddecker.com

**International Association of Plumbing
   and Mechanical Officials (IAPMO)**
Publishes *Uniform Plumbing Code*®
   and *Uniform Mechanical Code*®
909-472-4100
www.iapmo.org

International Code Council (ICC)
Develops residential and commercial
   building codes
Publishes *International Residential Code*®
888-422-7233
www.iccsafe.org

National Fire Protection Association (NFPA)
Publishes *National Electrical Code*® (NEC)
800-344-3555
www.nfpa.org

Photo Credits

Bruce Barker: 18 (bottom left and right), 50, 78, 109, 187, 207
City of Swainsboro: 10
iStock: 33 (left), 37 (bottom), 68 (top), 218
Moberg Fireplaces (www.mobergfireplaces.com): 102
Shutterstock: 22 (top right), 27, 32 (both), 33 (right), 60, 99 (both)

Index